THE CUISINE OF THE ROSE

Mireille Johnston was born in Nice and educated in France, England
and America. She is the presenter of twelve BBC2 television pro-
grammes on French regional cookery. She is the author of *The French
Family Feast, Cuisine of the Sun: Classical Recipes from Nice and Provence,
Central Park Country: A Tune Within Us* and various articles published
in France and in America. She is the translator and editor of the film
script for *The Sorrow and the Pity* by Marcel Ophuls and of Henri
Lefèvre's book *Criticism of Everyday Life*. She has taught comparative
literature at Yale University, Columbia University and Sarah Lawrence
College. She lives in Paris with her husband and their two daughters,
Margaret-Brooke and Elizabeth.

MIREILLE JOHNSTON

The Cuisine of the Rose

Classical French Cooking from Burgundy and Lyonnais

REVISED AND ANGLICIZED

ILLUSTRATIONS BY MILTON GLASER

PENGUIN BOOKS

PENGUIN BOOKS

Published by the Penguin Group
Penguin Books Ltd, 27 Wrights Lane, London w8 5tz, England
Penguin Books USA Inc., 375 Hudson Street, New York, New York 10014, USA
Penguin Books Australia Ltd, Ringwood, Victoria, Australia
Penguin Books Canada Ltd, 10 Alcorn Avenue, Toronto, Ontario, Canada m4v 3b2
Penguin Books (NZ) Ltd, 182–190 Wairau Road, Auckland 10, New Zealand

Penguin Books Ltd, Registered Offices: Harmondsworth, Middlesex, England

First published in the USA by Random House, Inc. 1982
First published in Great Britain by Penguin Books 1984
This revised edition first published 1992
1 3 5 7 9 10 8 6 4 2

Printed in England by Clays Ltd, St Ives plc
Set in 10½/13 pt Monophoto Garamond

Contents

Acknowledgements vii

Introduction 1

Ingredients 8

Les Soupes *Soups* 16

Les Hors-d'Oeuvres *Appetizers* 28

Les Salades *Salads* 44

Les Sauces *Sauces* 57

Les Poissons *Fish* 68

Les Oeufs *Egg Dishes* 86

Les Viandes *Meats* 99

Les Légumes *Vegetables* 155

Farineux *Pasta and Grain Dishes* 192

Les Plats de Festin *Festive Dishes* 198

Les Fromages *Cheeses* 211

Les Desserts *Desserts* 216

Les Boissons de Ménage *Home-made Beverages* 257

Le Vin *Wine* 264

Menus *Menus* 269

La Moutarde *Mustard* 274

Spécialités *Special Treats* 277

Index 281

Acknowledgements

I wish to thank Jason Epstein, *gourmet-en-residence*, who shared this effort to capture and transmit the joy of good living and fine eating of Burgundy and sustained it with unfailing flair and palate; Milton Glaser – undoubtedly a Bourguignon in one of his previous lives – who still displays the characteristics of the race: a sharp eye, salty humour and gargantuan appetite; Anne Freedgood, for her informed reading of the manuscript, her skilful help and her enthusiasm; Roberta Schneiderman, who tested every one of the recipes with expert thoroughness and precise taste; Barbara Sundahl, for her tasting and testing with patience and good cheer and the intricate deciphering of a most peculiar scribble; Tom, Margaret and Zabette, who have been known to eat pumpkin soup, pumpkin gratin and pumpkin cake along with pumpkin preserves in the same meal and with brave smiles.

Introduction

As one enters Burgundy there should be a warning sign, 'No one can come here if he is not ready to fall madly in love with life.' Burgundy stands in the heart of France as both a celebration and a challenge, for life always seems more intense and sunnier here. The whole province blooms like a fluffy rose, the incarnation of the sheer joy of being alive. But just as a rose is a rose is a rose, Burgundy is difficult to introduce formally. She is larger than life, and a bundle of tastes, smells and accents bursts forth whenever I think about her.

I remember the cattle fair in Digouin, the cream-coloured Charollais cows and the huge blond bulls tied on the town green. Heavy bargaining between the breeders, red cheeks and sparkling eyes, rolling rs, grey smocks over corduroy trousers. Later would come the truce – a hearty snack in a café, energy and laughter, piles of fritters and sausages, everybody commenting on the quality of some bull, the flavour of a wine, fast sales, shared treats, who did what how. And above this turbulent exchange, softly drifting from the back rooms, the intoxicating smell of wild boar marinating in earthen bowls.

I remember long walks in the woods of Morvan, the thick mat of leaves silvery with frost on the ground, the elder trees and the oak trees bare, the air smelling of burnt wood, and nearby a flight of partridges, a glimpse of deer. Then back to the village with the caramel-coloured roofs and, by the fire, a steaming glass of red wine simmered with clove and warm toast with hare pâté.

I remember the canal near Dijon with its long lines of symmetrical poplars, the lockhouses, the barges gliding slowly with flowerpots and drying linen on the deck, heavy with timber or sand – perhaps wine – the mellowest of sights.

Burgundy records only the rich hours. She seems to have a supplement of soul, an extra pinch of civilization given to her both by her past and by the rich nature she has been blessed with. She finds in her very old human identity and her diverse history – one of the oldest in Europe – the reason and the energy to believe in her future and to remain confident.

Rivers, canals and roads have crossed here for thousands of years carrying blood and energy through the whole country. All the strong moments of French history have left their traces. It is truly the mixed dreams and efforts of the Celts, the Romans, the Greeks and the Germans, and the spirit of the monks, merchants, pilgrims, sculptors, blacksmiths and wine-growers that have given Burgundy its vitality and its organic balance.

Civilization started here some twenty thousand years before Christianity spread over the country. One hundred thousand skeletons of wild horses have been found near Solutre dating to that period, and it is whispered that they have given Pouilly Fuissé wine its unique flavour. Reindeer and wild horses were hunted. The trade roads for tin, salt, amber and minerals crossed the region. Iron and timber were exploited; weaving, jewellery and sculpture flourished. There were rich markets and busy harbours long before the Romans arrived.

Then, when Caesar defeated the Gauls in Alesia, which is now Burgundy, a fruitful cooperation began. The Romans brought ceramics, olives, wines, and also law and order. They discovered a strong vine able to tolerate Burgundy's climate, and soon vineyards spread all along the rocky hillsides. Later, when the Burgundians – tall, heavy drinkers from Scandinavia – invaded the region, they were welcomed by the Gallo-Romans. They worked hard; forests were cleared and agriculture improved. A cohesive, busy community came into being.

In every branch of life this constant outpouring of energy flooded through Burgundy, but during the Middle Ages the region knew a spirituality and an explosion of artistic and political activity that have not been matched since. The apogee of the dukedom came in the fifteenth century, when Burgundy encompassed Flanders, Luxembourg, Artois, Franche-Comté and the provinces along the Rhône Valley down to the Mediterranean Sea. It became the vibrant, tumultuous centre of feudal Europe, and the great dukes of Burgundy were all lusty, earthy characters. Philip the Bold, John the Fearless and Philip the Good made the Burgundy court a model of fashion and manners all over Europe. Their appetite for life and irrepressible energy were felt in technology as well as in philosophy, sculpture, architecture and gastronomy. There was quality in every realm.

Today the pre-Roman crypts, Roman ruins, monasteries, fortified cities, castles, and Roman and Gothic cathedrals still seem to grow out of the land according to some natural law. The past lingers everywhere and enhances the present. A festive air blows over the province; mind and flesh mingle happily. There are as many Romanesque and Gothic works of art as wine and gastronomical Meccas. A fortress built in the third century shows how the region was already fascinated by food and sculpture equally: fishmongers, butchers and fruit merchants appear in elaborate stone carvings. And perhaps the most durable work of the dukes of Burgundy, heralded as 'lords of the best wines of Christendom', has been the standards they set for cuisine and wines. The splendour of their festivities, when guests spent nights and days at banquets, echoed throughout Europe. Each course contained ten dishes, and there were five to six courses, with acrobats and jugglers in between. Great attention was given to the production of wine. Farmers and monks created a unique vineyard under the vigilant eye of the dukes.

Even then, gastronomy reflected the formidable appetite and the respect for the past that prevail in Burgundy. Discoveries from other lands and other times were harmoniously mingled. The seasoning of garlic and parsley from Egypt became a favourite in Burgundy. The Romans brought olives and grapes. The Gauls favoured sauces and pork. Sugar, cinnamon, pepper, ginger, saffron and shallots, discovered during the Crusades in the Orient, were added and led to a truly inventive cuisine. The changing of plain beef into a fragrant *boeuf bourguignon* and the slow development of great *crus** that changed simple beverages into exquisite wines

* *Cru* means a vineyard of high quality, worthy of recognition under the laws of classification.

made every Bourguignon forever wish he 'had a throat shaped like a screw, so food would go down more slowly and be enjoyed more'.

The whole province has remained without a pause under the spell of food. High cuisine blossoms in Burgundy because it can rely on a rich countryside, a diversified and meticulous agriculture and a constant interest in taste. Here all the fruits of the land, rivers and woods are gathered in abundance. Throughout the province, open markets with crates of live snails, piles of vegetables and huge trays of cheese speak of a generous land.

Dijon, the capital of Burgundy, has been a true gastronomical centre since the days of the Gauls. It has a splendid ducal palace, whose kitchen walls are still lined with cooking devices of all sorts, ready to prepare sixty dishes a day. South is the Lyonnais region, and Lyon, now the second largest city in France and once the formal capital of Gaul, is where Rabelais wrote *Pantagruel* and *Gargantua*, where endless gourmets' clubs blossom, where legendary chefs and the famous Mothers, women chefs, offer true bourgeois regional cooking at its very best. It also claims the title of world capital of gastronomy.

But if Dijon and Lyon are the heart of the Burgundy rose, there are treats to be discovered under every petal. Beaune offers rich *oeufs en meurette*; Mâcon, *coq au vin* stewed in Chambertin wine and herbs, and *escargots* stuffed with butter, shallots and garlic; Morvan, a rich stew of wild boar and chestnuts and wild mushrooms; Charolles, its sumptuous beef with marrow; Auxerre, the famous pike-and-trout mousse and frog soufflé; Sens, its crispy *gougère*, its mushrooms stuffed with snails; and all along the Loire Valley, salmon and wild duck. In Franche-Comté there are corn dishes and carp stuffed with sorrel and simmered in cream and cheese. There are glorious gratins and walnut salads in Dauphiné; sausages with pistachios, raw ham, truffles and garlic in Lyon, and fritters and soups of all kinds. Permeating the whole region is the hearty fragrance of marinades, wild mushrooms and sumptuous sauces.

All the dishes here have developed slowly and carefully through the centuries. It has taken a constant taste for the good life to achieve this shared bliss in living. In medieval days the rich ate extravagantly; live birds under napkins and theatrical mixtures were

part of endless banquets. In contrast, the poor always had more nose than money and used all their tricks to transform their basic potato, rye and milk into tasty dishes. Out of these two repertories of cooking, the bourgeois middle class created an interesting balance. In each family, experiences and observations on recipes were recorded, different versions of a regional dish were kept, simplified versions of elaborate *haute cuisine* recipes were developed, and one of the most inventive and satisfying cuisines was born.

And so it is an artisan's heritage we have gathered here, a medley of memories, experiences, secrets and records of splendid meals enjoyed through the years. I have added a few comments because a dish seems better when one speaks about it. Eating involves palate, eyes, memory and wit to enjoy it fully.

I have transcribed old recipes only in a form suitable to today's appetite. Most dishes cannot be as hearty and rich as they once were, since we cannot, as the early Burgundy gourmets did, digest both snails and their shells. *Nouvelle cuisine* came and went but did teach us a few things. Yet since raw fish and crisp vegetables lack diversity, I offer a few dangerously rich recipes, sumptuous sauces and medieval alliances of sweet and salty. But I always emphasize the pungent, the light, the sharper version of a recipe.

Cooking becomes refined among people long civilized, and today gourmandise is still taught early through daily practice in Burgundy. Each flower, each root, bark and leaf has value and is picked to become tea, sauce, syrup, marinade, condiment. The children are responsible for little odd jobs, which give them the very spirit of Burgundy gastronomy. The fresh cheese in the cellar must be washed with salty water, brandy and wine; the pears and quinces drying on the cupboard have to be inspected; the blue cheese in its earthenware pot, stirred with fresh butter; the snails have to be gathered and fed with flour; the frog, caught in the pond; the mushrooms, dandelions, elderberries, beechnuts and hazelnuts, gathered regularly; the cream, skimmed off with a wooden spoon and kept until it becomes a rich ivory colour and has a nutty taste.

Young palates are educated gently with an after-school snack of rye bread covered with yellow velvety fresh cream sprinkled with garlic, or with warm chestnuts, or a coarse paste of pear wrapped in crisp warm pastry and, when a child goes to share a shepherd's day, with snails in their shells, new potatoes in their skins, and goat cheese wrapped in leaves, all cooked gently under the ashes. And so, of course, it is no surprise that food becomes the criterion of all values. When asked whom he likes best, his mother or his father, the spirited child is likely to answer, 'I like snails best, with plenty of butter and parsley.' At all times, the kind and witty ghosts of Rabelais, Brillat-Savarin and Colette walk beside him. He is part of a strong race of peasants, artists and wine-growers, who have transmitted to him the coherence of a heritage in which so many tendencies enrich each other.

Cooking acts as a catalyst; it awakens in the soul new potentialities. Whenever I think of the joy of living, the pleasure of a perfect dish served with a perfect wine and the deep joy that comes from perfect harmony, I see Burgundy; the light greens of the Charollais pastures with the cream-coloured cattle, the dark green of the Morvan wood, the pink and grey stones of the castles and cathedrals, the silver of ponds and creeks, the yellow gloss of the tiled roofs. I see the pink cheeks, the sparkling eyes crinkled as if they had faced the sun too much, the eloquent forceful faces.

The song of the world grabs me – I know I am in the right place to enjoy life. Burgundy is one of those perfect achievements in which nature and craft fulfil each other. It is reassuring to know there is an actual paradise in this world. Let the feast begin! *A table, que la fête commence!*

Notes on Measurements

The recipes are written in both metric and imperial measurements. In any one recipe follow only one set of measurements; do not mix them.

Spoons are standard cook's *level* measuring spoons, not just any household teaspoon or tablespoon.

Fractions of a pint are easy to measure: just remember that ⅕ pint equals 4 fl oz.

Ingredients

A serious meal depends largely on very serious shopping. You must learn how to smell, touch and select your ingredients and to demand freshness and quality. Although Burgundy and Lyonnais cooking uses a large variety of ingredients, most of them are easily available here.

The following is a descriptive list of all the basic Burgundy and Lyonnais ingredients used in this book.

Fonds de Cuisine
Staples to have in your kitchen at all times

Anchovies (*les anchois*)
Anchovies are used in salads and with beef (*boeuf marinière*), and can be bought packed in salt or oil. Before using the salt-packed variety, wash the fish thoroughly in cold running water. Cut along the back and pull out the bone, then remove the tail.

Bouquet garni
This is a small bundle of herbs wrapped in a piece of cheesecloth and used to enhance the seasoning of soups, stews and the like. The basis is 2 or 3 sprigs of parsley, a bay leaf and a sprig of thyme (or ¼ teaspoon of dried thyme); for a tastier bouquet garni, add a stalk of celery and a stalk of fennel. When the dish is ready, remove the bouquet garni.

Bread (*le pain*)

Stale bread, once a standby for the frugal housewife, is now a traditional ingredient of many dishes in one of several forms: breadcrumbs, *croûtons* or *chapons*. Sometimes a slice is soaked in milk, which is squeezed out before the bread is used for a sauce or for stuffing. You can buy so-called French or Italian bread, but home-baked is best. I prefer baking my own firm white bread with unbleached flour.

Breadcrumbs (*la panure, la chapelure*)

The ready-made kind is uniformly bad, so breadcrumbs simply have to be home-made.

To make a supply, either grate a few slices of stale bread or crumble them into a blender and blend at high speed for a few seconds. They will keep for at least two or three days in a jar and for three weeks in the freezer. When kept longer, they become mouldy, but you can still use them if you remove the mould.

Cheese (*le fromage*)

Always keep a large piece of Gruyère, tightly wrapped, in the refrigerator, grate it and sprinkle on soups, pasta and stews.

Goat cheese is used in some preparations and can be found in some supermarkets or in specialty shops.

Parmesan cheese keeps if it is wrapped in cling film; always have a large wedge of it on hand. Ricotta, although made with pasteurized cow's milk, can be used for *claqueret*. *Fromage frais* is now widely available in shops and supermarkets.

Where a recipe calls for blue cheese, use a crumbly one, such as Stilton or Roquefort, not a creamy one.

Chestnuts (*les marrons*)

You can buy canned chestnuts, already peeled and cooked. Keep a few cans for purée, stuffing and pastry. For other recipes, try to buy fresh ones, which are usually available in the autumn and early winter.

Country ham
This much-used ingredient is a raw, cured ham such as prosciutto, Bayonne ham or the Spanish Cerrano ham. This type of ham is available in many supermarkets, delicatessens and specialty shops. As an alternative you can use unsmoked gammon or bacon.

Cream (*la crème*)
You may use single or double cream, but to add taste and texture to a dish, try ½ double cream mixed with ½ soured cream.

Croûtons
These are used in many dishes in Burgundy and in Lyon. To make them, cut slices of good firm home-made bread in triangles and fry in butter or vegetable oil. You may, for a lighter touch, simply bake the *croûtons* at 180°C/350°F/Gas Mark 4.

Dried cod (*la morue sèche*)
Dried cod can be kept in a dry corner of your kitchen or in the freezer. It is sold in three forms. The dried whole fish (bone, skin and tail) requires about two days of soaking in cold water, with the water changed several times a day. Dried filleted cod requires an overnight soaking and four changes of water. Frozen fillets will require only about four hours' soaking with four changes of water.

You will probably have to go to French, Italian, Spanish or Greek shops to find it. Buy a great amount since so many of Lyon's light, tasty, inexpensive dishes are made from it – *morue à la lyonnaise*, *beignets de morue* and so on.

Flour (*la farine*)
Always use unbleached flour, available in many health-food shops.

Garlic (*l'ail*)
Since I use great quantities of garlic, I buy it in a wreath and hang it in a dry place in the kitchen. Red garlic is tastier and stronger than the white. All supermarkets carry some garlic in the vegetable department. Remember that a garlic clove whole is much less strong than a minced or crushed one.

Gherkins (*les cornichons*)
These little pickles originally came from India but have become an everyday staple in Burgundy cooking. They are called *cornichons* because they look like little horns (*corne*). They are eaten before they become mature. To make your own, choose very small (about 5-cm-/2-in.-long) cucumbers, all roughly the same size. Wash and dry them carefully and place them in a large bowl with rough salt or kosher salt. Let them stand for 24 hours, tossing them from time to time.

Dry them with a piece of soft cloth. Place them in a jar with a few pearl onions, a few cloves, 4 garlic cloves, a sprig of tarragon and 10 peppercorns. Boil enough red-wine vinegar to cover them and pour over the vegetables. Let stand overnight. In the morning pour the vinegar into a pan and bring it to a boil. Pour over the cucumbers. Let them soak another night. Repeat the boiling and soaking. Add a sprig of thyme and 2 bay leaves. Close the jar tightly. The *cornichons* will be ready in 1 month. Use in hors-d'oeuvres, with *boeuf mironton* and in various sauces. If you cannot make them yourself, you can buy them in gourmet and specialty shops.

Lean salt pork (*le petit salé*)
Sautéing with salt pork is the essential first step in making stews and fish dishes. Ask your butcher for salted belly of pork; if it is not available, use a solid cut (not rashers) of unsmoked streaky bacon. Always choose the leanest and keep a large piece in the refrigerator.

Mustard (*la moutarde*)
Always keep a large pot of Dijon-style mustard at hand.

Nuts (*les noix*; *les noisettes*; *les amandes*)
Keep walnuts, hazelnuts and almonds frozen for freshness.

Oil (*l'huile*)
For salad dressing I use either olive oil, or ½ peanut oil and ½ olive oil, or walnut oil. For cooking, I mostly use peanut oil. Many good brands of walnut oil and olive oil are available. Experiment

with them. Buy your favourite and keep it always in closed dark bottles. Refrigerate if you use it slowly.

Orange-flower water (*l'eau de fleurs d'oranger*)
This flavouring is used with fresh cheese or in desserts. It is available in dark blue bottles in specialty shops and some chemists (because it is supposed to calm nerves and put angry babies to sleep).

Pork caul (*la crépine*)
This thin, fatty membrane is sold by the kilo/pound in some butcher shops. If you cannot find it, substitute thin slices of streaky bacon. It is used for *caillettes* and to cover terrines.

Salt (*le sel*)
Kosher salt is coarse and tasty; I use it with *pot-au-feu* and also in cooking. *Sel gros* (rough sea salt) is excellent for cooking and available at some shops, but tends to be expensive. Since the amount of salt used depends on individual preference, I recommend tasting each dish at least twice to check the seasoning adequately.

Shallots
Available in many markets and supermarkets, they should always be kept on hand. They store well if they are kept in a dry part of your kitchen.

Stock
Use vegetable stock or a simple meat stock made by cooking bones and herbs in salted water, unless otherwise specified.

Vermouth
Dry white vermouth is good in sauces. The sweet red vermouth is acceptable, too. Take a sip of your vermouth before using, since cooking intensifies its flavour – good or bad.

Vinegar (*le vinaigre*)
Whether red or white, wine vinegar is available everywhere. Find a kind you like and keep a few bottles on hand. We use mainly red wine vinegar, preferably from an old wine.

Wine (*le vin*)
I use hearty red Burgundy to make stews and either a dry or sweet white wine or a dry or sweet white vermouth for fish, lamb or chicken sauces. Always taste before using and keep a few bottles of your favourite wines in your kitchen for cooking.

Les Herbes et les Épices
Herbs and spices

All the recipes in this book are made with fresh herbs unless stated otherwise. If fresh herbs are unavailable, use approximately ⅓ the quantity dried.

Aniseed (*les graines d'anis*)
Anise has a flavour somewhat like that of liquorice. The seeds are used in confectionery and pastry or with fish.

Bay leaf (*le laurier*)
Use it in stews (*boeuf bourguignonne*) and sauces, with fish and rice (*riz aux herbes*), and with cooked fruits (*fruits cuits au vin*).

Capers (*les câpres*)
Capers are the buds of the caper bush. They are kept in vinegar or salt and used in hors-d'oeuvres, with meat and in sauces.

Cayenne pepper
Pungent and lively.

Chives (*la ciboulette*)
Use the narrow big leaves, finely chopped, in omelettes and with vegetables and *fromage frais* (*claqueret*).

Clove (*le clou de girofle*)
Stick one clove into a large onion, sauté the onion on all sides, and add it to soups and stews.

Coriander seeds (*le coriandre*)
The round seeds of coriander look like peppercorns. This spice must be used with discretion because it is powerful. It is used in marinades and with pork.

Ginger (*le gingembre*)
Widely available, it was used often in old recipes, and *nouvelle cuisine* has fallen in love with it.

Mint (*la menthe*)
This is used in salads, with fish and as a garnish with strawberries or custard. Brewed as tea, it is supposed to rekindle an honest man's passion and a pretty woman's vigour.

Nutmeg (*les noix de muscade*)
Buy whole nutmeg and grate it when needed at the last moment with a sharp knife. Use in sauces with fish and meat.

Parsley (*le persil*)
This is the most commonly used of all herbs. Italian parsley, flat-leaved, is the most savoury and will keep in a plastic bag in the refrigerator. Because parsley is rich in vitamins A and C, which heat destroys, add it, finely chopped, at the last minute. Try to grow it (you might have a hanging basket in the kitchen), since there is a constant use for it – sprinkled on black olives, in omelettes, in sauces and with most meat and fish dishes. Always chop it as finely as possible so that it is almost a paste.

Pepper (*le poivre*)
White pepper made from the ripe berries of the pepper plant has a slightly milder flavour than the black, which is made from the dried, underripe berries. But the major difference is colour – add white pepper to dishes that should have a pale colour and black to others. Peppercorns are sometimes added to a simmering liquid and then removed when the dish is done. For sprinkling, always use peppercorns to make freshly ground pepper.

Saffron (*la safran*)

Use the stamens of Spanish saffron only. More expensive than the powdered kind, but well worth it.

Les Soupes

Soups

For centuries, soup was the core of a Burgundian meal. It was dinner as well as breakfast until World War I, when women decided that coffee and milk should replace it in the morning. *Faire la soupe* meant 'to cook dinner', and *venez souper* meant 'Come for dinner'. Every cook in Burgundy had a rich repertory of soups. Every woman learned how to create rich blends of flavours with ingredients as varied as plain sorrel, delicate crayfish and wild mushrooms.

Vegetable soups are prepared with leeks, turnips, asparagus, pumpkin, chestnuts and sorrel, often sautéed in butter and enriched with cream and egg yolks. *La porée à la ribelette* is the most famous. Vegetable purées – carrots, cauliflower, lentils, red kidney beans and turnips – are often served with *croûtons*.

Cereal soups are made with corn meal, barley, oatmeal or chestnut flour; *la soupe aux gaudes* is the classic among them.

The *mitonnées* are vegetable or meat soups in which pieces of bread are soaked to thicken the broth. The celebrated *gratinée lyonnaise* is the most sumptuous of them.

And then there are soups that are somewhere between stews and soups, such as *pochouse* and *potée*, and soups that are unique, such as the soup prepared with slices of thick custard of egg served with a hot broth, or the curious blend of frogs, leeks and turnips. Also somewhat strange are poached eggs sprinkled with truffles. There is a thick soup made with chicken and crayfish enriched with cream, and, finally, the beloved wine-cropper soup.

Most of the recipes included here from this rich repertoire will make delicious lunches as well as first-course dishes.

Potage de Porée à la Ribelette de Lard

A leek and potato soup seasoned with sautéd onions and pork, and served with croûtons

One of the oldest recipes in Burgundy, this is the kind of soup that evokes images of old copper dishes, a cat asleep by a high roaring fire and waxed oak furniture.

For 8 people

5 leeks, only the white part, chopped
40 g/1½ oz unsalted butter
1.4 l/2⅖ pt water
6 potatoes, peeled and diced
salt

freshly ground black pepper
85 g/3 oz lean salt pork, diced
2 onions, peeled and sliced
8 *croûtons*, fried in peanut oil and butter

Cook the leeks in the butter for a few minutes over low heat. When they are soft, add the water and potatoes, salt and pepper, and cook slowly.

After 30 minutes, sauté the salt pork and onions and add to the soup. Serve with *croûtons*.

Soupe à l'Oeuf

Broth served with an egg-yolk and stock custard

This Lyon speciality can be prepared with a beef or chicken stock, highly seasoned. It is a perfect lunch dish followed by a green salad and a light dessert.

For 8 people

8 egg yolks
1.8 l/3⅕ pt strong beef (or chicken) stock

Beat the egg yolks until foamy and slowly add 450 ml/16 fl oz of the stock while stirring. Pass through a sieve into a shallow dish.

Place the dish over a pan of boiling water and cook until the mixture is thick. Remove the dish from the heat and let it cool.

Heat the remaining broth. Cut the custard into slices. Place a slice in each soup plate and pour the hot stock over it. Serve at once.

Soupe à la Bressane

A tomato and chicken soup

Delicious and invigorating, this soup was traditionally prepared for weddings and brought to the bride's bedroom in the middle of her wedding night.

For 8 people

1 chicken back, neck and gizzard	2 onions, peeled and sliced
1 onion, peeled and chopped	2 tbsp lard
1 whole clove	6 tomatoes, quartered
1 celery stalk, chopped	2 egg yolks
5 peppercorns	3 tbsp double cream
thyme	3 tbsp finely chopped fresh herbs

Cover the chicken back, neck and gizzard with cold water. Bring to a boil, stirring from time to time. After 10 minutes, add the chopped onion, clove, celery, peppercorns and thyme. Cook, uncovered, for 1 hour. Strain through a sieve.

Sauté the sliced onions in the lard. Add the tomatoes and cook, covered, for 10 minutes. Pass the onions and tomatoes through a sieve into the hot chicken stock and cook for 20 minutes.

Meanwhile, whip the egg yolks and the cream. Remove the stock from the heat and stir in the egg mixture. Return to the burner over low heat, stirring vigorously for 5 minutes.

Sprinkle with fresh herbs and serve.

Soupe Arlequin

A rich vegetable soup with cream

A wonderful soup served cold, warm or hot.

For 8 people

2 small leeks, shredded (or ½
    onion, ½ spring onion)
25 g/1 oz unsalted butter
1 celery stalk, finely chopped
170 g/6 oz diced potatoes
400 g/14 oz diced peeled pumpkin
salt

freshly ground black pepper
freshly grated nutmeg
1.4 l/2⅖ pt milk
1 egg yolk
450 ml/16 fl oz double cream
1 tbsp chopped chives

Sauté the leeks in butter until soft. Add the celery and potatoes.
Sauté for 5 minutes longer. Pour into a saucepan with the pumpkin,
salt, pepper, nutmeg and milk and cook for 20 minutes. Pass
through a blender or food processor. Add the egg yolk and cream.
Return to the saucepan and reheat gently. Check the seasoning,
since pumpkin is very bland. Sprinkle with chives and serve.

Soupe au Chou

A cabbage, carrot and turnip soup enriched with cream and egg yolks

A wonderful soup. Enjoy it often with either of the two garnishes.

For 8 people

25 g/1 oz unsalted butter
1 tbsp vegetable oil
170 g/6 oz lean salt pork, finely
    chopped
1 onion, peeled and finely chopped
1 small cabbage (1.25 kg/3 lb),
    trimmed and coarsely chopped

4 carrots, peeled and quartered
2 turnips, peeled and quartered
salt
5 peppercorns, crushed

··············· Garnish I ···············	·············· Garnish II ··············
115 ml/4 fl oz single cream	4 garlic cloves, peeled and crushed
2 egg yolks	85 g/3 oz pork fat, finely chopped
	2 tbsp country ham, chopped

Heat the butter and oil and cook the salt pork over medium heat for about 3 minutes. Add the minced onion and sauté 3 minutes longer, then add the cabbage, carrots and turnips. Cook for 5 minutes, stirring from time to time, and sprinkle with salt and the crushed peppercorns. Add 1.8 l/3⅕ pt boiling water, then lower the heat. Simmer uncovered for 1½ hours.

Just before serving, add Garnish I. Beat the cream and egg yolks in a bowl and pour into the hot soup, stirring. Check the seasoning and serve.

For a heartier version, add Garnish II. Place the garlic and pork fat in a food processor or a mortar and make a thick paste. Add to the hot soup, along with the chopped ham, just before serving.

Soupe au Fromage I

A smooth cheese soup

For 8 people

1.6 l/2¾ pt chicken stock	70 g/2½ oz breadcrumbs
5 eggs	pinch of nutmeg
8 tsp grated Parmesan, Gruyère or Romano cheese	5 tsp finely chopped chives (or chervil)

Bring the stock to a boil. Meanwhile, beat the eggs, cheese, breadcrumbs and nutmeg together. Remove the pan from the burner and slowly beat some of the stock into the egg mixture; then slowly stir the egg mixture into the stock pan. Check the seasoning and correct. Sprinkle with the herbs and serve.

Soupe au Fromage II

A hearty cheese soup

For 8 people

8 potatoes, peeled and diced
2 large onions, peeled and
  chopped
1.8 l/3⅕ pt beef stock
450 g/1 lb Gruyère cheese, grated
2 tbsp grated Parmesan cheese
2 tbsp chopped chives

salt
freshly ground black pepper
225 ml/8 fl oz dry white wine
2 tbsp finely chopped parsley
5 slices of bread, diced
40 g/1½ oz unsalted butter

Prepare the vegetables while you bring the stock to a boil. Cook
them in the stock for 20 minutes. Crush them with a fork; they
should not be too smooth. Stir in the cheese and chives and reheat
on a low flame until the mixture is thicker. Season carefully. Pour
in the wine. Fry the bread dices in butter and serve the soup
sprinkled with parsley and *croûtons*.

La Soupe au Potiron

Pumpkin soup

La soupe au potiron tout rond (made with the very round French
cousin of the pumpkin) is a favourite in Burgundy. I have chosen
two of the most interesting versions: one spectacular and rich, in
the spirit of the Lyon Great Cook masters, and the other simpler,
easier.

For 8 people

·············· I · The rich version ··············

140 g/5 oz peeled, finely chopped
  shallots (or onions)
70 g/2½ oz unsalted butter
255 g/9 oz diced bread, toasted
salt
freshly ground black pepper

170 g/6 oz grated cheese (Gruyère,
  Parmesan or Romano)
1 2.75-kg/6-lb pumpkin
1.1 l/2 pt single cream
freshly grated nutmeg
2 bay leaves

Cook the shallots in 40 g/1½ oz of butter over low heat for 10 minutes. Add the bread and cook for 2 minutes longer. Sprinkle with salt and pepper and add the cheese. Set aside.

Preheat the oven to 200°C/400°F/Gas Mark 6.

Cut the top off the pumpkin with a strong, sharp knife. Reserve the lid. Remove all the seeds with a long-handled spoon or a wide knife. Sprinkle salt over both the inside and the outside of the pumpkin. Fill with the mixture of shallot, bread and cheese. Stir in the cream, salt, pepper, nutmeg and bay leaves. Replace the lid on top of the pumpkin.

Bake the filled pumpkin on a large ovenproof dish for 2 hours. Twice, while it is cooking, lift the top and stir vigorously, reaching into the pumpkin with a long-handled spoon.

When you are ready to serve, place the pumpkin over a folded napkin on a shallow serving plate. Check the seasoning, stir carefully, add the remaining butter and serve.

········ II · The simpler, lighter version ········

1 2.75-kg/6-lb pumpkin (or acorn, hubbard or butternut squash)
salt
freshly ground black pepper
2 bay leaves
1 large onion, studded with 1 clove
1.1 1/2 pt single cream

55 g/2 oz unsalted butter
170 g/6 oz diced bread, toasted
55 g/2 oz grated cheese (Gruyère, Parmesan or Romano)
2 tbsp finely chopped chives
aniseed
grated nutmeg

Remove the seeds of the pumpkin. Scoop out all the flesh, dice it, and boil it in a large pot of salted water with pepper, bay leaves and the onion. Drain it carefully. Purée it in a blender or a food processor. Add the cream and pour into a saucepan. Simmer for 20 minutes, uncovered. Check the seasonings – it must be highly seasoned – and add the butter.

Serve, sprinkled with the diced bread, grated cheese, chives, aniseed and a little grated nutmeg.

Soupe au Riz et au Chou

A rice and cabbage soup

A very hearty country soup I find easy to prepare in advance and reheat for chilly winter evenings.

For 8 people

140 g/5 oz cooked rice	1.4 l/2⅖ pt hot chicken or beef
900 g/2 lb cabbage, trimmed and	stock, well seasoned
quartered	salt
2 onions, peeled and chopped	freshly ground black pepper
25 g/1 oz unsalted butter	3 tbsp grated Gruyère cheese

Cook the rice and cabbage in salted water for 1 hour. Discard the water. Sauté the onions in hot butter for 5 minutes. Add to the rice and cabbage, then pour in the hot stock and bring to a boil. Season. Pass through a blender or a Moulinex mill. Sprinkle with grated cheese and serve.

Soupe au Vin

A rich wine and vegetable soup

This hearty soup does wonders on cold winter nights.

For 8 people

2 big onions, peeled and sliced	1 tbsp vegetable oil
3 carrots, peeled and diced	450 ml/16 fl oz hearty red wine
3 pink turnips (or 1 big waxy	1.4 l/2⅖ pt chicken stock
yellow one), peeled and diced	salt
2 leeks (or 2 white onions),	freshly ground black pepper
chopped	1 tbsp arrowroot
25 g/1 oz unsalted butter	2 tbsp finely chopped chives

Sauté the vegetables in butter and oil over medium heat for 5 minutes, stirring from time to time. Add the wine and bring to a boil, uncovered. Simmer for 20 minutes. Add the stock. Simmer for 10 minutes more, stir, and add salt and pepper. Dissolve the arrowroot in 3 tablespoons of water, then stir it into the soup. Simmer for 3 minutes, sprinkle with chives and serve.

La Soupe aux Gaudes

A smooth chicken soup with cream and corn meal

Although sweetcorn, or maize, was first used by the American Indians, it has been made into soups in Europe in regions where poor harvests or poverty made wheat a luxury item.

In Burgundy, men who enjoyed their corn soups were traditionally called 'yellow belts' and corn was called *gaudes*. This smooth soup should be served before a pungent dish such as *Travers de Porc aux Herbes* (p. 151).

For 8 people

6 yellow onions, peeled and thinly sliced
25 g/1 oz unsalted butter
1 tbsp vegetable oil
225 g/8 oz fine corn (maize) meal
900 ml/1⅗ pt chicken stock (or milk)

900 ml/1⅗ pt cream (single or double)
salt
freshly grated nutmeg
freshly ground white pepper
3 tbsp finely chopped chives or spring onions

Sauté the onions in butter and oil in a large frying-pan. Sprinkle them with a little salt and cook gently until soft and pale brown.

Pour the corn meal into a bowl filled with half of the stock (or milk). Stir, and add the rest of the stock. Beat carefully and add to the onions. Simmer for 30 minutes, then add the cream, salt, nutmeg and pepper. Check the seasoning.

Sprinkle with the fresh chives and serve at once.

Soupe Dauphinoise
An onion, carrot, turnip, sorrel soup enriched with cream

A fragrant velvety soup perfect for a light lunch or to start an elegant dinner.

For 8 people

2 veal bones
bouquet garni
85 g/3 oz unsalted butter
1 tbsp vegetable oil
3 onions, peeled and finely
　chopped
2 leeks (or 2 white onions),
　chopped
6 carrots, peeled and diced
2 turnips, peeled and diced

salt
freshly ground pepper
200 g/7 oz sorrel (or watercress),
　finely shredded
4 tbsp single cream
5 slices of bread (crusts removed),
　diced, and fried in 55 g/2 oz
　unsalted butter and 1 tbsp
　vegetable oil (optional)

Bring 1.8 l/3⅕ pt of water, bones and bouquet garni to a boil and continue to boil, uncovered, for 1 hour.

Heat half the butter and the oil in a large heavy-bottomed pan and sauté the onions, leeks, carrots and turnips for a few minutes, stirring. Add the hot stock and the seasonings and simmer for 30 minutes. Heat the remaining butter and sauté the sorrel (or watercress) for 5 minutes. Add to the soup. Discard the bones and bouquet garni. Stir in the cream, and check the seasoning. Pour into a warmed soup tureen and serve at once. For a richer soup, add *croûtons*.

Soupe Nevers
An unusual soup with Brussels sprouts

Named for Nevers, the city it comes from, this soup is also a never-ending delight with its abundance of flavours.

For 8 people

36 Brussels sprouts, trimmed and
 quartered
4 carrots, peeled and diced
40 g/1½ oz unsalted butter
1 tbsp vegetable oil

1.8 l/3⅕ pt chicken stock, hot
salt
freshly ground black pepper
3 tbsp finely chopped chives (or
 parsley or chervil)

Sauté the vegetables in the butter and oil, stirring for 5 minutes.
Pour them into a large saucepan. Add the hot stock and bring to a
boil. Cook for 35 minutes. Add salt and pepper, sprinkle with the
fresh herbs and serve at once. The Brussels sprouts should not be
overcooked.

Soupe Savoyarde

A hearty vegetable, cheese and salami soup

Made with fresh vegetables, simmered with bacon and served with
a crisp garnish, this soup is superb as a main dish for lunch on a
cold winter day.

For 8 people

25 g/1 oz unsalted butter
2 tbsp vegetable oil
5 carrots, peeled and diced
4 pink turnips, peeled and diced
3 leeks (or 3 white onions), peeled
 and chopped
1 small green cabbage, finely
 chopped
3 stalks celery, peeled and finely
 chopped
3 potatoes, peeled and diced
85 g/3 oz streaky bacon, chopped

1.4 l/2⅖ pt boiling water
225 ml/8 fl oz warm milk
salt
freshly ground black pepper
8 slices good bread, crusts
 removed
25 g/1 oz unsalted butter
170 g/6 oz Gruyère cheese
10 slices good Italian or Danish
 salami
2 tbsp chervil (or spring onions),
 finely chopped

Heat the butter and oil in a heavy frying-pan. Add the vegetables
and cook over moderate heat for 15 minutes, stirring. Add the
bacon and cover with the boiling water and milk. Bring to a boil.
Add salt and pepper and simmer for 30 minutes.

Butter the slices of bread, sprinkle them with cheese, cover with salami and then a little more cheese and grill them for 3 minutes, until golden. Cut them diagonally in half.

Sprinkle the soup with chervil and float the cheese toast on top. Or place a slice of toast in the bottom of individual soup bowls and pour the warm soup over it, then sprinkle with chervil and serve.

Soupe Verte
A creamy vegetable soup

A fresh and rather fancy soup, delicious whether you make it with sorrel, spinach or watercress (my favourite is sorrel). It can be eaten cold or warm.

For 8 people

1 kg/2½ lb sorrel, spinach or watercress, washed and dried (you may use ½ spinach and ½ sorrel)	freshly ground black pepper
	3 egg yolks
	225 ml/8 fl oz double cream
	freshly grated nutmeg
40 g/1½ oz unsalted butter	1 tbsp finely chopped chervil
1 large onion, finely chopped	8 slices good bread, cubed and
1.4 l/2⅖ pt chicken stock	fried in butter (optional)
salt	

Wash the sorrel (or spinach or watercress) under cold water and dry well.

Heat the butter in a heavy-bottomed pan, add the onion and cook for 3 minutes. Add the greens and cook for 5 minutes. Bring the stock to a boil, season with salt and pepper and then add the greens. Simmer for 10 minutes.

Drain the greens and put them through a food processor or a blender. Meanwhile, blend the egg yolks, cream and nutmeg in a large bowl and add the boiling stock, one cup at a time, stirring constantly. Next, stir in the purée. Pour the whole mixture into a saucepan and reheat very gently over low heat; do not boil. Check the seasoning and sprinkle with chervil. Add *croûtons* if you want a richer soup.

Les Hors-d'Oeuvres
Appetizers

Meals are carefully planned in Burgundy, and as a rule, since the main course is indeed the most serious part of the meal, hors-d'oeuvres are meant to be inviting, provocative, amusing, but always discreet so as not to compete with or overshadow what is to follow.

There are cold hors-d'oeuvres, such as *cerneaux* – fresh green walnuts kept for a few days in salt, pepper and wine vinegar, and nibbled with a glass of good red wine. There are plump *cèpe* mushrooms marinated in oil, vinegar, garlic and herbs, and cold fritters of little wild mushrooms. There are all kinds of pork delicacies: piles of sausages, dried, cured, smoked; big tripe sausages, simmered in white wine; small grilled chitterlings; crispy *gratons* made with the residue of fried pork fat; pâtés made of veal and sweetbread, eel, chicken liver, hare. There is tender asparagus served with a mustard cream-and-herb sauce.

There are warm pies: a leek tart, a rich meat pie, a thick pancake stuffed with cheese, egg and rum. There are stews of snails, there is a *rigodon* pastry made with diced ham and *corniottes* (little pouches filled with egg and cream), and finally, the most famous of all, *la gougère*, the best friend of red Burgundy wines.

Bersaudes

A highly tasty pork spread

For 8 people

1.8 kg/4 lb lean salt pork, cut into very small dice	2 bay leaves
25 g/1 oz lard	1 garlic clove, peeled and chopped
2 tsp thyme	1 onion, peeled and chopped
	salt
	freshly ground black pepper

Sauté the pork in the lard until crisp. Drain.

Place the pork in a saucepan with the thyme, bay leaves, garlic and onion, cover with cold water and cook over medium heat for 3 hours, covered. Drain. Season with black pepper. Place the mixture in pots and cover with lard.

Delicious on hot toast as an appetizer with a glass of cool white or rosé wine.

Crépinette aux Marrons

Fried cakes of pork, chestnuts and spices

These crisp little patties are perfect as an hors-d'oeuvre, warm or cold, in a buffet or to accompany a plain pork roast.

You will find chestnuts already peeled and blanched in cans if you are reluctant to go to the trouble of boiling and peeling them.

For 8 people

900 g/2 lb lean salt pork or country ham with some fat, finely chopped	1 tsp ground coriander
	450 g/1 lb cooked, peeled chestnuts, chopped
4 shallots, peeled and finely chopped	16 slices of streaky bacon (or one large pork caul cut in pieces)
6 tbsp finely chopped parsley	115 g/4 oz unsalted butter
salt	3 tbsp vegetable oil
freshly ground black pepper	

29

Mix the pork, shallots, half of the parsley, salt, pepper and coriander together. Add the chestnuts. You must have a finely ground mixture. Use a blender if you cannot chop it fine enough.

Place one-sixteenth of this mixture on a piece of bacon (or caul) and wrap it into a tight little ball. Flatten it with the palm of your hand so it will cook more evenly.

Heat the butter and oil in a large frying-pan. Sauté the patties, five or six at a time, for 15 minutes over medium heat, turning with a spatula or a pair of tongs.

Sprinkle with pepper and the remaining parsley.

Délices d'Endives
Chicory and ham, chopped and cooked with cream in individual dishes, then topped with a poached egg

Prepared in a few minutes, this is a lovely lunch dish or an elegant first course for a more elaborate meal. It should be eaten with a spoon.

For 8 people

4 large chicories or 8 small ones, trimmed and chopped or sliced	pinch of sugar
juice of 1 lemon	freshly ground black pepper
100 g/3½ oz unsalted butter	4 tsp single cream
1 large onion, peeled and finely chopped	pinch of nutmeg
salt	4 large slices country ham or smoked ham, shredded
	8 eggs

Trim and slice the chicory leaves. Bring a pot of salted water to a boil, add the lemon juice and the chicory and cook for about 5 minutes. Drain carefully.

Preheat the oven to 200°C/400°F/Gas Mark 6.

Put 55 g/2 oz of the butter in a saucepan, add the onion and cover. Cook for about 5 minutes over low heat. Add the chicory, salt, sugar, pepper, cream and nutmeg. Cover and simmer for 20 minutes. Remove the lid and cook for 5 minutes more, stirring. Add the shredded ham.

Pour the mixture into eight small ramekins or individual oven-proof dishes. Break an egg into the centre of each dish. Dot with the remaining butter, sprinkle with salt and bake for 5 minutes or until just set. Serve at once.

L'Enchaud

Patties of pork, herb and eggs

These can be served warm, but I find them tastier cold. A welcome addition to a picnic or a buffet meal.

For 8 people

1.25 kg/3 lb pork tenderloin (use 2 pieces if it is small)
25 g/1 oz unsalted butter
1 clove garlic
115 g/4 oz chopped pork or chicken liver
225 g/8 oz chopped lean salt pork (or country ham)
4 shallots (or small onions), peeled and chopped
2 garlic cloves, peeled and chopped

2 slices of bread, dipped in water, then squeezed
2 beaten eggs
3 tbsp finely chopped parsley
2 tbsp brandy
2 tsp chopped sage (or savory)
salt
freshly ground black pepper
1 lemon, halved
slices of streaky bacon (enough to cover the meat)
3 bay leaves
115 ml/4 fl oz stock

Preheat the oven to 190°C/375°F/Gas Mark 5.

Split the pork tenderloin lengthwise. Flatten each piece with a cleaver. Rub both sides with butter and garlic.

Put the chopped meats, shallots, garlic and bread into a large bowl. Stir in the eggs, parsley, brandy and sage. Season with salt, pepper, and more sage or savory, if needed. The mixture must be very pungent. Place some in the centre of each flattened piece of pork and roll it as you would a Swiss roll. Tie each roll with a string. Rub the surface with lemon, and wrap each roll in bacon strips. Place the rolls in an oiled dish, top with the bay leaves and bake for 2 hours, basting with stock from time to time. Let cool until the next day and slice before serving.

There is another version of *enchaud* that must be served warm. Slice open the pork loin in the centre, from top to bottom, leaving the sides untouched, creating a pocket.

Sauté the shallots, salt pork, garlic and parsley in butter for a few minutes. Add the eggs and wrap this stuffing with a slice of ham, then slide it into the pocket in the centre of the meat.

Wrap the piece of pork with the caul or slices of streaky bacon and bake for 2 hours at 180°C/350°F/Gas Mark 4. Meanwhile, peel and core 8 apples. Put 1 clove and 5 g/¼ oz unsalted butter in each apple and place them around the pork after 1 hour of cooking.

Serve warm.

Filets de Harengs

Marinated kippered herring fillets

These are easy to prepare and are used in salads with warm potatoes. They will keep, covered, in the refrigerator for at least one week.

3 thick kippered herring fillets	3 bay leaves
2 onions, peeled and sliced	10 peppercorns
1 carrot, peeled and sliced	olive oil
1 sliced lemon	

Place the herring fillets in the bottom of a dish. Cover with the onions, carrots, lemon, bay leaves, peppercorns and oil. Wrap in foil and refrigerate or leave in a cool place to marinate for at least two days before tasting.

Fricandeau

Chicken liver, pork and herb-spiced patties

These are variations on a theme found in each province of France – *gayettes, caillettes, crépinettes* – each housewife makes her very own creation. These are what I found to be the liveliest *fricandeau* in Burgundy. They are eaten warm but can be kept in an earthenware pot and used cold in summer with a little green salad.

For 8 people

225 g/8 oz chicken livers (or pork liver)
25 g/1 oz unsalted butter
3 shallots, peeled and chopped
225 g/8 oz lean salt pork, finely chopped
100 g/3½ oz sorrel leaves (or spinach), shredded
1 garlic clove, peeled and crushed

4 tbsp finely chopped parsley
1 tbsp chopped thyme
pinch of clove
2 tsp chopped sage
2 tbsp coarsely chopped pistachio nuts
about 20 slices of streaky bacon
85 g/3 oz lard, or more if needed

Sauté the chicken livers for a few minutes in butter, chop them, and set aside. Sauté shallots for a few minutes. Mix all the ingredients except the bacon and lard and form into egg-size balls. Flatten with your hands and tightly wrap each patty in slices of bacon.

Melt the lard in a large frying-pan and sauté the patties on all sides, using a spatula to turn them. After 5 minutes cover the pan and cook for 1 hour. Serve at once or let cool and put in an earthenware pot. Pour the cooking fat over the patties and store in a cool place. Serve cold with a bitter green salad of dandelion, endive or watercress.

Sometimes the little dumplings are dipped in beaten egg, rolled in breadcrumbs and baked at 180°C/350°F/Gas Mark 4 for 1 hour.

Gâteau de Foies Blonds

Chicken-liver Soufflé

This light chicken-liver soufflé is at its best when made with fresh Bressan chicken livers; in order to replace that unobtainable treat here, I have decided to marinate the livers. A delicious first course served in individual dishes, or a good luncheon main course, it is often served unmoulded but then requires ten eggs. I find this version lighter.

For 8 people

8 fresh chicken livers	85 g/3 oz lean salt pork, finely
115 ml/4 fl oz good sherry or port	diced
1 tbsp vegetable oil	thyme
5 g/¼ oz unsalted butter	4 tbsp double cream
1 tbsp flour	1 garlic clove, peeled
salt	15 g/½ oz finely chopped parsley
freshly ground black pepper	3 eggs, separated
3 shallots, finely chopped	freshly grated nutmeg

Rinse and dry the livers. Put them in a bowl, cover with sherry (or port), and marinate for at least 2 hours.

Heat the oil and butter in a heavy frying-pan. Drain the livers and sprinkle them with flour, salt and pepper and sauté them in the butter and oil. Add the shallots and salt pork and cook over low heat for 10 minutes, turning the livers with tongs from time to time.

Sprinkle with thyme and the marinade, add cream, garlic and parsley. Cook a few more minutes, and remove from the heat to cool.

Preheat the oven to 180°C/350°F/Gas Mark 4.

Put the cooled mixture in a blender or food processor with the egg yolks and nutmeg and make a thick paste. Put into a bowl.

Beat the egg whites until stiff and gently fold them into the liver mixture. Check the seasonings. The mixture must be highly flavoured and heavy on pepper and nutmeg.

Pour into a buttered soufflé dish and place the dish in a large ovenproof pan. Add hot water to the pan to come halfway up the side of the dish. Cover with foil and bake for 45–60 minutes.

Serve in its own dish with a bowl of tomato *coulis* (p. 58) or a bowl of onion purée. A strong red wine or a chilled dry white wine goes well with this.

La Gougère
A seasoned cheese pastry

This glorious cheese hors-d'oeuvre tastes and smells as wonderful as it looks. It can be made into a fluffy golden crown or individual little puffs.

You can have it as an appetizer with a chilled Kir (p. 259), as a main course for lunch, or with a good red wine to start an important meal. It was originally eaten only to enhance the taste of Burgundy wines.

For 8 people

170 ml/6 fl oz milk
170 ml/6 fl oz water
115 g/4 oz unsalted butter
155 g/5½ oz plain flour
salt
cayenne pepper
freshly ground white pepper

freshly grated nutmeg
6 large eggs
200 g/7 oz Gruyère cheese, cut
   into 6-mm/¼-in. dice
1 tbsp Dijon-style mustard
1 tbsp milk

Preheat the oven to 200°C/400°F/Gas Mark 6.

Place the milk and water in a saucepan and bring to a boil; add the butter. Remove from the heat and stir in the flour, salt, cayenne, pepper and nutmeg all at once. Stir vigorously with a big wooden spoon.

After a few minutes, the mixture should come away from the sides of the pan and form a ball. Add the eggs one by one, beating with the spoon after each addition. Pour in 170 g/6 oz of the diced cheese. Taste for seasoning – *it must be highly seasoned.*

Butter a large, heavy baking sheet and, with a tablespoon, pile the dough high in the shape of a 23-cm/9-in. wide crown with a 5-cm/2-in. hole in the centre, or fill buttered tins with 2 tablespoons of dough in each mould, if you prefer individual puffs.

Smooth the top, brush lightly with milk and sprinkle with the remaining diced cheese.

Bake the crown for 45 minutes, the little puffs for 20 minutes. Do *not* open the oven door during the baking.

After baking, open the door and leave the *gougère* in the oven for 5 minutes. It should then be firm to the touch, though it will collapse a little when out of the oven.

Serve warm or lukewarm with a dry white wine, a strong rosé or a hearty red wine.

Jambon Persillé

Aspic of ham, parsley, garlic and vinegar

A traditional part of New Year's Eve or Easter dinner, this is also glorious for a buffet or a summer lunch. Make large quantities of it, since it will keep a week in the refrigerator.

For 20–25 people

1 4.5-kg/10-lb mild-cured butt or ready-to-cook ham, with bone in and most of the fat and rind removed

1–1.25 kg/2–3 lb veal bones (or a 10-cm/4-in. piece of veal knuckle)

1 calf's foot, split

3 large onions, each studded with 2 cloves

8 carrots

1 garlic clove

10 peppercorns

3 tbsp tarragon

3 tbsp thyme

900 ml/1⅗ pt dry white wine

680 ml/1⅕ pt stock

3 egg whites, beaten

300 g/10½ oz parsley, finely cut with scissors

8 tbsp wine vinegar

8 garlic cloves, peeled and finely chopped

salt

freshly ground black pepper

Place the ham in a large pan with the veal bones, calf's foot, onions, carrots, garlic clove, peppercorns, tarragon, thyme, wine, stock and enough water to cover by 2.5 cm/1 in. Bring to the boiling point, reduce the heat and simmer covered for 5 hours. (You may prefer, after it has reached the boiling point, to cover it with a piece of foil and bake it on a middle shelf in the oven at 170°C/325°F/Gas Mark 3 for about 4 hours.)

When the ham is cooked and you can easily pierce it with a fork, remove from the heat and let it cool completely in the stock for about 1 hour.

Discard the veal bones and calf's foot. Remove the ham from the pan and place it on a board or a table. Remove the bone, then tear the meat with your fingers, shredding it into small pieces and discarding any gristle you may find. Put the ham in a bowl, mix it vigorously with a fork and set aside.

Reduce the stock over a high heat to about 3 1/6⅔ pt. Skim off the fat. Correct the seasoning; it should be highly flavoured. Remove the onions, crush them, and add them to the bowl of ham. Pass the rest of the stock through a sieve covered with 2 or 3 layers of cheesecloth.

Add the beaten egg whites to the stock and bring to a boil, stirring. Simmer for 15 minutes, remove from the heat, and let cool. The stock should be clear. Pour one-third of it into a 4.5-1/8-pt porcelain bowl. Sprinkle with a thin layer of parsley, then add a layer of ham, then vinegar, chopped garlic, salt and pepper. Add a little stock and repeat until all the ham, parsley, vinegar and garlic are in the bowl, ending with a layer of parsley. Press the mixture hard with your hands, add a little more stock and cover with a plate weighted with a large can. Chill for at least 24 hours. Chill the rest of the stock in a separate bowl.

Serve in its own mould, or if you prefer, unmould it on to a large flat serving dish, slice and serve with some of the chopped aspic (congealed stock) spread around it as garnish.

Note: In Burgundy the rind and outer layer of fat are chopped and added to the dish. I have omitted them from the recipe because I have noticed that they are always pushed aside by my guests, but you may add them if you like their crunchy texture and taste.

Petites Brochettes

Little cubes of cheese and ham dipped in egg and breadcrumbs and deep-fried

Wonderful for children or for buffets and prepared in a jiffy, these come from the Jura and should be served with a chilled white wine.

For 8 people

8 slices country or plain ham, cut into 5-cm/2-in. strips
680 g/1½ lb Gruyère cheese, cut into 2.5-cm/1-in. cubes
2 eggs, beaten with 1 tbsp

vegetable oil and 1 tbsp mustard
140 g/5 oz breadcrumbs
about 450 ml/16 fl oz oil for deep-frying

Wrap the strips of ham over the cheese cubes. Dip into the beaten egg mixture, then roll in the breadcrumbs. Using 8 metal skewers, put 6 cubes on each skewer.

Heat the oil until it is very hot and deep-fry for about 1 minute, or until golden. The cheese should be partially melted.

Drain on paper towels, sprinkle with pepper and serve at once with a tossed green salad.

Les Petits Paniers

Warm dumplings, some stuffed with chopped beef, vegetables, herbs and eggs, some with cream and onion

A good first course, these little baskets are also perfect for a picnic or a buffet.

For 8 people

·············· Dough ··············

340 g/12 oz plain flour
2 small eggs
115 g/4 oz unsalted butter, melted

2 tbsp vegetable oil
salt

·············· Filling I ··············

2 tbsp vegetable oil
2 shallots, peeled and finely
   chopped
½ green pepper, chopped
5 mint (or tarragon) leaves,
   chopped

225 g/8 oz chopped beef
2 small egg yolks
3 tbsp spinach, cooked, drained
   and chopped
1 tbsp rice, cooked and drained
3 sprigs parsley, finely chopped

·············· Filling II ··············

6 onions, peeled and finely
   chopped
40 g/1½ oz unsalted butter
1 tsp crushed coriander seeds

4 tbsp soured cream
115 ml/4 fl oz milk
55 g/2 oz grated Gruyère cheese

Put the flour on a floured surface, add the eggs, melted butter, oil and salt, and mix. Add 3 tablespoons of water and knead until smooth. Cover with a kitchen towel and refrigerate for at least 30 minutes.

Filling I
Heat the oil and cook the shallots and green pepper for a few minutes. Add the mint or tarragon. In a large bowl, mix together the beef, shallots and green pepper, egg yolks, spinach, rice and parsley.

Filling II
Sauté the onions in the butter for a few minutes. Add the coriander and stir into the soured cream.

Preheat the oven to 200°C/400°F/Gas Mark 6.
   Roll the dough as thin as you can and cut into 13-cm/5-in. squares. Fill each square with 1½ tablespoons of stuffing. Fold the dough in half over the filling and press with your fingers all around the dumpling. Place on a buttered baking sheet, sprinkle with a little milk and grated cheese and bake for 15 minutes.

Le Régal Aillé
A garlic treat

When cooked, garlic becomes sweet and nutty and adds a superb touch to a first course. (*Régal* means a treat.)

For 8 people

6 tbsp vegetable oil
85 g/3 oz unsalted butter
50 garlic cloves (preferably red garlic), unpeeled
salt
freshly ground black pepper
340 ml/12 fl oz dry white wine
8 slices toasted bread, halved
8 tbsp finely chopped parsley and chives

Heat the oil and butter in a pan and sauté the garlic for 5 minutes.

Add salt, pepper and the wine and bring to a boil. Simmer 15 minutes, uncovered.

Pass the garlic cloves through a Moulinex mill or crush them with a fork, discarding the skins, and spread the paste on the pieces of toast. Sprinkle with the parsley and chives and serve.

Roulade au Fromage
Cheese and mint pork rolls

A lively spring dish, this is at its best when goat cheese and fresh mint are in season. It can be prepared ahead of time.

For 8 people

1.25 kg/3 lb potatoes, peeled
40 g/1½ oz goat cheese
2 tsp peppercorns, coarsely crushed
2 tsp thyme
150 g/5½ oz unsalted butter
8 13-mm-/½-in.-thick slices (about 1.1 kg/2½ lb) of pork shoulder butt (remove as much fat as possible and pound with a cleaver)
salt
10 tbsp fresh mint, cut fine with scissors
115 ml/4 fl oz warm milk
115 ml/4 fl oz single cream
3 tbsp grated Gruyère cheese

Cook the potatoes in salted water. Mix the goat cheese with pepper, thyme and 55 g/2 oz of the butter in a bowl. Sprinkle each slice of pork with salt and spread a thick layer of the cheese mixture on it. Roll each slice tightly and secure it with a piece of string. Mix 8 tablespoons of the mint with 55 g/2 oz of the butter.

Preheat oven to 190°C/375°F/Gas Mark 5.

Mash the potatoes into a purée, add the milk, cream and 25 g/1 oz of butter. Whip vigorously and put over medium heat. Add the grated cheese, stirring.

Butter an ovenproof dish. Pour the puréed potato into it. Place the pork rolls on top, then spread the mint-and-butter mixture on top. Bake for 15 minutes and dot with 15 g/½ oz of butter. Bake for 30 minutes more. Serve piping hot in its cooking dish sprinkled with the remaining mint.

Roulades au Céleri

Celery hearts wrapped in ham and baked in a cheese and mustard sauce

This is made in a jiffy and will do for a light lunch or hors-d'oeuvre.

For 8 people

8 celery hearts, cut in half lengthways	freshly ground pepper
55 g/2 oz unsalted butter	1 egg yolk
4 tbsp flour	3 tbsp single cream
450 ml/16 fl oz warm milk	1 tbsp Dijon-style mustard
2 bay leaves	8 slices good ham (boiled or country), cut in half
freshly grated nutmeg	55 g/2 oz grated Gruyère cheese
salt	2 tbsp breadcrumbs

Cook the celery hearts in boiling salted water for 30 minutes. Drain.

Melt half of the butter in a saucepan and briskly stir in the flour. Stir in the milk, bay leaves, nutmeg, salt and pepper. When the mixture thickens, beat together the egg yolk and cream and add them. Remove from the heat and add the mustard.

Preheat the oven to 180°C/350°F/Gas Mark 4.

Wrap each celery piece with a slice of ham and place them side by side in a buttered ovenproof dish. Pour the warm sauce over the ham, and sprinkle with cheese and breadcrumbs. Dot with the remaining butter and bake for 20 minutes.

Saucisson Chaud Lyonnais

Sausage with potatoes seasoned with white wine and mustard

If it is difficult to find *saucisson à cuire*, Polish kielbasa or the Italian cotechino make good replacements.

For 8 people

about 1.8 kg/4 lb *saucissons à cuire* (or kielbasa or cotechino)
1.8 kg/4 lb potatoes, boiled in their skins
4 tbsp dry white wine
2 tsp Dijon-style mustard

140 ml/5 fl oz peanut or olive oil
4 tbsp red wine vinegar
salt
freshly ground black pepper
2 tbsp chopped parsley and chives

Prick the sausages with a fork, place them in cold water and bring to a boil. Cook for 25 minutes.

Meanwhile, cook the potatoes and then, holding them in a tea-towel, peel them while warm and slice them. Place them in a warm shallow serving dish.

Mix the wine, mustard, oil, vinegar, salt and pepper and pour over the potatoes. Toss gently.

Slice the sausages, place on a serving dish, sprinkle with the parsley and chives and serve. You can also serve the sliced warm sausages with a very light *Gratin Dauphinois* (pp. 169–70).

Terrine de Canard

Duck pâté

This can be made with the addition of truffles, calf's liver, or goose liver, but the following version, though less extravagant to prepare, is one of the finest I have ever tasted. Prepare two days in advance.

For about 10 people

1 2.25-kg/5-lb duck
55 ml/2 fl oz cognac (or any other
  brandy)
115 ml/4 fl oz Madeira
1 tbsp oil
15 g/½ oz lard
450 g/1 lb lean salt pork, chopped
450 g/1 lb pork breast, chopped
450 g/1 lb chicken livers

1 duck liver
3 garlic cloves, peeled and
  chopped
4 bay leaves
4 tsp thyme (or savory)
1 egg
freshly ground black pepper
rashers of streaky bacon

Remove as many bones as you can from the duck with a little sharp knife. Strip away the fat and cut the meat into 13-mm/½-in. pieces. Marinate the duck meat in the cognac and Madeira for 2 hours.

Meanwhile, heat the oil and lard in a frying-pan and sauté the salt pork for 3 minutes, stirring; add the pork breast and cook for 5 minutes; then add the livers and sauté for another 5 minutes. Remove from the heat and add the garlic, bay leaves and thyme (or savory). Let cool.

Remove the bay leaves, add the egg and blend the mixture in a food processor or blender briefly. It must be smooth but keep some consistency. Correct the seasoning; the mixture should be flavourful.

Drain the duck from its marinade and sprinkle it with pepper.

Line an ovenproof dish with rashers of streaky bacon. Place the duck pieces on the bottom and cover them with the liver mixture. Cover everything with more strips of bacon, press hard with your hands, cover with foil and refrigerate overnight.

Preheat the oven to 190°C/375°F/Gas Mark 5. Place the foil-covered dish in a larger ovenproof dish filled with 225 ml/8 fl oz of hot water. Bake for 1 hour and 40–50 minutes.

Let cool, then cut a piece of wood or cardboard that will just cover the top of the pâté. Wrap this cover in kitchen foil and place on top of the covered pâté. Weight it down with full cans and refrigerate for at least 8 hours. Serve cold, in slices, from the dish.

Les Salades

Salads

The Romans started it all with their mixed salads, blending green lettuce with onions, eggs and olives or leeks, lettuce and mint, and cooks have not stopped displaying a rich variety in tastes and textures up to today's *nouvelle cuisine*, which has created the most disconcerting marriages – some legitimate, some less so. In fact, too often anything goes in a salad, and it is easy to display virtuosity at the expense of the final taste.

There are cold salads and warm salads. The dressing can be a simple vinaigrette, a mixture of cream and mustard or plain single cream seasoned with herbs.

A cold salad might include lettuce, chopped sautéd chicken livers, and a rich sauce of egg yolk, mustard, oil and vinegar; or sliced potatoes marinated in white wine and tossed with mussels, celery and truffles; or crayfish, green peppers and avocado seasoned with a light tomato sauce; or a cheerful mixture of nasturtiums, dandelion greens and lamb's lettuce, seasoned with verjuice.

Among the warm salads are shredded white cabbage sautéd with pork and seasoned with warm vinegar, or dandelions seasoned with sautéd brain, garlic and a mixture of mustard and warm vinegar. They also include lentils and white beans in lightly seasoned mixtures.

Cold tossed salads are usually served to refresh the palate between courses or to accompany a meat dish, but lately they, along with the warm salads, are served as a first course or as a main course in a light lunch.

Laitue Bourguignonne

Green salad seasoned with garlic, butter and lemon

A delicate, most unusual way of serving fresh greens.

For 8 people

40 g/1½ oz unsalted butter
1 garlic clove, peeled and crushed
salt
juice of 1 lemon

freshly ground white pepper
3 tbsp finely chopped parsley
young round lettuce or Little Gem
    lettuce

Melt the butter until it is soft and lukewarm. Add the garlic, salt, lemon juice, pepper and parsley. Mix thoroughly.

Wash and dry the lettuce leaves carefully. Place them in a large glass or china bowl. Pour the sauce over them, toss gently and serve at once.

Salade à la Menthe

Lettuce seasoned with mint marinated in oil, garlic and wine vinegar

Mint is often used in Burgundy for health as well as for flavour. It brings an unusual freshness to this salad, and one quickly becomes addicted to it.

For 8 people

4 mint sprigs or about 18 fresh
    mint leaves, finely chopped
3 chive leaves, finely chopped
8 tbsp vegetable oil
salt
freshly ground black pepper
4 tbsp wine vinegar

2 heads of round lettuce, trimmed,
    washed and dried
1 head of Batavian endive,
    trimmed, washed and dried
2 garlic cloves, peeled and finely
    chopped

Place the mint and the chives in a bowl with the oil and set aside for 30 minutes. Add the salt, pepper and vinegar, and mix thoroughly.

Place the lettuce and endive leaves in a large bowl, sprinkle with garlic and pour the sauce over them. Toss well and serve.

Salade au Chou

Sautéd strips of cabbage seasoned with bacon, vinegar, oil and spices

Choose tender cabbage and don't overcook it. This salad has a wonderful taste and texture.

For 8 people

2 Savoy cabbages	salt
25 g/1 oz unsalted butter	freshly ground black pepper
7 tbsp olive or peanut oil	2 garlic cloves, finely chopped
225 g/8 oz streaky bacon, diced	2 tbsp finely chopped parsley (or
4 tbsp wine vinegar	chives)
1 tbsp Dijon-style mustard	

Trim the cabbage and cut it into very narrow strips.

Heat the butter and 1 tablespoon of the oil in a large frying-pan, add the diced bacon and sauté on all sides until crisp. Add 2 tablespoons of the vinegar, then the cabbage. Cook briefly over high heat, until the cabbage is just wilted.

Meanwhile, mix together the mustard, 2 tablespoons of vinegar, 6 tablespoons of oil, salt and pepper. Pour over the cabbage and bacon and stir carefully.

Add the garlic and parsley to the salad just before serving.

Salade aux Griaudes

Crisp diced pork seasoned with vinegar and herbs

For a buffet, a snack or a summer hors-d'oeuvre, this is a simple dish to prepare but a very interesting one.

For 8 people

450 g/1 lb lean salt pork, cut into
    very small dice
115 ml/4 fl oz red wine vinegar
freshly ground black pepper
1 garlic clove, finely chopped
2 tbsp finely chopped parsley

Slowly heat the pork in a frying-pan until all the fat has melted and the meat is crisp. Put the pork in a bowl and discard the fat. Add the vinegar to the pan for 1 minute, then pour it over the crisp pork. Sprinkle with pepper, garlic and parsley and serve as a side dish.

Salade aux Noix

Green salad with walnuts, lemons, mustard and cream

For 8 people

3 heads of young round lettuce
16 walnuts, cut in half
1 tbsp Dijon-style mustard
juice of 1 lemon

cayenne pepper
225 ml/8 fl oz double cream
salt

Trim the lettuce, wash and dry them and place them in a glass or china bowl. Sprinkle with the walnuts.

In another bowl, mix the mustard, lemon juice, cayenne, cream and salt. Pour it over the lettuce and serve.

Salade de Céleri

Celery hearts seasoned with walnuts, cheese, vinegar and oil

A very rich salad, perfect for a winter meal.

For 8 people

4 celery hearts, finely chopped
15 g/4 oz coarsely chopped
   walnuts
225 g/8 oz Roquefort or other blue
   cheese

2 tbsp brandy
freshly ground black pepper
2 tbsp red wine vinegar
6 tbsp walnut (or peanut) oil
salt (optional)

Place the celery hearts in a bowl with the walnuts. Crush the cheese in the brandy, add the pepper, vinegar and oil and beat with a fork. Pour over the celery and walnuts. Check the seasoning and add salt if desired. Stir well and serve.

Salade de Haricots Verts

A green bean salad with shallots and mushrooms

This lovely dish is usually made with fresh truffles, but with fresh mushrooms it remains a treat if you don't overcook the beans.

For 8 people

1 kg/2½ lb green beans, trimmed and washed	peeled and finely chopped
450 g/1 lb white mushrooms, washed, dried and thinly sliced	3 tbsp walnut oil
	1 tbsp red wine vinegar
3 shallots (or little white onions),	salt
	freshly ground black pepper

Steam the beans, or cook them in a large pot of salted water for 10–15 minutes. Drain and place them in a large shallow bowl. Sprinkle with mushrooms and shallots.

Vigorously stir together the oil, vinegar, salt and pepper and pour over the vegetables. Mix gently and serve lukewarm or cold.

Salade de Lentilles

A lentil salad with vegetables, herbs and bacon

A hearty winter dish, a good buffet dish.

For 8 people

800 g/1¾ lb dried brown or green lentils	salt
	freshly ground black pepper
4 carrots, peeled and cut in quarters	225-g/8-oz piece of smoked streaky bacon
2 onions, peeled and studded with 1 clove each	3 tbsp chopped parsley
1 garlic clove, peeled	4 slices bread, cut in triangles for *croûtons*
3 bay leaves	40 g/1½ oz unsalted butter
3 sprigs of thyme	

·············· Sauce ··············

2 tbsp Dijon-style mustard
8 tbsp olive or peanut oil
4 tbsp red wine vinegar
3 tbsp finely chopped chives
3 garlic cloves, peeled and crushed

3 red onions, peeled and finely
  chopped
salt
freshly ground pepper

Wash and prepare the lentils according to the directions on the package. Place them in a large pot of cold water with the carrots, onions, garlic, bay leaves, thyme, salt and pepper. Cover and simmer for about 35 minutes, or until the vegetables are tender.

Prepare the sauce, blending all the ingredients in a large bowl. Stir well.

Drain the lentils and carrots, discarding the bay leaves, thyme and onions with cloves. Cut the bacon into thin slices, then cut the slices into strips and fry them. Drain on paper towels. Pour the lentils and carrots into the sauce. Add the bacon strips and stir gently. Sprinkle with parsley and check the seasoning. Fry the triangles of bread in the butter.

Serve lukewarm (in a dome shape) in a shallow dish surrounded with the *croûtons*.

Salade de Lyon

A tossed green salad with herring and boiled eggs

For 8 people

3 herrings, cut in 2.5-cm/1-in.
  pieces
70 ml/2½ fl oz oil
pepper
2 onions, sliced

·············· Dressing ··············	······· Greens and Garnish ·······
2 tbsp wine vinegar	chicory, washed and sliced
2 tbsp Dijon-style mustard	lengthways
salt	watercress, trimmed and washed
freshly ground black pepper	endive, trimmed and washed
3 tbsp finely chopped parsley	round lettuce, trimmed and
	washed
	celery hearts, cut in thin strips and
	washed
	4 hard-boiled eggs, peeled and
	quartered

A day or so ahead, cut the herrings and marinate them in oil with pepper and onion.

To prepare the dressing, combine in a bowl the oil in which the herrings have been marinated with the vinegar, mustard, salt and parsley.

Place the well-drained greens in a large bowl. Place the cut herrings on top and the quartered eggs around. Pour on the dressing and serve. Toss after the dish has arrived at the table.

Salade de Nevers

Green salad with a Dijon mustard, Roquefort, bacon, garlic, egg and vinaigrette sauce

You need very tender young dandelions or equally tender endive for this pungent, invigorating salad.

For 8 people

1 kg/2½ lb dandelion greens, very carefully washed, trimmed and dried.

2 tbsp oil

170 g/6 oz lean salt pork, diced quite small (12-mm/½-in. pieces)

3 tbsp wine vinegar

1 tbsp Dijon-style mustard

2 tbsp Roquefort or blue cheese

salt

freshly ground black pepper

3 garlic cloves

about 3 slices of good bread cut into 12-mm/½-in. pieces

2 tbsp minced parsley (or chives)

4 hard-boiled eggs, shelled and quartered lengthways

While you clean and trim the greens, warm a large salad bowl and heat 1 tablespoon of oil in a frying-pan. Add the salt pork and cook over medium heat until crisp.

Meanwhile, mix the vinegar, the mustard and the cheese into a soft paste.

Place the greens in the warm bowl, add salt, pepper, the vinegar-mustard-cheese mixture, and the pork. Sauté the garlic cloves in 1 tablespoon of oil in the pan for 2 minutes and discard them. Add the pieces of bread to this garlic-scented oil and, when they are golden on all sides, add them to the salad. Stir carefully. Sprinkle with parsley or chives and place the hard-boiled egg quarters all around the bowl. Serve at once. The salad should be warm.

Note: It is more efficient to use two frying-pans at once, cooking the salt pork in one and the garlic and *croûtons* in the other. Your dandelion salad will be warmer this way.

Salade de Pissenlits
A dandelion salad with bacon and garlic croûtons

The best dandelions come early in spring, after the snow has melted. The plants should be tender and pale green, but if they are not, use only the young, inner leaves. Wash and dry thoroughly.

For 8 people

340 g/12 oz lean salt pork, diced very small or cut in thin strips
1 kg/2½ lb dandelion greens (or Batavian endive or endive)
4 tbsp wine vinegar

freshly ground black pepper
4 slices good bread, toasted or fried in butter
2 garlic cloves, peeled

Melt the salt pork slowly. Place the dandelion greens in a warm bowl. Pour the pork fat over the leaves. Add vinegar to the pork in the pan, and pour over the leaves. Sprinkle with pepper and serve at once with toasted slices of bread rubbed with garlic.

Salade de Pommes de Terre
A warm potato salad seasoned with wine, mustard and herbs

This is served with boiled sausage or kippered herring.

For 8 people

16 potatoes
6 tbsp white wine
2 tsp dried thyme or chopped fresh
thyme
10 tbsp vegetable oil (walnut or
olive oil)
2 tbsp red wine vinegar

2 tbsp Dijon-style mustard
2 shallots, finely chopped
1 garlic clove, finely chopped
3 tbsp fresh parsley or chives
salt
freshly ground black pepper

Wash and boil the unpeeled potatoes in salted water. Holding them with a thick kitchen mitt or a towel, peel and cut them into thick slices. Bring the wine and thyme to a boil and pour over the potatoes.

Bring 8 tablespoons of oil and the vinegar to a boil, add the mustard, shallots and garlic and pour over the potatoes.

Sprinkle with the herbs, salt and pepper and dribble 2 tablespoons of oil over the top. Serve lukewarm or at room temperature.

Salade des Vendangeurs
Tossed green salad with ham, fresh herbs and warm vinegar

A wonderful salad with a great variety of greens and fresh herbs.

For 8 people

dandelion, endive, watercress and
cos lettuce
freshly ground black pepper
15 g/½ oz lard (or tbsp oil)
340 g/12 oz streaky bacon (or lean
salt pork), cut into 12-mm/½-in.
cubes
2 tbsp vegetable oil (optional)
3 tbsp wine vinegar

85 g/3 oz thin strips (25- x 12-
mm/1 x ½-in. pieces) of sliced
country ham or prosciutto
1 tbsp finely chopped chives
1 tbsp finely chopped tarragon
1 tbsp finely chopped chervil
1 tbsp finely chopped parsley (or
mint or basil)
1 garlic clove, peeled and crushed

Wash, trim and dry the greens and place them in a large bowl. Sprinkle with pepper. Heat the lard in a frying-pan, lower the heat and sauté the diced bacon until crisp. Pour the bacon and the fat over the greens. (You can add 2 tablespoons of vegetable oil if the bacon does not yield enough fat.) Add the vinegar to the pan, heat for 2 seconds and pour over the greens. Add the ham, herbs and garlic and mix thoroughly.

Serve at once.

Salade Dijonnaise

A lettuce, egg, ham, celery, walnut, mustard and herb salad

Superb for a buffet or a picnic, this salad can be made with olive, peanut or walnut oil.

For 8 people

6 hard-boiled eggs, shelled
450 g/1 lb boiled ham, diced (12-mm/½-in. pieces)
225 g/8 oz salami, diced (12-mm/½ in. pieces)
2 celery hearts, diced (12-mm/½-in. pieces)
12 walnuts, coarsely chopped
450 g/1 lb Gruyère cheese, diced (12-mm/½-in. pieces)
4 Granny Smith apples, peeled and diced (12-mm/½-in. pieces)
4 tbsp strong Dijon-style mustard
2 tbsp wine vinegar
8 tbsp olive, peanut or walnut oil
salt
freshly ground white pepper
2 large heads of round lettuce washed
3 tbsp chopped chervil

Separate the yolk from the white of the hard-boiled eggs. Dice the egg white, and mix in a large bowl with the diced ham, salami, celery, walnuts, Gruyère cheese and apples.

Crush the egg yolks with the mustard, vinegar and oil. Stir well and add salt and pepper.

Place the lettuce leaves around the edges of a large glass or white china bowl, add the diced ingredients and pour the sauce over everything. Chill.

Remove from the refrigerator 1 hour before serving. Just before serving, toss gently and sprinkle with chervil.

Salade Rouge et Verte

A green pepper with red beetroot salad served with a celery and shallot salad seasoned with oil, vinegar, mustard and fresh herbs

You must prepare the two salads separately and keep them refrigerated until ready to use. This is a beautiful dish, full of flavour and colour.

For 8 people

·············· Green Pepper and Beetroot Salad ··············

2 green peppers, cut in very small
   strips
115 g/4 oz cooked red beetroot,
   peeled and diced

3 tbsp vegetable oil
1 tbsp red wine vinegar
1 garlic clove, finely crushed
2 tbsp finely chopped parsley

·············· Celery Hearts and Shallot Salad ··············

4 celery hearts, diced
1 or 2 shallots (or 1 white onion),
   finely chopped
3 tbsp vegetable oil

juice of 1 lemon
1 tbsp Dijon-style mustard
salt
freshly ground black pepper

·············· Garnish ··············

3 tbsp chopped fresh herbs (chives,
   mint, chervil)

Prepare the two salads in separate bowls, tossing them delicately in their sauces, made by thoroughly mixing all the ingredients except the vegetables.

When you are ready to serve, place the pepper and beetroot salad on a shallow dish with the celery salad all around. Sprinkle with the fresh herbs and serve.

Le Saladier Lyonnais

A pungent salad of chicken livers, eggs, herrings, meat, herbs and vinaigrette sauce

This is a crowd pleaser from Lyon. Highly seasoned, it is a wonderful summer lunch, the core of a country buffet or the first course of a hearty informal meal.

There are many variations of the *saladier*. Sometimes poached eggs are placed on top. Sometimes the whole salad nests on a bed of chicory, watercress and dandelion greens. If you use a mutton foot (a must in Lyon, but not easily available everywhere), split it and carefully remove all the hair growing underneath in the centre before you cook it in *court bouillon*, then dice it.

It is better to prepare this salad 1 hour in advance to increase the flavour.

For 8 people

4 chicken livers
25 g/1 oz unsalted butter
1 tbsp vegetable oil
340 g/12 oz cold meat (boiled beef or chicken or ham), diced
4 large herrings, cut in 12-mm/1-in. pieces and marinated in 70 ml/ 2½ fl oz oil with pepper and 2 sliced onions
1 mutton foot, trimmed, cooked and diced (optional; see introductory note)
2 tbsp finely chopped chive

4 tbsp finely chopped tarragon (or chervil)
2 tbsp finely chopped parsley
8 tbsp peanut or olive oil
3 tbsp red wine vinegar
3 tbsp Dijon-style mustard
salt
freshly ground black pepper
pinch of coriander
4 hard-boiled eggs, shelled and quartered lengthways
1 tbsp fresh herbs (tarragon or chives)

Sauté the livers in the butter and oil. Quarter or dice them.

Remove the fat (if any) from the cold meat and dice. Put the livers, meat, herrings, mutton foot if available, chives, tarragon and parsley in a large bowl.

Mix the oil, vinegar, mustard, salt, pepper and coriander and pour into the bowl. Stir gently. Place the quartered eggs all around and sprinkle the fresh herbs on top.

Salade Verte à la Crème

Tossed green salad with a cream, egg yolk, vinegar and herb sauce

For 8 people

3 tsp salt
2 tsp freshly ground white pepper
2 egg yolks
2 tbsp wine vinegar (or lemon
  juice)
4 tbsp single cream

3 tbsp finely chopped fresh herbs
  (chervil, chives, mint, basil,
  parsley)
4 lettuce hearts or Little Gem
  lettuces, washed and dried

Pour all the ingredients for the sauce except the cream and the herbs into a large bowl and mix vigorously. Stir in the cream and herbs.

Place the lettuce leaves in a glass or china bowl and pour the sauce over them. Toss gently and serve at once.

Les Sauces

Sauces

Rich, sumptuous sauce recipes have been handed down for generations, but less flour is used now, and cream, vegetables and wine are added to natural juices instead. The sauces are made to enhance flavour, not to mask it.

The red-wine sauces (*bourguignonne, matelote*), the white-wine sauces (*lyonnaise, pauchouse*) and the sauces made with highly seasoned stock are always thickened with vegetables like onions or tomatoes and fresh cream. They are seasoned with garlic, mustard, coriander, pepper, shallots and vinegar, and embody the spirit of Burgundy.

Beurre Bourguignon

A butter, garlic, shallot and parsley sauce

For snails, mussels, clams or green beans, a wonderful pungent sauce.

Enough for 6 dozen snails

450 g/1 lb unsalted butter,
  softened
6 garlic cloves, peeled and finely
  chopped
3 shallots, peeled and finely
  chopped

70 g/2½ oz chopped parsley
4 tbsp salt
freshly ground black pepper

Put all the ingredients in a large bowl. Crush and mix them. Cover in cling film and keep in the refrigerator until ready to use. The butter will remain fresh and tasty for about 2 weeks.

Beurre d'Escargot
Snail butter

What do beef and snails have in common? This lively butter sauce. It gives spirit to roast beef or turns the simplest steak into a Burgundy treat, especially if you serve it with a *Gratin Dauphinois* (pp. 169–70) or a *Paillasson* (p. 181). You may like to use this *beurre d'escargot* with grilled fish (particularly swordfish) as well.

Enough butter for 8 people

4 shallots, peeled and finely chopped	salt
1 garlic clove, finely chopped	freshly ground black pepper
3 tbsp finely chopped parsley	115 g/4 oz butter, softened

The simplest way to make this butter is to mix everything except the butter in a food processor, then add the butter and mix for 1 second. Cover and leave at room temperature.

Place dots of the butter between slices of beef or on top of fish and serve at once.

Coulis de Tomates
A warm tomato sauce

The secret here is to cook the sauce briefly to avoid a bitter taste. It can be poured into a jar, covered with a little oil and kept for a week in the refrigerator.

For 570 ml/1 pt of sauce

2 onions, peeled and finely
  chopped
2.25 kg/5 lb ripe tomatoes
2 tbsp olive oil
2 garlic cloves, peeled and crushed
20 g/¾ oz chopped parsley

1 tsp dried herbs (oregano, thyme)
bouquet garni
2 tsp sugar
salt
freshly ground black pepper

Squeeze the onion in a towel to remove excess moisture. Pass the tomatoes through a Mouli food mill and discard the skins.

Heat the oil in a heavy-bottomed frying-pan, add the onions, half of the garlic, the parsley, herbs and bouquet garni. Cook for 10 minutes.

Place the tomato purée in a heavy-bottomed pan, add the sugar and simmer, uncovered, for 10 minutes. Pour it into the onion and herb mixture and heat, uncovered, for 5 minutes.

Remove from the heat, add the remaining garlic, salt and pepper. Discard the bouquet garni.

Marinade

For beef, pork, rabbit or chicken

This can also be made with white wine. Meat should be marinated for 2 days before being cooked.

For 1.8 l/3⅓ pt of marinade

1 carrot, peeled and sliced
2 onions, peeled and sliced
2 garlic cloves, peeled and crushed
20 g/¾ oz parsley, stems and
  leaves
1 celery stalk
thyme
2 bay leaves

5 peppercorns
2 cloves
900 ml/1⅗ pt hearty red wine
225 ml/8 fl oz wine vinegar
225 ml/8 fl oz brandy
2 tbsp vegetable oil
salt

Mix all the ingredients and it is ready to use.

Sauce à la Menthe

A warm, unctuous sauce made with egg yolks, vinegar, butter and fresh mint

This lively sauce is superb with poached trout.

For 450 ml/16 fl oz of sauce

6 egg yolks
1½ tbsp wine vinegar
salt
freshly ground black pepper

115 g/4 oz unsalted butter, melted
2 tbsp fresh mint leaves, cut up
   with scissors

Place the egg yolks, vinegar and seasoning in a blender. Blend for a few seconds. Add the butter and blend at top speed for a few seconds more. Keep the sauce over tepid water until ready to use. Add the mint just before serving.

    This sauce can be made by hand by mixing the egg yolks and butter together energetically, stirring in the vinegar and cooking the mixture over low heat for a few minutes.

Sauce au Beurre Rouge

A red wine, vinegar, shallot and butter sauce

This superb, highly flavoured sauce is served with fish poached in a *court bouillon*.

For 340 ml/12 fl oz of sauce

4 tbsp shallots, peeled and finely
   chopped
115 ml/4 fl oz red wine vinegar
55 ml/2 fl oz red wine
salt

freshly ground pepper
4 tbsp water
170 g/6 oz unsalted butter, chilled
   and cut into cubes

Cook the shallots, vinegar and wine over low heat until they become a paste. Season to taste with salt and pepper.

    In another pan, heat the water and add the butter, whipping and stirring constantly. It must not reach the boiling point. Add the shallot paste little by little, stirring constantly. Check the seasoning. Transfer to a tepid serving bowl and serve. (If you must keep it for a while, place it over a bowl of barely warm water.)

Sauce Bourguignonne
A red wine, bacon and onion sauce

This hearty sauce can be reheated and will improve in the process. Sautéd mushrooms are often added to it.

For 1 bowl of sauce

1 large chunk streaky bacon with rind removed (or country ham), cut into strips 6 mm/¼ in. thick and 4 cm/1½ in. long
1 carrot, peeled and diced
1 onion, peeled and diced
25 g/1 oz unsalted butter
1 tbsp vegetable oil
freshly ground nutmeg

1 clove
450 ml/16 fl oz red wine
1 tbsp tomato purée
1 tbsp flour
1 tbsp Dijon-style mustard
5 peppercorns, crushed
25 g/1 oz unsalted butter (optional)

Sauté the strips of bacon for 3 minutes. Remove from the pan and set aside.

Sauté the vegetables in the hot butter and oil for a few minutes until soft. Add a pinch of nutmeg and the clove, then stir in the wine and the tomato purée. Cook, uncovered, for 20 minutes – until it reduces by half. Put the sauce through a sieve, add flour and return it to the stove. Add the strips of bacon. Allow the mixture to heat for a few minutes, then remove from the heat and add the mustard and peppercorns.

If you want to keep the sauce and reheat it later, add 25 g/1 oz butter.

Sauce Bourguignotte

A good sauce for eggs and fish

For 450 ml/16 fl oz of sauce

115 g/4 oz unsalted butter
2 tbsp flour
450 ml/16 fl oz hearty red wine
10 shallots, peeled and finely
  chopped

2 tbsp finely chopped parsley
2 tsp thyme
2 bay leaves
4 garlic cloves, peeled and crushed

Heat half the butter in a heavy-bottomed pan. Add the flour, stirring, then the wine, shallots, herbs and garlic. Let the sauce reduce for a few minutes, uncovered. Discard the bay leaves and put the sauce through a sieve into a warm bowl. Add the remaining butter bit by bit while stirring; correct the seasoning if necessary and serve.

Sauce de Sorges

A lively herb sauce made with eggs and oil and seasoned with mustard and lemon

A tart sauce to serve with boiled artichokes, asparagus, celery root or a boiled meat.

For 170 ml/6 fl oz of sauce

1 tbsp Dijon-style mustard
juice of 1 lemon
peel of 1 lemon, grated
salt
freshly ground black pepper
3 tbsp vegetable oil

2 warm hard-boiled eggs, yolks
  and whites separated
1 tbsp finely chopped shallots
2 tbsp chervil, cut with scissors
1 tbsp finely chopped tarragon
1 tbsp finely chopped chives

Put the mustard, lemon juice, lemon peel, salt and pepper in a large bowl. Pour the oil in gradually, stirring (as you would for a mayonnaise). Add the egg yolks, shallots and the fresh herbs, mashing the yolks as you stir. Crush the egg whites through a sieve into the sauce. Check the seasoning.

Sauce Dorée

A light mayonnaise seasoned with shallots, wine, herbs and cream

Wonderful with boiled beef, boiled poultry, raw fennel or celery root.

For 570 ml/1 pt of sauce

2 tsp finely chopped shallots
10 g/⅓ oz unsalted butter
115 ml/4 fl oz white wine
15 g/½ oz chopped tarragon
  leaves

3 tbsp single cream
450 ml/16 fl oz home-made
  mayonnaise (see next recipe)

Cook the minced shallots in the butter until limp. While stirring, add the wine, tarragon and cream. Stir the hot mixture into the mayonnaise.

Serve lukewarm or cold.

Sauce Mayonnaise

Home-made mayonnaise is easy and quick to prepare.

For 450 ml/16 fl oz of sauce

2 egg yolks, at room temperature
1 tbsp Dijon-style mustard (or 1
  tsp, according to taste)
450 ml/16 fl oz oil (½ peanut and
  ½ olive oil, or all peanut), at
  room temperature

1 tbsp red wine vinegar (or 2 tbsp
  lemon juice)
salt
freshly ground white pepper

If you make this by hand, slip a kitchen towel under the bowl to prevent it from sliding while you beat the egg yolks and mustard together. Then add the oil in a slow, steady stream, whisking constantly until firm.

Bring the vinegar to a boil and stir it into the sauce while beating (or use cold lemon juice instead, according to taste). Add salt and pepper.

If you use a blender, place 1 tablespoon of oil in the bowl with the rest of the ingredients, cover and blend on low speed for 2 minutes; stop, then add the rest of the oil in a steady flow and blend slowly.

Place the mayonnaise in a covered bowl and refrigerate. It will keep three to four days. If the egg yolks separate from the oil, place a fresh egg yolk in a new bowl, add 1 teaspoon of mustard and stir well. Slowly add the curdled mixture, stirring until it is firm and silky. Correct the seasoning.

Sauce Meurette

A rich sauce made with red wine and vegetables and seasoned with herbs.

This is Burgundy's national sauce, mostly used with eel, pike, trout and carp, although it can also be served with poached eggs or lamb's brains.

Enough for 8 servings

25 g/1 oz unsalted butter
2 large onions, peeled and
    chopped
3 carrots, peeled and chopped
4 garlic cloves, peeled and crushed
2 whites of leeks, chopped (or 4
    shallots, peeled and chopped)
900 ml/1⅗ pt hearty red wine
2 bay leaves, crushed

2 tsp thyme
salt
freshly ground black pepper
1 tsp sugar
3 tbsp flour thoroughly mixed
    with 70 g/2½ oz softened
    unsalted butter
2 tbsp brandy (optional)
2 tbsp redcurrant jelly

······· Additional garnishes ·······

225 g/8 oz sautéd mushrooms
16 pickling onions
8 small *croûtons* sautéd in oil and
    rubbed with garlic

Heat the butter and sauté the onions for a few minutes. Add the carrots, garlic and leeks and cook until soft. Add the wine, herbs and seasoning and bring to a boil. Lower the heat and simmer, uncovered, for 40 minutes.

Discard the bay leaves. Pass the mixture through a sieve, crushing the vegetables with a wooden spoon. Add the flour-and-butter paste to the wine–vegetable mixture. Put it back on the heat and simmer for 2 minutes, stirring. Pour in the brandy. Ignite. Beat in the redcurrant jelly and serve.

Sauce Mousseline Dijon

A warm, frothy egg, butter, lemon and mustard sauce

A lovely tart sauce for poached eggs, poached or grilled fish and boiled vegetables.

For 225 ml/8 fl oz of sauce

3 egg yolks	freshly ground black pepper
juice of 1 lemon	115 g/4 oz unsalted butter, cut in
1 tsp cold water	small pieces
salt	2 tbsp Dijon-style mustard

Put everything but the mustard in a pan over simmering water. Whip steadily until frothy and thick. Add the mustard and check the seasoning. Serve lukewarm in a warm bowl.

Sauce Moutarde I

Mustard sauce

To serve with pork chops, veal or boiled vegetables.

For 450 ml/16 fl oz of sauce

55 g/2 oz unsalted butter	4 tbsp Dijon-style mustard
4 tbsp flour	1 tbsp wine vinegar
340 ml/12 fl oz warm milk (or stock)	2 tbsp single cream
2 egg yolks	salt
	freshly ground pepper

Heat the butter and add the flour, stirring briskly with a whisk, then add the warm milk or stock. Cook, stirring, until the mixture thickens. Remove it from the heat and, stirring vigorously, add the egg yolks. Return the sauce to low heat for a few minutes.

Remove it from the heat and add the mustard, vinegar, cream, salt and pepper. Check the seasoning. Keep warm at a simmer until ready to serve – don't let it come to a boil.

Sauce Moutarde II
Mustard sauce

To be served with grilled meat.

For 570 ml/1 pt of sauce

2 onions, peeled and finely
    chopped
2 shallots, peeled and finely
    chopped
40 g/1½ oz unsalted butter
1 tbsp vegetable oil
1 tbsp flour
450 ml/16 fl oz white (or red)
    wine

2 tbsp red wine vinegar
1 tbsp tomato purée
salt
freshly ground pepper
2 tbsp Dijon-style mustard
2 tbsp finely chopped parsley

Sauté the onions and shallots in the butter and oil over medium heat until golden. Sprinkle with the flour and cook, stirring, a few minutes longer. Stir in the wine, vinegar, tomato purée, salt and pepper and simmer over low heat, uncovered, for 30 minutes. Check the seasoning.

Just before serving, stir in the mustard and parsley.

Sauce Tomate Crue

A raw tomato sauce

This comes from the South. It is served with cold dishes.

450 ml/16 fl oz of sauce

2.25 kg/5 lb very ripe tomatoes,
   peeled
2 onions, peeled and quartered
2 garlic cloves, peeled
3 tbsp chopped parsley

3 tbsp chopped basil (optional)
3 tbsp olive oil
salt
freshly ground black pepper

Put half of the tomatoes in a blender with half of the onions and 1 garlic clove. Blend at high speed for 5 minutes and pour into a bowl. Blend the rest of the tomatoes, onion and garlic along with the parsley (and basil) and oil. Blend for 5 minutes and add it to the first batch in the bowl. Season with salt and pepper and stir well.

    Covered in the refrigerator, this sauce will keep for four to five days.

Les Poissons
Fish

Because of its many creeks, rivers, ponds, waterfalls and lakes, Burgundy is blessed not only with a vast population of good-natured fishermen adding a peaceful note to its countryside, but also with an abundance of salmon, eel, trout, pike, carp, barbel, bream, herring, perch, frogs, crayfish and the rarest freshwater treat – *l'omble chevalier*.

Most fish in Burgundy, Lyonnais and Savoy are cooked in wine and herbs, enriched with cream and often with mustard. But the recipes are as varied as they are numerous. In Burgundy the *matelote* is usually called a *pauchouse* when prepared with white wine, and a *meurette* when red wine and more than one kind of fish are used. Pike may be larded, grilled with butter, white wine and mustard, or baked with cream and vinegar. It may be served on a purée of sorrel and tarragon, or cooked covered with shallots, garlic and mushrooms and sprinkled with nutmeg. Frogs are sautéd, then cooked gently with snails, garlic, herbs and white wine. Carp are often marinated, then stuffed with their roe, herbs and mushrooms and served with an oil, vinegar and hard-boiled-egg sauce.

Trout are sometimes cooked *au bleu*, briskly in a fragrant *court bouillon* or stuffed with mushrooms, herbs and cream, or made into *quenelles*. Crayfish (which are best from June to September, and must be cooked alive) are cooked with cream, brandy, wine mustard and Spanish saffron or quickly cooked in a highly seasoned *court bouillon* made of white wine. They are also mixed with cream and cheese for a succulent gratin.

Salmon may be stuffed with vegetables and cooked in wine and mustard, or simply cooked in *court bouillon* and served with a mustard, egg yolk, spice and chive sauce. It can also be eaten raw with herbs and oil.

Shad is simmered on top of chopped sorrel and shallots and sprinkled with brandy and wine before it is baked, or stuffed with its roe and sorrel to be marinated and grilled.

Snails deserve a whole chapter to themselves, but I have included them here in a few delectable preparations.

Generally, no seawater fish are used, since, in Burgundy, they were mostly thought of as punishment served only during Lent. The children still sing the little ballad:

No more herring
Bad smelling, foul tasting
Give us good ham instead!

Remember, always spend almost as much time *choosing* a fish as cooking it. The eye must be clear and bulging, the gills red, and the scales must adhere firmly to the skin and have a sheen. When you serve lemon – unless it is done only to please the eye – peel and dice it so that its taste is clear and sharp.

Anguille en Matelote
Eel cooked in wine and herbs

Despite their unfortunate resemblance to snakes, eels have refined tastes and a delicate flesh. They love clear water; they hate mud. They feed on snails and grasshoppers when they are on land, and on fish when they swim in rivers. Their flesh is considered a delicacy in Burgundy.

They must be killed in a rather rigorous fashion with a sharp blow on the head; they are then hung on a hook on a wall with a ring tied around the neck. Before cooking an eel, one must grip the skin with a piece of cloth, pull it down and peel it off. The head, fins and tail must also be removed, along with the entrails. Dry the eel carefully with paper towels.

This recipe will reheat well and should be served with plain boiled potatoes.

For 8 people

2 onions, peeled and chopped	1.4–1.8 l/2⅖–3⅕ pt red (or red and
55 g/2 oz unsalted butter	white) wine
1 tbsp vegetable oil	parsley
salt	2 bay leaves
freshly ground black pepper	thyme
16 thick slices of eel, peeled	1 carrot, peeled and chopped

1 tsp fennel seeds

2 garlic cloves, peeled and crushed

2 tbsp flour

16 *croûtons*, sautéd in butter

Sauté the onions in half the butter and the oil. Sprinkle with salt and pepper. Add the pieces of eel and sauté on all sides, then cover with wine. Add the herbs, carrot, fennel seeds and garlic and simmer until the fish is done, about 15–25 minutes. If it flakes easily from the bone, it is ready. Discard the bay leaves. Mix the remaining butter and the flour and drop this paste into the fish sauce, stirring. Cook for a few minutes. Correct the seasoning. The sauce should be glossy and coat the pieces of fish. For a smoother sauce, pass the fish liquid through a sieve before adding the butter–flour paste, but I rather like the rough texture of the *matelote*.

Serve in a warm serving dish surrounded with *croûtons*. Some people like to add brandy to the sauce and ignite it.

Carpes en Meurette

Sautéd carp cooked with garlic, onions, herbs and wine

Carp are found in ponds or rivers all over Burgundy. When a pond has not been emptied, the fish can reach over five pounds. Carp are usually served stuffed and cooked in wine and cream. They can be stuffed with bread, bacon, carp roe, parsley and egg, and cooked in white wine and chopped vegetables or red wine. They can be stuffed with a thick cream sauce consisting of mushrooms, thyme, carp roe, and cream, and basted while baking with a mixture of cream and white wine. In Morvan they are stuffed with a light puff pastry enriched with diced Gruyère cheese. They can be sautéd in butter and seasoned with garlic, parsley, butter and lemon, or parboiled in herbs and white wine and served with an egg-yolk-and-cream sauce seasoned with chopped gherkins. They can be served baked with wine, fresh spices and butter and seasoned with capers. The following recipe is a classic and can also be done with eel, perch, whitefish or bass.

For 8 people

450 g/1 lb lean salt pork, diced	2 900-g/2-lb carp, trimmed and cut
2 tsp vegetable oil	in slices 4 cm/1½ in. thick
10 garlic cloves, peeled and	1.4 l/2⅖ pt red wine
crushed	40 g/1½ oz unsalted butter
2 onions, peeled and chopped	3 tbsp flour
2 bay leaves	16 *croûtons*, sautéd in butter
2 tsp thyme	

Sauté the salt pork in the oil; add the garlic cloves, onions, bay leaves, thyme, slices of carp and the wine, and simmer, uncovered, for 30 minutes, stirring from time to time. Knead the butter and flour together and add to the sauce, stirring for another 30 minutes. Discard the bay leaves.

Serve with *croûtons* sautéd in butter and, if you like, rubbed with garlic.

Les Escargots
Snails

Snails roam Burgundy throughout spring and summer, chewing fresh grass. In the autumn, when they are plump enough, they close their shell openings with a sand and chalk mixture, which looks like plaster, and sleep from October to March. This period of hibernation goes roughly from Halloween to Easter and is the best time to eat them.

Snails were always considered a delicacy in Burgundy, and throughout the centuries barges loaded with snails would glide along canals and rivers, bringing their precious cargo to the various castles and monasteries. The Romans, who were fond of snails, kept them and fed them herbs.

In Burgundy during the Middle Ages snail parks were the property of monasteries and convents. The best snails were fed in vineyards. Real gourmets have always been against the practice of making the snails fast just before eating them, because while it may indeed cleanse the snails' stomachs of dangerous weeds, it also makes them dry and hard. So snails should be kept for about eight days in an enclosed place and fed with lettuce, thyme and clean water.

They can be sautéd in olive oil with diced lean salt pork, crushed walnuts and diced anchovy fillets and served on cooked spinach. They can be stuffed in mushroom caps, then covered with *beurre escargot* and grilled.

Dredged with flour, salt and pepper, they can be lightly sautéd in hot butter, then poured into beaten eggs to make a really marvellous omelette.

Preparation of snails

You can buy canned snails with a bag of clean shells attached. Leave them overnight in a good broth made of salted water, a clove, a garlic clove and a bouquet garni, and use them in the recipes that follow.

If you use fresh snails, remove the protective membrane at the opening of the shell. Wash them several times and let them stand in clean cold water with salt, vinegar and a pinch of flour for about 2 hours. Rinse them in cold water and blanch them in a large pot of boiling water for six minutes. Drain them and remove them from their shells. Take off and discard the black tip of the tails and replace the snails in their shells. Cook them with carrots, onions and herbs (and a handful of ashes, if you have them) in a mixture of half white wine and half water to cover them completely. Add salt and cook over a low heat for three hours. Let them cool in their liquor and remove them from their shells when cold.

Boil the empty shells in water with a pinch of bicarbonate of soda for 30 minutes to cleanse them, and dry them in a low oven.

Escargots à la Bourguignonne
Snails baked with butter, garlic, shallots and parsley

Allow about one dozen snails for each guest. Serve with a dry white wine.

For 8 people

450 g/1 lb unsalted butter
5 garlic cloves, peeled and finely
    chopped
2 shallots, peeled and finely
    chopped
1 large bunch parsley, finely
    chopped
salt

freshly ground black pepper
juice of 1 lemon
100 snails and their shells, cooked
    according to the directions
    under 'Preparation of snails'
    (p. 73)
115 ml/4 fl oz dry white wine

Preheat oven to 200°C/400°F/Gas Mark 6.

Mix butter, garlic, shallots, parsley, salt, pepper and lemon juice into a soft paste and fill half of each shell with it. Put one snail in each shell and put a little more of the butter mixture on top of it. Place the shells on a snail plate and pour a little wine over each. The wine will mix with the hot butter, which will melt in the bottom of the dish as it cooks.

Bake for 6 minutes and serve hot with bread.

Escargots au Vin Blanc
Marinated snails stuffed and baked

Once the snails are cleaned and cooked according to the directions given under 'Preparation of snails' (p. 73), they can be prepared in various ways. Snails can be fried and seasoned with oil and vinegar. They can be cooked with cream and garlic in a pastry shell for a *tarte aux escargots*. Chopped with shallots and parsley, they can be used to stuff large mushrooms. They can be sautéd in butter, then covered with cheese and more butter and baked. They can be dipped in butter and breadcrumbs and cooked on skewers. They can be cooked with wine, mushrooms and herbs in a casserole. They can be sautéd in butter and put back in their shells with butter, parsley and a little white wine. They can be chopped and sautéd with frogs' legs. They can be deep-fried, then sprinkled with garlic and parsley.

The following recipe is a particularly enticing one.

For 8 people

8 dozen snails
115–225 ml/4–8 fl oz dry white
  wine
2 tbsp good brandy
2 tsp thyme
3 bay leaves
450 g/1 lb unsalted butter
5 shallots, peeled and finely
  chopped

4 garlic cloves, peeled and finely
  chopped
140 g/5 oz hazelnuts, finely
  chopped
parsley, finely chopped
salt
freshly ground black pepper
16 *croûtons*, sautéd in butter and
  rubbed with 1 clove of garlic

After preparing the snails according to the directions given under 'Preparation of snails' (p. 73), marinate them for 24 hours in the wine, brandy, thyme and bay leaves, stirring and basting three or four times.

Knead the butter with the shallots, garlic, hazelnuts, parsley, salt and pepper.

Twenty minutes before the meal, preheat the oven to 200°C/ 400°F/Gas Mark 6. Fill each shell with one snail and some of the butter-and-herb mixture. Bake for 10 minutes and serve with the *croûtons*.

Filets au Safran

Baked fish fillets, cooked with chicory and seasoned with saffron

Medieval Burgundy cooking used many spices, but this recipe, although high in flavour, is very delicate. You can prepare it with any light fish such as pike, whiting or sole.

For 8 people

head and bones of one fish
1 carrot, peeled and sliced
1 onion, peeled and sliced
2 bay leaves
1 sprig of thyme
225 ml/8 fl oz dry white wine
salt
8 chicories, trimmed and sliced

170 g/6 oz unsalted butter
freshly ground pepper
10 sole fillets
large pinch of Spanish saffron
  stamens
juice of 1 lemon
3 tbsp finely chopped chervil

Bring the fish bones, carrot, onion, bay leaves, thyme, wine and about 450 ml/16 fl oz of water to a boil, add salt, and simmer for 20 minutes.

Sauté the chicory in 55 g/2 oz of the butter. Sprinkle with salt and pepper, cover and cook over low heat for 15 minutes, stirring twice.

Slice the chicory into a large ovenproof dish. Place the sole fillets on top. Season with salt and pepper. Pour half of the fish stock through a sieve into the dish. Bake for 6 minutes.

Meanwhile, bring the rest of the stock to a boil and reduce by half. Crush and sprinkle the saffron into it. Add the remaining butter cut in large pieces, stirring constantly over low heat. Check the seasoning and add the lemon juice.

Pour over the sole fillets and serve sprinkled with chervil.

Filets de Brochet Mâcon

Marinated pike fillets baked with mushrooms and enriched with cream,
wine and herbs

Pike have firm, delicate flesh, although they are cruel, gluttonous animals. The following recipe can also be made with bass.

For 8 people

2 good-sized pike fillets
450 ml/16 fl oz dry white wine
1 large onion, peeled and chopped
8 shallots, peeled and finely
    chopped
1 bunch parsley, stems and leaves
    chopped
2 bay leaves

10 peppercorns, crushed
225 g/8 oz mushrooms, trimmed
    and thinly sliced
salt
freshly ground black pepper
225 ml/8 fl oz single cream
55 g/2 oz unsalted butter

Place the fillets in a dish and cover with the wine, onion, shallots, parsley, bay leaves and peppercorns. Cover with a piece of grease-proof paper and let marinate overnight.

Drain the fillets and place them in an ovenproof dish. Spread the sliced mushrooms over them.

Pour the marinade into a saucepan, bring it to a boil and reduce for 20 minutes.

Preheat the oven to 180°C/350°F/Gas Mark 4.

Discard the bay leaves; pass the sauce through a sieve and dribble it over the fish. Sprinkle with salt and pepper, add the cream and bake for 30 minutes, basting two or three times. Add the butter, stirring a little, just before serving.

Filets de Poisson aux Pâtes

Fish fillets baked with sherry, cream and sorrel, and served with noodles

For 8 people

10 fillets of any fresh firm fish	115 ml/4 fl oz dry white sherry
2 bay leaves	225 ml/8 fl oz single cream
15 g/½ oz unsalted butter	200 g/7 oz shredded sorrel
salt	1 large dish of home-made
freshly ground black pepper	noodles, barely cooked (p. 194)

Preheat the oven to 190°C/375°F/Gas Mark 5.

Place the fillets side by side in an ovenproof dish with the bay leaves on top of them. Dot the fillets with butter. Bake for 10 minutes; sprinkle with salt and pepper, and turn the oven off. Cover the fish with kitchen foil.

Pour the sherry into a saucepan. Over medium heat, add the cream and let it reduce, stirring until the sauce thickens and coats the spoon. Season with salt and pepper. Add the shredded sorrel and bring to a boil. Place the fillets in a warm serving dish. Spoon the sauce over them and serve with home-made noodles.

Gratin de Morue

A dried-codfish gratin

'Crayfish are fine, and lobsters are fine, but when I prepare a codfish gratin for you, then you will know what fine cooking really means' – so goes the saying. This inexpensive dish can be prepared ahead of time and is a treat.

For 8 people

900 g/2 lb dried codfish fillets
900 g/2 lb potatoes, peeled and
    thinly sliced
salt (if needed)
freshly ground white pepper
freshly grated nutmeg (to taste)

1.4 l/2²⁄₅ pt milk
3 egg yolks
115 ml/4 fl oz single cream
1 garlic clove, peeled
55 g/2 oz unsalted butter

Leave the codfish in cold water according to the instructions on the package, or soak in several changes of cold water for 24 hours to remove the salt.

Place the sliced potatoes in a deep saucepan. Season them with salt, pepper and nutmeg, and cover with milk. Bring to a boil and simmer for 20 minutes.

Meanwhile, beat the egg yolks and cream in a bowl. Remove the potatoes from the heat and, while stirring, add the egg mixture. Check and correct the seasoning.

Preheat the oven to 180°C/350°F/Gas Mark 4.

Place the codfish fillets in a large pan of cold water. Bring it to a boil and cook for only 2 minutes. Drain. Remove the skin and bones and shred the fish finely.

Rub an ovenproof dish with the garlic clove, then with butter. Pour half of the potatoes into the dish, cover them with shredded codfish and then add the remaining potatoes. Dot with butter and bake for 30 minutes. Serve in its baking dish.

Grenouilles au Vin Blanc

Frogs' legs sautéd and served with a white wine, garlic, cream and herb sauce

Frogs' legs are best in the autumn, when they are light. Only the back legs are served. They can be fried, cooked with wine or used in fritters.

For 8 people

2 tbsp flour
48 frogs' legs
225 g/8 oz unsalted butter
2 tbsp vegetable oil
2 garlic cloves, peeled and crushed
3 tbsp white wine

6 tbsp single cream
salt
freshly ground black pepper
4 tbsp chives, parsley, and chervil,
  finely chopped

Sprinkle the flour on the frogs' legs. Sauté them in the butter and oil on all sides. Remove and keep warm. Add the garlic to the pan, then the wine and reduce by half. Remove from the heat and add the cream, salt and pepper. Pour the mixture over the frogs' legs. Sprinkle with the herbs and serve at once.

Morue à la Lyonnaise

Salt codfish boiled, then sautéd with onions and potatoes and seasoned with warm vinegar

For 8 people

900 g/2 lb salt codfish, poached
  and flaked
1 tsp thyme
1 bay leaf
7 onions, peeled and sliced
115 ml/4 fl oz vegetable oil
8 potatoes, peeled, boiled and
  sliced 6 mm/¼ in. thick

115 g/4 oz unsalted butter
2 garlic cloves, peeled and finely
  chopped
20 g/¾ oz parsley, minced
5 tbsp red wine vinegar
2 tsp freshly crushed coriander
freshly ground black pepper

Soak the codfish in cold water according to the directions on the package, then poach it in unsalted cold water, with the thyme and bay leaf, boiling it for 5 minutes. Remove all skin and bone and flake the fish.

Sauté the onions in the oil until golden, add the potatoes and the codfish and cook for 5 minutes. Add the butter. Sprinkle with garlic and parsley. Pour into a warm shallow dish. Briefly heat the vinegar in the hot pan and dribble it over the fish and potatoes. Sprinkle with coriander and pepper and serve at once.

Morue en Beignets
Codfish fritters

Salt codfish is sold in fillets. Choose the thickest part, near the tail. Since all codfish is not salted to the same degree, follow the instructions on the package.

An overnight soaking is best done in a colander immersed in a large pan of cold water. Change the water often. Usually dried codfish is poached briefly before being used in a recipe. Cover the fish with cold water and place over high heat. As soon as it comes to a boil, lower the heat and leave the fish for 10 minutes in the water. Remove the bones and skin with tweezers.

For 8 people

900 g/2 lb salt codfish, trimmed, boiled and finely shredded	salt
450 g/1 lb potatoes, boiled and puréed	freshly ground black pepper
	parsley
4 eggs	oil for deep-frying

Blend the shredded cod and puréed potatoes in a blender. Add the eggs, salt, pepper and parsley and make little balls 5 cm/2 in. wide. Flatten them and deep-fry them.

Serve with fried fresh parsley all around.

Perche à la Charollaise
Fish baked with a wine and cream sauce

This is the easiest way I know to prepare a firm-fleshed fish and transform it into a Burgundy treat.

For 8 people

1 1.8-kg/4-lb perch or any firm-fleshed fish, cleaned and trimmed	salt
	freshly ground black pepper
6 shallots, peeled and chopped	225 ml/8 fl oz single cream
450 ml/16 fl oz dry white wine	25 g/1 oz unsalted butter
	115 ml/4 fl oz soured cream

Preheat the oven to 200°C/400°F/Gas Mark 6.

Place the trimmed fish on top of a layer of chopped shallots. Pour the wine over it. Sprinkle with salt and pepper and add the single cream. Dot with butter and bake for 25 minutes.

Test for doneness. Add the soured cream and stir it into the juices lightly. Bake for 5 more minutes and then serve.

Petits Poissons à la Bourguignotte
Whitebait grilled, then marinated with herbs, wine and vinegar

This is also often made with baby pike, but it can be made with almost any fresh firm-fleshed fish. It needs to be prepared three days in advance.

For 8 people

1.8 kg/4 lb whitebait	3 tbsp parsley
salt	2 tsp thyme
freshly ground black pepper	3 bay leaves
4 tbsp vegetable oil	225 ml/8 fl oz red wine vinegar
6 onions, peeled and chopped	

·············· Garnish ··············

1 bowl of mayonnaise
55 g/2 oz chopped walnuts

Sprinkle the fish with salt and pepper and with 2 tablespoons of oil. Grill for a few minutes until it is cooked and flakes easily.

Lay the fish in a shallow dish. Cover it with the chopped onions, parsley, thyme and bay leaves. Heat the vinegar and pour it over the fish. Add salt, pepper and the remaining oil and cover the dish with a lid or a sheet of foil. Let it marinate for three days.

Serve cold with a bowl of mayonnaise and a bowl of chopped walnuts.

Poisson à la Moutarde

Slices of fish seasoned with a mustard, wine and cream sauce

Served with spinach or sorrel, a light dish.

For 8 people

3 tbsp flour
8 thick slices of any lean firm-
  fleshed fish (about 225 g/8 oz
  each)
4 tbsp oil
85 g/3 oz butter

4 tbsp Dijon-style mustard
1 tsp dry white wine
450 ml/16 fl oz single cream
salt
freshly ground white pepper

Sprinkle the flour on the slices of fish and sauté them in oil and 25 g/1 oz of butter for 4 minutes on each side. Set them aside, but keep them warm.

Mix the mustard with the wine and heat until reduced by half. Add the cream and reduce by two-thirds. Remove from the heat and add the remaining butter, whipping briskly. Season to taste.

Pour the sauce over the slices of fish and serve at once.

Poisson en Meurette

Fish cooked in a red wine, vegetable and bacon sauce

This is also called *matelote* and is made with a hearty red wine and freshwater fish.

For 6–8 people

1.8 kg/4 lb freshwater fish (carp,
  pike, eel, trout, perch)
2 tbsp oil
85 g/3 oz streaky bacon (or lean
  salt pork), cut into small dice
225 ml/8 fl oz red wine
2 garlic cloves, peeled and crushed
2 large onions, peeled and sliced
2 cloves

3 tsp thyme
2 bay leaves
salt
freshly ground black pepper
3 tbsp brandy
4 bread slices, cut into triangles
butter
1 clove garlic

Scale, clean and chop the fish. Sauté it in oil with the bacon for a few minutes and set aside. Bring the red wine, garlic, onions, cloves, thyme and bay leaves to a boil and reduce by half over medium heat. Run the wine through a sieve into a heavy-bottomed pan. Add the fish, salt and pepper and bring to a boil. Remove from the heat, add the brandy, and ignite. Place over low heat and simmer, uncovered, for 30 minutes. Check and correct the seasoning.

Prepare the slices of bread and fry them in butter. Rub them with a clove of garlic.

Place the fish in a warm shallow dish, pour the sauce over it and place the bread triangles all round.

Some people like to add 40 g/1½ oz butter kneaded with 2 tablespoons of flour to thicken the sauce, but I think a light pungent sauce is better.

Saumon en Papillotte
Salmon cooked with fresh mint and tomatoes

The Loire Valley has delicious salmon, and lots of mint grows on the river banks. This is a superb dish, but make sure both the salmon and the mint are very fresh.

For 8 people

1.25 kg/3 lb skinless, boneless fillets of salmon	salt
8 tomatoes (fresh or canned), thickly sliced	freshly ground black pepper
	freshly ground coriander
55 g/2 oz mint leaves	225 ml/8 fl oz Béarnaise sauce (optional)

Blanch the salmon in a *court bouillon* for 5 minutes. Let it cool in its juice.

Preheat the oven to 180°C/350°F/Gas Mark 4.

Put 8 25-cm/10-in. squares of kitchen foil on an oiled ovenproof baking sheet. On each square place 3 slices of tomato sprinkled with a few mint leaves, then a fillet of barely cooked salmon. Sprinkle with salt, pepper and coriander, add more tomato slices and, finally, the rest of the mint leaves.

Close each square of foil, leaving as much air space inside as possible. Bake for 15 minutes.

When you are ready to serve, slide each foil pouch on to a warm serving dish, then open and roll down the sides of the pouches.

Béarnaise sauce is a good, though not essential, accompaniment for this dish.

Saumon aux Herbes

Raw salmon marinated with herbs, lemon and oil

The salmon from the Loire Valley is usually stuffed with sorrel or coated with cream sauce, but this is a lighter dish – perfect as a lunch dish or as part of a summer buffet.

For 8 people

680 g/1½ lb salmon	2 tsp freshly ground black pepper
6 tbsp good olive oil	juice of 1 lemon
2 tsp crushed green peppercorns	3 tbsp finely chopped chervil

Remove all skin and bones from the salmon with tweezers and cut paper-thin fillets.

Brush the surface of the fillets with olive oil and place them in the refrigerator for 2 hours to make the flesh firmer. Cut 5-cm/2-in. strips widthways and spread them on a large serving plate. Sprinkle with green and black pepper, lemon juice and the chervil.

Serve with warm, buttered toast or a green tossed salad.

Truite Farcie aux Herbes

Trout stuffed with greens, cream and shallots, and baked with wine, herbs and cream

The fresh trout of the Morvan region are famous in Burgundy. They can be stuffed with salmon and cream and cooked in red wine, or sautéd with butter. The following recipe is a truly delicious way to prepare this fish.

For each person

1 trout, about 225 g/8 oz
1 tbsp chopped sorrel or spinach
15 g/½ oz unsalted butter
4 tbsp cream
freshly grated nutmeg
salt

freshly ground black pepper
2 tbsp finely chopped shallots
70 ml/2½ fl oz dry white wine
1 tsp mustard
1 tsp lemon juice

Open the trout at the back, slicing it all along to clean it, and clip the backbone at each end with scissors to remove it. Place the sorrel or spinach and the butter in a saucepan and cook over low heat. Add 1 tablespoon of the cream and the nutmeg. Season the trout with salt and pepper and stuff it with the sorrel or spinach mixture. Lay it on its side in a buttered ovenproof dish.

Preheat the oven to 190°C/375°F/Gas Mark 5.

Spread the chopped shallots on the trout. Add the wine and heat on the top of the cooker, then cover with a sheet of greaseproof paper and bake for 10 minutes, or until the flesh flakes easily.

Pour the cooking liquid into a saucepan. Reduce it by half, then add the remaining cream, mustard and lemon juice. Check the seasoning. Place the trout on a warm serving dish and spoon the sauce over it.

Les Oeufs

Egg Dishes

If *les oeufs en meurette* is one of the most celebrated dishes, there are also, in most regions of Burgundy, elegant and imaginative varia-tions on fried, poached, stuffed and baked egg. From poached eggs covered with a crayfish sauce to scrambled eggs prepared with wild mushrooms and cream, or hard-boiled eggs stuffed with snails and shallots, the repertory is rich.

There are delicious omelettes as well. The Romans used to season theirs with honey and pepper, and since then imagination has never lacked in that realm. There are flat omelettes made with onions, parsley, garlic and fresh pork blood. There are mountain omelettes made with potatoes, chervil, cream and Gruyère cheese, or with rich wild mushrooms, country ham and herbs. Then there are the fancier rolled omelettes – some stuffed with walnuts and snails, some with dandelion greens and onion, a favourite at Easter time. There are elaborate omelettes stuffed with calf's brains and sweetbreads and some with the tender flesh of crayfish.

There are omelette cakes – several omelettes piled high, filled with chives, sorrel, goat cheese, and coated with a cream, herb and lemon juice sauce.

I have chosen here the recipes I thought would be most likely to please the modern palate. I will not dwell on how to make an omelette, since one should not have to think twice about the technique. Remember only that for four eggs you must use a 25-cm/10-in. frying-pan, heavy-bottomed, well greased and very hot, and that the eggs should be beaten for only a few seconds before being poured into the pan.

Faux Escargots
Fake snails

An easy way to serve eggs Burgundy style. If one-half garlic clove per person seems too much, use one-third. Allow one ramekin per person.

For each person

½ garlic clove, peeled and crushed
15 g/½ oz softened unsalted butter
1 tbsp finely chopped parsley

salt
freshly ground black pepper
1 or 2 eggs

Crush the garlic and add the butter, parsley, salt and pepper to make a paste.

Preheat the oven to 180°C/350°F/Gas Mark 4.

Butter each ramekin. Break 1 or 2 eggs into each and bake for 5 minutes (or cook for 3 minutes on top of the cooker). Top with the garlic–butter mixture and serve at once.

Oeufs à la Dijonnaise
Baked stuffed eggs

Dijon mustard made with dry white wine transforms this classic stuffed-egg recipe into a pungent dish.

For 8 people

8 hard-boiled eggs
2 tbsp Dijon-style mustard
3 tbsp double cream
1 tbsp wine vinegar
2 shallots, finely chopped
3 tbsp finely chopped fresh herbs
  (chives, chervil and tarragon)

salt
freshly ground white pepper
25 g/1 oz unsalted butter, softened
1 tbsp wine vinegar

Preheat the oven to 180°C/350°F/Gas Mark 4.

Shell and halve the hard-boiled eggs lengthways. Mix the egg yolks, mustard, cream, vinegar, shallots, herbs, salt and pepper into a paste and fill the white halves of the eggs with it. Place in an ovenproof porcelain dish. Dot with butter and vinegar and bake for 10 minutes. Serve warm.

Oeufs au Civet

Fried eggs seasoned with onions, wine and herbs

This treatment of fried eggs is truly inspired.

For 8 people

40 g/1½ oz unsalted butter	freshly ground black pepper
2 tbsp vegetable oil	4 tbsp wine vinegar
8 onions, peeled and thinly sliced	juice of 1 lemon
340 ml/12 fl oz dry white wine	8 eggs
salt	3 tbsp finely chopped parsley

Heat 15 g/½ oz of butter and 1 tablespoon of oil in a thick frying-pan. Add the sliced onions and cook until golden. Add the wine, salt, pepper, vinegar and lemon juice and, stirring occasionally, cook, uncovered, for 20 minutes. The liquid should be reduced by half.

Meanwhile, heat the remaining butter and oil in another pan and fry the eggs. Pour the onion-and-wine mixture into a warm serving dish and slide the fried eggs on top.

Sprinkle with chopped parsley and serve at once.

Oeufs au Nid

Eggs baked in a nest of mashed potatoes and sprinkled with cheese

This is a good dish for children. You can add left-over chicken or meat or simply prepare it with mashed potatoes and grated cheese.

For 8 people

170 g/6 oz finely chopped ham
   and/or left-over chicken
1.25 kg/3 lb mashed potatoes,
   whipped with milk and butter
salt

freshly ground black pepper
freshly grated nutmeg
25 g/1 oz unsalted butter
8 eggs
4 tbsp grated cheese

Preheat the oven to 200°C/400°F/Gas Mark 6.

Add the meat to the mashed potatoes, mixing in salt, pepper and nutmeg. Arrange the mixture in a buttered baking dish, making a deep hole for each egg. Place a dab of butter in each hole and break an egg into it. Add salt and pepper. With a fork, make a deep groove circling each egg to make a nest. Sprinkle with cheese and bake for 15 minutes.

Oeufs Crémés

Baked eggs with cheese

Prepared in a jiffy, this mountain recipe is a children's favourite. Choose a pretty ovenproof dish, since it will be brought to the table.

For 8 people

55 g/2 oz unsalted butter
225 g/8 oz Gruyère cheese, thinly
   sliced
8 large eggs
115 g/4 oz Gruyère cheese, grated

3 tbsp double cream
freshly ground nutmeg
freshly ground white pepper
salt

Preheat the oven to 190°C/375°F/Gas Mark 5.

Butter an ovenproof dish and cover the bottom with the sliced cheese. Bake for 4 minutes until the cheese starts melting. Remove from the oven and carefully break the eggs into the dish, side by side. Sprinkle with the grated cheese. Dribble cream over the top and sprinkle with nutmeg, pepper and a little salt. Bake for 10–12 minutes, until the whites are set and the yolks are still moist.

Oeufs en Cassolette Dijonnaise

Poached eggs covered by a shallot, lemon, cream and butter sauce, and seasoned with herbs

A lovely lunch dish, quick to prepare and most elegant.

For 8 people

2 tbsp Dijon-style mustard	8 eggs
4 tbsp double cream	85 g/3 oz unsalted butter
2 tbsp lemon juice	salt
6 tbsp dry white wine	freshly ground white pepper
4 shallots, peeled and finely chopped	2 tbsp finely chopped parsley
2 tbsp finely chopped tarragon (or chervil or chives)	

Preheat the oven to 120°C/250°F/Gas Mark ½.

Pour the mustard, cream, and lemon juice into a bowl with the white wine and stir well. Add the shallots and tarragon. Pour into a saucepan and cook over low heat, stirring, for 10 minutes. Remove from the heat.

Meanwhile, heat a wide, shallow saucepan of salted water to the boiling point. Reduce the heat to a gentle boil and, breaking each egg into a saucer, gently slide it into the water. Cook for 3 minutes. Trim the whites of the eggs so that each egg looks pretty and place them in individual buttered ramekins. Cover with a sheet of kitchen foil and leave the ramekins in the oven to keep warm.

Cut the butter into small pieces and add to the warm sauce. Stir vigorously off the heat. Add salt and pepper and pour this thick sauce over the individual eggs.

Sprinkle with parsley and serve very hot.

Oeufs en Cocotte

Baked eggs with shallots, mushrooms and cream

For 8 people

85 g/3 oz unsalted butter
6 shallots (or white onions), peeled
    and finely chopped
225 g/8 oz mushrooms, washed,
    dried, and chopped

340 ml/12 fl oz single cream
salt
freshly ground white pepper
5 tbsp chives, finely chopped
8 large fresh eggs

Heat half the butter in a heavy-bottomed frying-pan. Add the shallots and cook over low heat for 2 minutes. Add the mushrooms and cook over low heat, stirring with a wooden spoon, for 3 minutes. Pour in 225 ml/8 fl oz of the cream and let it thicken, stirring from time to time with a wire whisk. Season with salt, pepper and 1 tablespoon of the chives.

Preheat the oven to 180°C/350°F/Gas Mark 4.

Butter 8 individual china ovenproof ramekins and pour the mixture into them evenly. Carefully break one egg into each dish. Divide the remaining cream among them and sprinkle with 3 tablespoons of the chives.

Place the ramekins in a large ovenproof dish, adding enough hot water to the larger dish to reach half the height of the ramekins. Bake 10–15 minutes, or until the egg whites are opaque. Sprinkle with the remaining chives and serve.

Oeufs en Meurette

Eggs poached in a wine, onion and herb sauce

This traditional dish has a questionable name in Burgundy: it is called 'donkey's balls'. It is a hearty dish. I tried to make it lighter for modern appetites, and since I did not want to thicken the sauce with flour and could not thicken it with pork blood, I reduced the wine and the onions. Prepared a day in advance, *meurette* sauce improves greatly. Cooled, it is also easier to degrease.

These tangy, light *oeufs en meurette* are high in flavour and should be served with a bitter dandelion or watercress tossed salad.

For 8 people

70 g/2½ oz unsalted butter
255 g/9 oz streaky bacon (or lean salt pork), cut into 2.5-cm/1-in. pieces
3 large onions, peeled and finely chopped
2 or 3 shallots, peeled and finely chopped
2 garlic cloves, peeled and finely chopped
1.4 l/2⅖ pt hearty red wine
1 clove

1 tsp sugar
salt
freshly ground black pepper
2 bay leaves
2 tsp thyme (or a large sprig of fresh thyme)
8 large eggs
8 slices of stale bread, with crusts removed
1 tbsp vegetable oil
8 tbsp chopped parsley

Heat 25 g/1 oz of butter in a heavy-bottomed frying-pan, add the bacon (or lean pork) and cook for 5 minutes. Add the onions, shallots and garlic, and cook over low heat for 5 minutes. Add the wine, clove, sugar, salt, pepper, bay leaves and thyme, and cook, uncovered, for 40–60 minutes, reducing and thickening the sauce.

Discard the bay leaves and thyme. Remove the bacon and set aside. Pass the hot sauce through a Mouli mill or a food processor and check the seasonings. Remove as much fat as possible from the sauce.

Put the puréed sauce in a large frying-pan and bring it to a boil. Reduce the heat to very low and slip in the eggs, two or three at a time. Cook for about 3 minutes. Meanwhile, fry the slices of bread in the remaining butter and oil. Drain the eggs and place them on the slices of bread. Add the bacon to the sauce and pour over the eggs. Sprinkle with the parsley and serve.

Oeufs Savoyard

Eggs baked on a layer of sliced potatoes and cheese with cream

For 8 people

1.25 kg/3 lb potatoes, peeled and
 sliced
25 g/1 oz unsalted butter
1 tbsp vegetable oil
salt

freshly ground black pepper
130 g/4½ oz grated Gruyère
 cheese
8 eggs
8 tbsp single cream

Preheat the oven to 180°C/350°F/Gas Mark 4.

Sauté the sliced, dried potatoes in the butter and oil in a large frying-pan for 15 minutes. Place them in an ovenproof dish and sprinkle with salt, pepper and cheese. Break the eggs, one by one, on top of the potatoes and sprinkle with salt and pepper. Pour the cream over the eggs and bake for 10–15 minutes. Serve in the baking dish.

This recipe can also be made by substituting sautéd sliced mushrooms for half the amount of potatoes.

Omelette à la Mie

A breadcrumb, cream and herb omelette

For each person

70 g/2½ oz breadcrumbs
115 ml/4 fl oz cream
2 eggs, beaten
salt

freshly ground black pepper
1 tbsp chopped fresh herbs
15 g/½ oz unsalted butter
1 tbsp oil

In a bowl, mix all ingredients except the last two. Heat the butter and oil in a frying-pan and pour in the mixture. Lower the heat and cook for about 5 minutes on one side. Invert the omelette on a flat plate, slide it back into the pan and cook for about 3 minutes.

Omelette à la Crème

A fluffy cream omelette

A glorious, soufflé-like omelette, perfect for an elegant lunch. Soured cream is more interesting than double cream; you may want to try it both ways.

For 4 people

6 eggs, separated
3 tbsp soured cream (or 2 tbsp soured cream and 1 tbsp double cream)
salt
freshly ground black pepper

heavy pinch of freshly grated nutmeg
55 g/2 oz unsalted butter
1 tbsp vegetable oil
1 tbsp chervil (or any fresh herb), finely chopped

Whip the egg whites until stiff. Beat the egg yolks, soured cream, salt, pepper and nutmeg. Heat 40 g/1½ oz of butter and the oil in a 23-cm/9-in. frying-pan and pour in the egg-and-cream mixture. Lower the heat and delicately fold in the beaten egg whites. Cover and cook for about 7 minutes on one side. Invert the omelette on to a flat plate and return it to the pan. Cook the other side for 3 minutes longer.

Soften the remaining butter and spread over the top, sprinkle with herbs and serve on a warm dish.

Omelette à la Moutarde

Mustard, cream and chive omelette

This is an invigorating omelette that would make for a cheerful lunch served with a tart green salad. It's truly interesting in both texture and flavour.

For 4 people *

55 g/2 oz unsalted butter	2 tbsp single cream
2 tbsp finely chopped chives	salt
8 eggs	freshly ground white pepper
2 tbsp Dijon-style mustard	

Heat 15 g/½ oz of the butter in a frying-pan and cook the chives over low heat for 2 minutes.

Preheat the oven to 180°C/350°F/Gas Mark 4.

Whip 3 egg whites until stiff. Pour the remaining eggs and yolks into a bowl, add the mustard, cream and cooked chives, and stir until lightly foamy. Add the egg whites, salt and pepper.

Heat 25 g/1 oz of the butter in the frying-pan, pour in the eggs and heat for 1 minute. Put the pan in the oven for 3–4 minutes.

Gently place the omelette on a warm serving dish, spread the remaining butter on it and serve at once.

Omelette aux Croûtons
A croûton *omelette*

For each person

1 slice of bread	salt
40 g/1½ oz unsalted butter	freshly ground black pepper
2 eggs	1 tbsp oil

Dice and sauté the bread in 25 g/1 oz of the butter. Beat the eggs in a bowl and add salt and pepper and the *croûtons*. Heat the oil and the remaining butter in a frying-pan and pour in the egg–*croûton* mixture. Lower the heat and cook for about 5 minutes on one side. Invert the omelette on to a flat plate, slide it back into the pan and cook for about 3 minutes.

* For eight people, double the ingredients and use two frying-pans.

Omelette aux Foies

A chicken liver omelette

For each person

70 g/2½ oz chicken livers
25 g/1 oz unsalted butter
2 tbsp vegetable oil

salt
freshly ground black pepper
2 eggs

Sauté the livers in half of both the butter and oil. Season with salt and pepper. Beat the eggs in a bowl and add the livers. Heat the remaining butter and oil in a frying-pan and pour in the egg–liver mixture. Lower the heat and cook for about 5 minutes on one side. Invert the omelette on to a flat plate, slide it back into the pan and cook for about 3 minutes.

Omelette de Savoie

A baked cheese, country ham and cream omelette

This is the best omelette in the world for lunches or first courses. One quickly becomes totally addicted and fiercely loyal to it.

For 4 people

8 eggs
115 g/4 oz Gruyère cheese, grated
115 g/4 oz country ham or
  prosciutto, diced
3 tbsp single cream

salt
freshly ground black pepper
40 g/1½ oz unsalted butter
1 tbsp vegetable oil

Beat the eggs in a large bowl. Add half the grated cheese, the diced ham, cream, salt and pepper.

Preheat the oven to 180°C/350°F/Gas Mark 4.

Heat the butter and oil in the frying-pan and pour the egg mixture into it. Cook over high heat for 3 minutes. Fold the omelette in half and slide it on to an ovenproof dish.

Sprinkle it with the rest of the grated cheese and bake for 2 minutes.

Serve at once. The top should be golden and crisp and the inside creamy.

Omelette d'Escargot
A snail omelette

For each person

1 garlic clove, peeled and finely chopped

6 snails, cooked according to directions under 'Preparation of snails' (p. 73)

2 walnuts, chopped

40 g/1½ oz unsalted butter

2 eggs

1 tbsp oil

1 tsp finely chopped parsley

Sauté in a frying-pan the garlic, snails and walnuts in 25 g/1 oz of the butter. Beat the eggs in a bowl and add the contents of the pan. Wipe the pan and heat the oil and the remaining butter in it. Pour in the mixture. Lower the heat and cook for about 5 minutes on one side. Invert the omelette on to a flat plate, slide it back into the pan and cook for about 3 minutes. Sprinkle the parsley on top and serve.

Omelette du Morvan
A country ham and mushroom omelette

For each person

85 g/3 oz country ham, diced

25 g/1 oz mushrooms, quartered

40 g/1½ oz unsalted butter

2 tbsp vegetable oil

2 eggs

salt

freshly ground black pepper

Sauté the ham and mushrooms in 25 g/1 oz of the butter and 1 tablespoon of the oil. Beat the eggs and add salt and pepper and the ham–mushroom mixture. Wipe the frying-pan and heat the remaining oil and butter in it. Pour in the omelette mixture. Lower the heat and cook for about 5 minutes on one side. Invert the omelette on to a flat plate, slide it back into the pan and cook for about 3 minutes more.

Omelette Machon

An onion, cream and vinegar omelette

The *machon* (a Lyon word for something to chew on) is a little snack, eaten mid-morning or mid-afternoon.

For 4 people

25 g/1 oz unsalted butter
1 tbsp vegetable oil
3 large onions, chopped
6 eggs
salt
freshly ground black pepper

1 tbsp single cream
4 tbsp chopped parsley
3 tbsp red wine vinegar
1 tbsp chopped chives or spring
  onions

Heat the butter and oil in a frying-pan. Add the chopped onions and cook over low heat until soft. Meanwhile, beat together in a bowl the eggs, salt, pepper and cream. Add the parsley and pour the egg mixture over the cooked onions. Stirring gently, cook the omelette on one side for 5 minutes, then gently slide it (cooked side down) on to a plate. Brush the pan with a little oil and replace the omelette (raw side down) in it and cook for 2 minutes.

Slide the omelette on to a warm serving dish. Pour the vinegar into the hot pan and bring it to a boil. Pour it over the omelette, sprinkle with pepper and chives and serve at once.

Les Viandes

Meats

Meat is abundant and of the highest quality in Burgundy: superb Charollais cattle in the south, chicken and ducks from Bresse, pigs and game from Morvan.

Some of the dishes rely on beef and tenderloin, but most regional treats use rather inexpensive cuts carefully prepared, enhanced by wine, vegetables and herbs. Beef, lamb, rooster and even turkey are often sautéd, then cooked with red wine, brandy, herbs and garlic as in the heady *boeuf bourguignon* or the pungent *coq au vin* described here. Chicken, goose, duck and veal are often sautéd, then cooked with white wine, herbs, mustard and cream.

I have chosen only a few wild boar, hare and wild duck recipes, since game is not always easily available, but I have selected many pork recipes. In Burgundy all of the pig is used. The casing for its intestines – washed in vinegar and water, brushed, stretched and shredded – is eaten cooked with shallots and white wine; the casing is also used for making sausages. The pig's blood is collected and mixed with onions, spices, herbs, diced fat and chestnuts and put in a piece of intestine casing. Ears, feet (the front ones are more tender because they support less weight) and tail are all prepared with great care. Hams kept forty-five days in brine and three days in a well to become desalted are simmered with shallots and vinegar or cooked with mustard and cream. Pork is boiled, grilled, cooked with prunes or leeks and prepared in a hundred ways. It is perhaps Burgundy's main meat, and there is no end to the variations in its preparation.

Blanquette de Veau

Veal simmered with vegetables, wine and herbs, egg yolks, cream and lemon juice

A delicious Lyon treat to serve with plain rice or noodles. Make sure it is lemony and quite heavily seasoned.

For 8 people

1.8 kg/4 lb veal shoulder and
    breast, cut into 5-cm/2-in.
    pieces, some with bones, some
    without
1.8 l/3⅕ pt dry white wine
2 onions, peeled, with 1 clove
    stuck in one of them
bouquet garni
4 carrots, peeled and cut in sticks
4 leeks (only the white part),
    peeled and sliced (optional)

2 celery stalks
salt
freshly ground pepper
85 g/3 oz unsalted butter, softened
115 g/4 oz flour
115 ml/4 fl oz single cream
4 egg yolks, beaten
juice of 2 or 3 lemons
capers

Place the pieces of meat in a pan and cover with wine and about 1.8 l/3⅕ pt of water. Bring to a boil. Remove the foam on top and add the onions, the bouquet garni, carrots, leeks, celery, salt and pepper and simmer for 1 hour. Pass the stock through a sieve.

Meanwhile mix the soft butter and flour into a paste. In another pot, over low heat, slowly add three-quarters of the cooking stock to the paste and simmer, stirring, for 15 minutes. Pour into the meat pan.

Stir the cream into the beaten egg yolks. Add the lemon juice, stirring, then slowly add a ladle of the warm sauce, stirring all the time, and pour into the meat pan. Don't let it boil. Check the seasoning.

Sprinkle with a few capers and serve at once.

Boeuf à la Mâcon

A gratin of cooked meat baked with onions, wine, herbs and mustard

An old recipe that comes from Mâcon to be made whenever the *potée*, the *pot-au-feu* or the boiled ham has been too abundant and you are faced with left-overs.

For 8 people

55 g/2 oz unsalted butter
1 tbsp vegetable oil
4 onions, peeled and thinly sliced
salt
1 tbsp flour
340 ml/12 fl oz white wine
freshly ground black pepper
pinch of freshly ground nutmeg
2 bay leaves

1.25 kg/3 lb boiled meat (beef, pork, poultry, ham), diced or sliced
3 tbsp wine vinegar
2 tbsp Dijon-style mustard
3 tbsp finely chopped parsley (or chives)
juice of 1 lemon (optional)

Preheat the oven to 180°C/350°F/Gas Mark 4.

Heat 25 g/1 oz of the butter and the oil in a large frying-pan. Add the onions, sprinkle with salt and sauté over low heat for 10 minutes, until soft. Sprinkle with flour, stirring, then add the white wine, salt, pepper and nutmeg and cook over low heat for 15 minutes.

Butter an ovenproof dish and line it with half the onion mixture. Sprinkle with crumbled bay leaves. Layer the boiled meat on top, sprinkle with salt and pepper and cover with the rest of the onions. Dot with the remaining butter and bake for 15 minutes.

Meanwhile, mix the vinegar and mustard. Dribble it over the dish just before serving. Sprinkle the top with parsley (or chives). You may also sprinkle lemon juice over the parsley.

Boeuf à Sauvage

Marinated slices of beef served with a rich wine and vegetable sauce

This turns an ordinary piece of beef into an interesting dish. It is good for a dressy dinner, and you can prepare almost everything at the last minute. Serve with *Gratin Dauphinois* (pp. 169–70) or *Gâteau de Pommes de Terre* (p. 167). The beef must marinate for three days to be properly enhanced by the flavour of all the herbs.

For 8 people

1 fillet of beef or 1 large sirloin tip, sliced (2.5 cm/1 in. thick)	2 bay leaves
salt	2 tsp thyme
freshly ground black pepper	hearty red wine, enough to cover the meat
2 carrots, peeled and finely chopped	2 tbsp vegetable oil
2 onions, peeled and sliced	100 g/3½ oz unsalted butter
1 tomato, quartered	1 tbsp red wine vinegar
1 garlic clove, unpeeled, crushed	4 tbsp finely chopped chervil

Sprinkle the slices of beef with salt and pepper and place them in a shallow dish. Add the carrots, onions, tomato, garlic, bay leaves and thyme, and cover with red wine. Let the meat, covered with a sheet of kitchen foil, marinate for 3 days on the lowest shelf of your refrigerator.

An hour before you are ready to serve your meal, preheat the oven to 150°C/300°F/Gas Mark 2 and drain the carrots, tomato and onions. Heat 1 tablespoon of the oil and 15 g/½ oz of butter in a large frying-pan and sauté the vegetables for 10 minutes, stirring with a wooden spoon. Add the vinegar and two-thirds of the marinade and simmer until the vegetables are tender and the marinade is reduced to 225 ml/8 fl oz. Pass through a sieve, pressing hard, and set aside.

While the marinade simmers, dry the pieces of meat with kitchen towels and sauté them in 55 g/2 oz of the butter and 1 tablespoon of the oil on both sides. Place them in a warm serving dish, cover with a sheet of kitchen foil, and leave them in the oven with the door slightly open as you finish the sauce.

Pour the remaining one-third of the marinade into the frying-pan, scrape up the juices coagulated on the bottom, add the remaining butter and stir vigorously. Add the vegetable purée and pour it over the slices of meat. Sprinkle with pepper and chervil before serving.

Boeuf aux Légumes

Sautéd beef baked with vegetables, herbs, wine and spices

An easy dish, since it can be entirely prepared ahead of time, and ingredients are available everywhere all year round.

For 8 people

15 g/½ oz unsalted butter
1 tsp vegetable oil
1.8 kg/4 lb rump pot roast (or lean boneless chuck or sirloin tip), cut into 5-cm/2-in. cubes
1 onion, chopped
1 celery heart, coarsely chopped
3 carrots, sliced
salt
freshly ground pepper

4 pink turnips, peeled and sliced (optional)
20 g/¾ oz chopped parsley
680 ml/1⅕ pt red wine
2 tsp tomato purée
1 garlic clove studded with 2 cloves
3 bay leaves
2 tbsp finely chopped chives (or parsley or basil)

Heat the butter and oil and sauté the pieces of meat on all sides. Add the onion and sauté for 5 minutes longer, then add the celery heart, carrots, salt and pepper and, after 5 minutes, the turnips.

Preheat the oven to 180°C/350°F/Gas Mark 4.

Cook over medium heat for 10 minutes, stirring once. Check the seasoning and pour the mixture into an ovenproof dish.

Blend the parsley, wine, tomato purée, garlic with cloves, and bay leaves; pour over the meat and vegetables. Cover with kitchen foil and bake for 2 hours.

Remove the foil and, with a ladle, skim off the fat floating on the top. Sprinkle with fresh herbs and serve in the baking dish, along with noodles or rice or any vegetable purée.

This is better prepared a day in advance because it is easier to remove the fat. If the dish is to be used the next day, bake only 1½ hours in the oven; reheat for 30 minutes before serving.

Boeuf Beaujolais

Steak sautéd with a shallot, herb and wine sauce

A quick, pungent way to prepare a plain steak. Cooked on the stove and kept warm in the oven, it is served with a sharp sauce. A *Gratin Dauphinois* (pp. 169–70) would be lovely with this or a *Flan de Pommes de Terre* (p. 163) and *Champignons de Dijon* (p. 160).

For 3 people

35 g/1¼ oz unsalted butter
1 tbsp vegetable oil
1 thick T-bone steak
2 shallots, finely chopped
1 tbsp peppercorns
finely chopped parsley
thyme

2 bay leaves
1 celery stalk, finely chopped
225 ml/8 fl oz good red Burgundy wine
1 garlic clove, finely chopped
1 tbsp good cognac

Preheat the oven to 150°C/300°F/Gas Mark 2.

Heat 25 g/1 oz of butter and the oil in a heavy frying-pan and cook the steak for 4 minutes on both sides over high heat. Place it in a dish, cover with kitchen foil and put it in the oven.

Over high heat, add the shallots, peppercorns, parsley, thyme, bay leaves, celery and red wine to the pan and cook, uncovered, for 10 minutes, until the sauce has reduced by two-thirds. Add the minced garlic, the cognac and the remaining butter.

Cut the meat and pour the sauce over it. Serve at once.

Note: For a smoother sauce, pass it through a sieve before pouring over the meat.

Boeuf Blond

Beef cooked with a sweet white wine and large whole yellow onions

This blond beef comes from the Charollais region, where the large cream-coloured cattle are bred. It is simmered with a sweet white wine and large yellow onions.

Choose a Sauterne-like sweet wine and serve it with the meal along with *Purée de Fenouil* (p. 188), or *Purée de Choux* (p. 188) or home-made noodles (p. 194).

For 8 people

2 tbsp oil

about 115 g/4 oz lean salt pork (or streaky bacon), cut into thin narrow strips

about 115 g/4 oz lean veal, cut into thin, narrow strips

1 1.8-kg/4-lb piece of rump pot roast, as lean as possible, tied with a string to keep its shape

20 whole yellow onions, peeled

450 ml/16 fl oz sweet white wine (or sweet white vermouth)

2 garlic cloves, each studded with 1 clove

3 bay leaves and 2 sprigs of thyme (or 3 sprigs thyme)

900 ml/1⅗ pt (approximately) hot stock or hot water

salt

freshly ground black pepper

2 tbsp arrowroot, blended with 2 tbsp sweet white vermouth

3 tbsp finely chopped chives

2 tbsp finely chopped parsley

Preheat the oven to 180°C/350°F/Gas Mark 4.

Heat the oil in a large, heavy-bottomed pan on top of the cooker. Add the lean salt pork (or bacon) and stir for 3 minutes. Add the veal, lower the heat, and add the beef. Sauté on all sides over low heat for 15 minutes. Add the yellow onions, then the sweet white wine, and cook, uncovered, over medium heat for 20 minutes.

Add the garlic cloves, bay leaves and thyme and place everything in a deep ovenproof dish. The meat should be surrounded by the whole onions and covered with the white wine and herbs. Add enough water (or stock) to cover it almost completely. Sprinkle with salt and pepper and cover with a lid or sheet of kitchen foil. Bake for 3 hours.

Remove as much fat from the top as you can, discard the bay leaves and garlic cloves (and the cloves, if you find them).

Place the meat and onions, covered with foil, in the turned-off oven while you reduce the cooking stock to about 340 ml/12 fl oz. Then add the arrowroot–vermouth mixture to the liquid and simmer for 5 minutes.

Slice the meat and the onions delicately with a very sharp knife and place them in a warm serving dish. Pour the reduced, thickened stock over them. Sprinkle with chives, parsley and pepper and serve at once with sweet white wine.

This dish can, of course, be prepared ahead of time. Cover and keep in the refrigerator. Remove the fat and reheat for about 20 minutes prior to serving.

Boeuf Marinière I

For centuries, before the railway came, bargemen would go down the Rhône carrying fishing boats to the South and would come back home, up the river, drawn by twenty or more horses. They gave Burgundy the famous *matelote* and these two versions of *boeuf marinière*. This recipe is better done a day or so in advance and re-heated.

For 8 people

1.8 kg/4 lb of beef, cut into 5-cm/ 2-in. cubes
70 g/2½ oz unsalted butter
2 tbsp vegetable oil
5 onions, peeled and thinly sliced
salt
freshly ground black pepper
1 tbsp arrowroot

1 tsp coarsely crushed coriander seeds
3 bay leaves
3 tsp thyme
225 ml/8 fl oz white wine
5 garlic cloves, peeled
2 anchovy fillets, trimmed and washed
3 tbsp chopped parsley (or chives)

Preheat the oven to 200°C/400°F/Gas Mark 6.

Dry the cubes of beef thoroughly with kitchen towels.

Heat 25 g/1 oz of butter and the oil in a heavy frying-pan and sauté the meat on all sides for 5 minutes, using a pair of tongs. Do it in three batches and put the sautéd meat aside in a large bowl.

Add the onions to the pan, sprinkle with salt and pepper and cook over low heat for 5 minutes, stirring from time to time. Add the meat to the onions, sprinkle with arrowroot and put the pan in the oven for 15 minutes to brown the arrowroot.

Remove from the oven, add the coriander, bay leaves, thyme and wine. Cover and simmer for 2½ hours.

Crush the garlic, anchovies and remaining butter together into a paste and stir in with a long wooden spoon just before serving. Sprinkle with parsley or chives.

Boeuf Marinière II

This is a splendid dish for a large family dinner. It can be served with home-made noodles (p. 194), or *Purée de Haricots Blancs* (p. 189) or *Pommes de Terre aux Herbes* (p. 184).

For 8 people

1.8 kg/4 lb lean beef	freshly ground black pepper
40 g/1½ oz unsalted butter, at room temperature	2 tbsp wine vinegar
	5 anchovy fillets, crushed
2 tbsp arrowroot or flour	5 garlic cloves, peeled and crushed
2 tbsp oil	2 tbsp Dijon-style mustard
1.25 kg/3 lb onions, thinly sliced	4 tbsp finely chopped parsley
salt	

Slice the meat into thin 5-cm/2-in. strips. Mix the butter and arrowroot into a paste. Put the oil in a heavy-bottomed saucepan, add a layer of sliced onions, salt and pepper, a layer of sliced meat, salt and pepper, and dot the top with the butter–arrowroot paste.

Cover tightly and cook very slowly for 2 hours, checking from time to time.

Put the vinegar, anchovies, garlic, mustard, parsley and pepper into a blender, food processor or mortar and make a paste.

Just before serving, add the anchovy paste to the saucepan, stir and pour it into a warm shallow serving dish after checking the seasoning. The onion and meat must be almost melted when you add the paste.

Variation

Another way to prepare this recipe is to omit the paste made with garlic, anchovies and mustard and gently stir 2 tablespoons of brandy into the sauce before serving.

Boeuf en Daube Charollaise

A beef stew

Daube was a festive dish often served at Easter or at weddings. It was also carried by the grape pickers for their lunch and eaten cold in thick slices.

As a child, I remember quarters of beef marinating in large barrels with fowls and herbs and vegetables before special family gatherings. The mere sight was intoxicating.

In a sixteenth-century archive I found a staggering recipe served for a wedding. It included 14 kilogrammes/30 pounds of Charollais beef, 8 large fowls, 2 veal heads, 40 pigs' feet, 18 litres/4 gallons of red wine, 1 litre/2 pints of old brandy and a variety of herbs and spices.

This lighter and more appropriate version of *daube* is for 8 persons. Prepare it in advance: it is always better reheated.

For 8 people

1.4 l/2⅖ pt red wine	1 piece of pork rind (about 450 g/
115 ml/4 fl oz brandy	1 lb), cut into pieces
1 onion, peeled and quartered	1 veal knuckle
3 bay leaves	3 carrots, peeled and quartered
20 peppercorns	3 onions, peeled and studded with
2 5-cm/2-in. wide pieces of orange	2 cloves each
peel	6 garlic cloves, peeled
2.75 kg/6 lb of top round (or	3 tomatoes, fresh or canned
bottom round, chuck shoulder	2 tsp thyme
or tip of roast beef), cut into	nutmeg
5-cm/2-in. cubes	salt
1 tsp oil	1 tsp sugar
170 g/6 oz diced lean salt pork	

Mix the first six ingredients together to make the marinade. Put the beef in a large bowl with the marinade, cover and let stand a few hours (or overnight on the lowest shelf of the refrigerator).

Dry the meat carefully. Heat the oil in a heavy-bottomed pot and add the salt pork, sautéing on all sides for 5 minutes. Remove the salt pork and set aside. Add the meat and sauté on all sides for 5 minutes.

Line a *doufeu** with the pork rind. Add the beef, veal knuckle, carrots, onions, garlic cloves, tomatoes, thyme, nutmeg, salt and sugar and cover with half of the marinade. Cover and let stand for 2 hours.

Add the rest of the marinade and cook on top of the cooker (or in the oven at 170°C/325°F/Gas Mark 3) for about 2 hours. Remove the herbs, orange peel, rind and cloves. Let cool overnight.

Remove as much fat as possible from the top. Check the seasoning. Reheat over low heat and serve with noodles or boiled potatoes or *Purée de Fenouil* (p. 188).

Boeuf en Gelée Vézulienne

Marinated beef braised with vegetables and served cold in its aspic

A spectacular country treat, which must be prepared 2 days ahead of time but is well worth it.

For about 8 people

1.6–1.8 kg/3½–4 lb rump of beef, cubed	3 onions, peeled and sliced
680 g/1½ lb lean salt pork, diced	2 garlic cloves, peeled and crushed
2 tbsp brandy	parsley
dry white wine, enough to cover the beef and salt pork	salt
1 onion	freshly ground pepper
bouquet garni	1 calf's foot
2 tbsp vegetable oil	1 pig's foot
5 carrots, peeled, sliced and cooked (about 20 minutes)	1 onion stuck with 2 cloves
	2 5-cm-/2-in.-square pieces of pork rind
	3 tbsp finely chopped chives

Put the meats in a large bowl, add the brandy and cover with the wine. Add the onion and the bouquet garni and marinate for 12 hours.

* The *doufeu* is the best of cast-iron casseroles. It comes either round or oval, and has a recessed cover, which is filled with a little water. The even distribution of heat makes it perfect for stews and dishes such as *boeuf bourguignon* and *coq au vin*.

Preheat the oven to 150°C/300°F/Gas Mark 2.

Heat the oil in a heavy-bottomed pan. Dry the beef and lean salt pork and sauté them on all sides for 10 minutes.

Reserve about half of the carrots. Then place a layer of beef, pork, carrots, sliced onions, garlic, parsley, salt and pepper in an ovenproof dish. Add the calf's and pig's feet, then another layer of meat and vegetables.

Meanwhile, add the clove-studded onion to the marinade and bring the marinade to a boil and cook, uncovered, for 20 minutes. Pass through a sieve onto the meat and vegetables. Sprinkle with salt and pepper and put the pork rind on top. Cover and bake for 5 hours, adding water twice, as needed.

Remove the meats. Discard the bones and pork rind. Strain the cooking juices. Chill, then scrape the fat off the top. Reheat.

Decorate the bottom of a large shallow dish with the remaining sliced carrots. Place the pieces of meat on top. Pour in the juices and place in the refrigerator.

Serve unmoulded, sprinkled with chives.

Boudin Blanc et Pruneaux

White sausages cooked in butter and served with stuffed prunes and tart apples

You will find these veal or chicken sausages in most German shops. Serve this dish with a rich red wine or a chilled dry white wine.

For 8 people

20 large prunes	salt
450 ml/16 fl oz warm tea	freshly ground white pepper
225 g/8 oz unsalted butter	11 veal or chicken sausages
1.8 kg/4 lb Granny Smith or other tart apples, peeled, cored and sliced	140 g/5 oz almonds, finely chopped
freshly grated nutmeg	2 tbsp finely chopped dill (optional)

Leave the prunes in the warm tea for 1 hour, then drain them and carefully remove the pits so that the prunes retain their shape.

Melt 25 g/1 oz of the butter in a frying-pan and add the apples.

Sprinkle them with nutmeg, salt and pepper, and cook them, shaking them from time to time. Keep warm.

Preheat the oven to 230°C/450°F/Gas Mark 8.

Prick the sausage skins with a fork. Remove the skins of 3 sausages and slice them so you have 20 pieces. Roll the pieces in the almonds and stuff the prunes with them.

Brown the other sausages in butter in a large frying-pan for a few minutes, then place them with the stuffed prunes in an oven-proof dish. Dot with butter and bake for about 10 minutes.

The sausages are very delicate, so be careful not to bake them too long. Place them on a warm serving dish with the cooked apples in the centre and serve at once. You may sprinkle the dish with dill.

Boulettes Dorées de Montagne

Beef, cheese, onions and herbs – little balls sautéd and seasoned with coriander

Wonderfully easy and perfect for a buffet or for children's parties. Cook in two frying-pans at the same time.

For about 8 people

170 ml/6 fl oz and 1 tbsp vegetable oil
15 g/½ oz unsalted butter
3 onions, finely chopped
900 g/2 lb chopped beef
2 thick slices of bread, moistened in milk and squeezed
2 eggs
55 g/2 oz finely chopped parsley (and any fresh herbs you can find – chervil, basil, mint, etc.)

salt
freshly ground black pepper
pinch of nutmeg
2 tsp thyme or savory
flour for dredging
225 g/8 oz Gruyère cheese, sliced and cut into small pieces
2 tbsp crushed coriander

Heat 1 tablespoon of the oil and the butter in a heavy frying-pan, add the onions and cook slowly for 5 minutes. Remove and set aside.

Mix the meat, onions, bread, eggs, parsley, salt, pepper, nutmeg and thyme with your hands. Divide into about 20 little balls and roll them in 4 tablespoons of the oil, then in flour.

Heat the remaining oil in the frying-pan and sauté the balls on all sides for 10 minutes, turning with kitchen tongs or two wooden spoons.

Press a piece of cheese, carefully, on top of each ball. Cover the pan and cook for 3 minutes.

Sprinkle with coriander and serve at once.

Canard à la Menthe
Duck roasted with mint and apples

There are three main varieties of duck in France. The Nantais, which is the fleshiest, the Rouennais and Canard de Barbarie.

This is a fresh, lively way to prepare a Rouennais duck. Very tart apples and fresh mint make it a splendid dish. Serve with fresh new peas or apple purée, *Petits Navets en Ragoût* (p. 182), *Purée de Choux* (p. 188) or *Raisiné* (p. 250).

For 8 people

2 free-range ducks, about 1.8 kg/4 lb each (if you can find only larger ducks, you will need to cook them longer)
1 lemon, halved
salt
freshly ground pepper
3 tsp thyme
85 g/3 oz unsalted butter

40 g/1½ oz finely chopped fresh mint
8 large crisp apples (preferably Granny Smith), peeled, cored and quartered
115 ml/4 fl oz sweet white wine (or sherry)
juice of 1 lemon

Preheat the oven to 220°C/425°F/Gas Mark 7.

Pull out as much fat from the ducks as you can near the neck and tail and in the cavity. Discard it. Prick the wings, thighs, back and under the wings with a fork.

Wipe the ducks with kitchen towels and rub them with the cut lemon, salt, pepper and thyme. Stuff the inside with 55 g/2 oz of the butter and 25 g/1 oz of the chopped mint. Truss the birds and place them in a shallow baking dish. Bake for 15 minutes and remove the fat.

Reduce the temperature to 190°C/375°F/Gas Mark 5 and turn the ducks on their sides. After 30 minutes, turn them on the other side and remove the fat once more. Cook for another 30 minutes.

Place the apples in the baking dish. Dot them with the remaining butter and let them cook around the ducks for 30 minutes.

Prick the thighs of the ducks; the juices should be yellow (or rosy, if you like your duck undercooked).

Cut the ducks into serving pieces, reserving the mint-and-butter stuffing, and place in a warm serving dish and surround with the apples. Add wine (or sherry) to the cooking pan, scraping the coagulated brown juices with a fork. Add the mint-and-butter stuffing and stir. Check the seasonings and pour over the pieces of duck. Sprinkle the lemon juice, mint and a little pepper over both ducks and apples and serve.

Canard Sauvage à la Diable
Wild duck baked with lemon, mustard, shallots and wine

Better choose a grain-fed shallow-water duck than a wild diving duck that feeds on fish and has too strong a taste. Frozen ducks can turn very dry, and to keep them moist you will have to lay strips of streaky bacon over their breasts and thighs.

This recipe comes from Franche-Comté and uses sharp seasonings for a truly devilish effect. Serve with rice or a vegetable purée or *Paillasson* (p. 181), along with *Raisiné* (p. 250).

For 8 people

2 wild ducks, fresh or defrosted (reserve the livers)	juice of 1 lemon
	2 tbsp Dijon-style mustard
salt	8 shallots, minced
freshly ground black pepper	5 tbsp chopped parsley
sage	115 ml/4 fl oz red wine
55 g/2 oz unsalted butter	thyme
peel of 1 lemon, chopped	savory

Preheat the oven to 200°C/400°F/Gas Mark 6. Season the cavity of the birds with salt, pepper and sage. Spread half of the butter all over the outside of the ducks and sprinkle with salt and pepper. Truss the ducks.

Bake in a shallow dish for 20 minutes (if you have defrosted birds, lay strips of streaky bacon on top to keep them moist). The flesh should be pink and underdone when you remove the birds from the oven. Let them stand for 5 minutes before cutting them into serving pieces.

Reduce the oven heat to 180°C/350°F/Gas Mark 4.

Mix the chopped lemon peel with the lemon juice and the mustard. Put the duck livers through a sieve and add to the lemon-mustard mixture.

Heat the remaining butter and sauté the shallots until soft. Add 3 tablespoons of the parsley and spread in an ovenproof dish. Place the pieces of duck on top. Sprinkle with salt and pepper. Cover with a sheet of kitchen foil and bake for 10 minutes. Transfer to a warm serving dish, and cover with the foil to keep warm.

Pour the wine into the oven dish and scrape the coagulated juices with a spoon. Season with salt, pepper, thyme and savory. Bring to a boil on top of the cooker and simmer for 10 minutes. Add the mixture of liver, mustard and lemon, stir vigorously and pour over the pieces of duck.

Sprinkle with the remaining parsley and serve.

Civet de Dinde

A turkey stewed in red wine and herbs

In Burgundy this dish brings luck: 'Such a good *civet* for dinner, fate can't harm me.' Curiously, in Nivernais a chopped eel is often added to the stew for a more velvety sauce.

Serve with *Terrine de Navets* (p. 190), steamed rice, *Pouti*, which is a potato and chestnut purée (p. 186), or home-made noodles (p. 194).

For 8 people

1 5.5-kg/12-lb turkey, cut into
    serving pieces (about 16 pieces)
3 tbsp vegetable oil
15 g/½ oz unsalted butter
6 onions, peeled and chopped
85 g/3 oz chopped lean salt pork
    (or streaky bacon)
3 garlic cloves, peeled and crushed
1 tbsp flour

enough red wine (preferably a
    hearty Burgundy) to cover the
    meat
salt
freshly ground black pepper
3 tbsp thyme
2 bay leaves
3 tbsp chopped fresh tarragon or
    parsley

Preheat the oven to 170°C/325°F/Gas Mark 3.

Sauté the pieces of turkey in the oil and butter on all sides until golden. Add the onions, then the pork and, 5 minutes later, the garlic. Sprinkle with flour. Pour in enough red wine to cover the meat and bring to a boil on top of the cooker. Add salt, pepper, thyme and bay leaves; cover and bake for 1½ hours.

Check the meat. If the joints are still pink, continue cooking. Remove pieces (thighs last) as they complete cooking and place in a warm serving dish. Cover and keep warm in the oven while you degrease the cooking juices. Discard the thyme and bay leaves. Crush the garlic with a fork, check the seasoning, add salt and pepper. Pour the sauce over the turkey. Sprinkle with tarragon or parsley and serve at once.

Civet de Porc
Pork slowly cooked with onions, red wine and herbs

This old recipe used to be made often in Burgundy, and the sauce was thickened with fresh pork blood. I have chosen other thickeners, but it is still a rich, tasty dish, superb with a purée of fresh apples, a purée of celery, a *Paillasson* (p. 181) or a *Gratin de Chou* (p. 171).

For 8 people

1.8 kg/4 lb pork shoulder, boned
   and cut in 5-cm/2-in. cubes
25 g/1 oz unsalted butter
1 tbsp vegetable oil
115 g/4 oz streaky bacon, cut into
   small dice
5 large onions, minced
450 ml/16 fl oz red Burgundy
   wine
salt

freshly ground black pepper
1 tbsp sage
2 tsp thyme (or a sprig of fresh
   thyme)
3 bay leaves
1 tbsp arrowroot mixed with 1
   tbsp water to make a paste
2 tbsp finely chopped chives (or
   parsley, or any other fresh
   herb)

Dry the cubes of pork with kitchen towels. Sauté them for about 5 minutes in butter and oil in a large frying-pan, turning them on all sides until golden. Add the bacon and onions and sauté for 10 minutes more.

Drain off all excess cooking fat. (You may wish to save it for other dishes.) Add the wine and vigorously scrape the bottom of the pan. Sprinkle the meat with salt, pepper, sage and thyme. Add the bay leaves, cover and simmer for 1½ hours, stirring from time to time. Stir in the arrowroot paste 10 minutes before the end of the cooking time.

Check the seasonings. Remove as much fat as you can with a long-handled spoon and pour the *civet* into a warm serving dish. Sprinkle with fresh herbs.

Cochon de Lait Vigneron
Stuffed suckling pig cooked with vegetables and herbs

A glorious festive dish. In Burgundy grape pickers love to eat it cold after the harvest, but I prefer it hot and crispy. It is best served with cooked apples, baked tomatoes, *Gratin d'Oignons* (p. 171), *Gâteau de Pommes de Terre* (p. 167) or *Paillasson* (p. 181).

Suckling pig can be ordered in many butcher's shops.

For 10 people

1 pork liver (or 140 g/5 oz chicken livers)	3 garlic cloves, peeled and crushed
1 tbsp vegetable oil	40 g/1½ oz chopped parsley
570 g/1¼ lb onions, peeled and chopped	2 tbsp dry white wine
170 g/6 oz diced lean salt pork (or boiled ham)	115 ml/4 fl oz pork blood (optional)
7 tsp thyme	1 suckling pig (about 4.5 kg/10 lb)
2 tsp sage	25 g/1 oz unsalted butter
3 eggs	1 garlic clove, peeled
2 tbsp single cream	2 carrots, peeled and sliced
salt	2 onions, peeled and sliced
freshly ground black pepper	2 bay leaves
	115 ml/4 fl oz white wine

Soak the pork liver in cold water for a few hours. Drain and chop.

Preheat the oven to 190°C/375°F/Gas Mark 5.

Heat the oil in a pan and sauté the onions, then the liver, then the salt pork. Add 5 teaspoons of the thyme, the sage, eggs, cream, salt and pepper, garlic and parsley and cook for about 10 minutes, stirring. Add the wine and pork blood (if available).

Fill the suckling pig with the cooked stuffing and sew it up carefully. Tie the legs with a string and rub the entire pig with butter and a garlic clove. Put a piece of wood in its mouth to keep it open.

Place the suckling pig in an uncovered, buttered ovenproof dish. Wrap the ears and tail with kitchen foil, sprinkle with salt and pepper and scatter the carrots, onions, bay leaves and remaining thyme around it. Bake for 15 minutes. Reduce the oven heat to 180°C/350°F/Gas Mark 4 and bake for 3 hours or more. Baste every 15 minutes with pan drippings. During the last half hour, add the white wine.

Place the pig on a warm serving dish. Remove the foil from the ears and tail and replace the wood in its mouth with a small apple or lemon.

Serve whole, surrounded by the vegetables. Slice at the table, removing forelegs and hams, then dividing the meat down the centre of the back. Make sure everyone has a piece of crackling skin. Degrease the cooking juice and pour it over the cut slices.

Coq au Vin Bourguignon
Sautéd chicken cooked with onions, herbs, red wine and mushrooms

A very old treat in Burgundy. There are as many versions as there are cooks, and it all started with the Gauls, who, being attacked by the Romans, sent a rooster to Julius Caesar carrying the ironic message *'Bon appétit!'* Caesar answered with a concoction made from their rooster cooked with herbs and Roman wine. This was, perhaps, the beginning of a great friendship and of interesting culinary exchanges.

For this *coq au vin bourguignon*, the wine should be as hearty and tasty as possible.

For 8 people

24 small white onions (or 12 larger white onions)
85 g/3 oz unsalted butter
1 tsp sugar
salt
170 g/6 oz lean salt pork, cut into small dice
6 tbsp vegetable oil
170 g/6 oz mushrooms, halved or quartered
1.4 l/2⅖ pt red wine (hearty Burgundy type)

3 1.25-kg/3-lb chickens, each cut into 6–8 pieces
freshly ground pepper
2 large onions, peeled and finely chopped
4 tbsp finely chopped parsley
55 ml/2 fl oz cognac
2 bay leaves
2 garlic cloves, peeled and left whole
2 tsp thyme
3 carrots, chopped
4 slices of bread, cut into triangles

Peel the white onions and cook them whole for about 10 minutes with 25 g/1 oz of the butter, sugar and a pinch of salt in enough water to cover them. Remove from the heat and set aside. (If you use large onions, cook for 20 minutes, until soft.)

Sauté the salt pork in 1 tablespoon of the oil on all sides until crisp. Remove and set aside. Sauté the mushrooms in the hot fat on all sides, sprinkle them with salt, remove and set aside.

Bring the wine to a boil and let it reduce, uncovered, for 10 minutes.

Sprinkle the pieces of chicken with salt and pepper. Heat 40 g/ 1½ oz of butter and 2 tablespoons of oil in a large frying-pan and sauté the chicken pieces on all sides until golden. After 10 minutes, add the chopped onions and cook for 20 minutes more. Add half the parsley and the salt pork, then pour the cognac over the chicken, turn off the heat and ignite. Then pour the hot wine over the chicken. Add the bay leaves, whole garlic cloves, thyme and carrots; cover and simmer for 1 hour. Then uncover and continue cooking for 15 minutes.

Meanwhile, heat 3 tablespoons of oil and the remaining butter in a frying-pan and, when it is very hot, sauté the triangles of bread until crisp and golden.

Warm a large serving dish.

When the chicken is ready, remove the bay leaves and the thyme. Check the seasoning, add the whole onions and mushrooms and pour into the serving dish. Dip the *croûtons* in the sauce, then in the remaining parsley, and place around the dish. Serve at once.

Côte de Boeuf Bourguignon

Rib steak with a shallot, wine and herb sauce

Wonderful with a *Gâteau de Pommes de Terre* (p. 167), a *Gratin d'Oignons* (p. 171) or a *Flan de Pommes de Terre* (p. 163).

For 4 people

2 thick rib steaks	1 garlic clove, peeled and finely
2 tbsp vegetable oil	chopped
130 g/4½ oz unsalted butter	5 tbsp dry sherry (or other wine)
freshly ground pepper	salt
freshly ground coriander	4 tbsp finely chopped chives (or
4 shallots, peeled and finely	parsley)
chopped	

Take the steaks out of the refrigerator 1 hour before you intend to use them.

Preheat the oven to 180°C/350°F/Gas Mark 4.

Heat 1 tablespoon of the oil and 40 g/1½ oz of the butter in two heavy frying-pans (or prepare in two batches). Sear the steaks quickly on each side, then lower the heat and continue cooking for

6–8 minutes, depending on their thickness.

Turn off the oven. Sprinkle the steaks with pepper and coriander. Slide them on to a large baking dish, cover with kitchen foil and leave in the open while you prepare the sauce.

Heat 25 g/1 oz of the butter and 1 tablespoon of oil in one of the pans, add the shallots and cook for 5 minutes. Add the garlic, then the sherry, and cook for another 5 minutes. Add coriander, salt and the chives.

Remove the meat from the oven. Sprinkle it with salt and pepper and turn it over.

Add the remaining butter to the sauce, stirring vigorously. Cut the meat into individual portions and pour the sauce over it so the flavour will penetrate the meat.

Côtes de Porc au Vinaigre
Pork chops cooked with garlic, herbs, onions, vinegar and mustard

A lively way to deal with pork chops and make them both digestible and delicious. Serve with *Purée de Choux* (p. 188) or braised chicory, or *Terrine de Navets* (p. 190).

For 8 people

1 tbsp vegetable oil	2 bay leaves
35 g/1¼ oz unsalted butter	4 onions, peeled and finely
8 pork chops, at least 2.5 cm/1 in.	chopped
thick	8 shallots or spring onions, finely
1 tbsp flour	chopped
salt	3 tbsp red wine vinegar
freshly ground black pepper	3 tbsp Dijon-style mustard
2 garlic cloves, peeled and crushed	55 g/2 oz chopped cornichons

Heat the oil and 25 g/1 oz of the butter. Sprinkle the chops with flour, salt and pepper and sauté them on both sides for about 10 minutes in several batches, turning them twice. Add the garlic and bay leaves and cook over low heat, uncovered, for 10 minutes. Remove the chops to a dish and cover with kitchen foil to keep them warm.

Add the onions, shallots, vinegar, remaining butter and mustard to the pan, scraping up the coagulated juices with a fork. Simmer, uncovered, for a few minutes. Add the chops and pickles for a few minutes and slide on to a warm serving dish.

You may want to add 2 tablespoons of tomato purée for a thicker sauce.

Côtes de Porc Farcies

Pork chops stuffed with ham, cheese and sage, and served with a cabbage purée

This is an easy way to transform plain pork chops into a surprisingly fancy and flavourful dish. Serve this with cabbage-and-potato purée and a dry white wine.

For 8 people

8 slices country ham (or good boiled ham), finely chopped	4 tbsp vegetable oil or 55 g/2 oz lard
170 g/6 oz Gruyère cheese, grated	salt
3 tsp sage	2 whole garlic cloves, peeled
freshly ground black pepper	1 green cabbage, trimmed and quartered
8 large, thick pork chops	3 potatoes, peeled
3 tbsp flour	25 g/1 oz unsalted butter

Mix the chopped ham, cheese, sage and pepper.

Trim the loose fat from the chops. Pat them dry. Make a slit in each chop until the tip of your knife reaches the bone. Fill this little pocket with some of the ham–cheese mixture. Push the filling in and secure it with wooden cocktail sticks if necessary. Dredge the chops with flour.

Heat the oil in a large frying-pan. Sauté the chops and sprinkle them with salt. Add the garlic cloves, lower the heat, cover and cook for 40–45 minutes.

Meanwhile, cook the cabbage and potatoes in a large saucepan of salted water for 30 minutes. Pass through a Mouli mill or food processor. Season with salt, pepper and butter.

Place the stuffed chops around the edge of a warm serving dish and put the vegetable purée in the centre.

Côtes de Veau Dijonnaise
Veal chops baked with onions and wine

This elegant and light lunch dish can be prepared ahead of time. I have used Parmesan to replace the dry strong sheep or goat cheese generally used in Burgundy.

For 8 people

8 veal chops (2 cm/¾ in. thick)
1 tbsp vegetable oil
55 g/2½ oz unsalted butter
850 g/1⅞ lb onions, peeled and finely chopped
salt
freshly ground black pepper

2 tbsp thyme
2 tsp coriander
115 ml/4 oz freshly grated Parmesan cheese
225 ml/8 fl oz dry white wine
115 ml/ 4 fl oz stock

Preheat the oven to 180°C/350°F/Gas Mark 4.

Sauté the chops on both sides in a frying-pan in the oil and half the butter until brown. Remove and set aside. Add the remaining butter to the pan and cook the onions until soft.

Butter an ovenproof dish and cover the bottom with half of the cooked onions. Sprinkle with salt, pepper and 1 tablespoon of the thyme. Place the chops on the layer of onions. Sprinkle with salt, pepper and coriander and cover with the rest of the onions. Sprinkle with salt, pepper, the remaining thyme and grated cheese.

Pour the wine and stock into the dish, dot with butter and bake for 25 minutes.

Check the seasoning and serve in the baking dish.

Croquettes aux Herbes

Pork, bacon and herb patties

These used to be cooked in summer over open fire-pits. Baked in an oven, they are made in a jiffy. Serve them with *Purée de Choux* (p. 188), chicory or *Crozets* (p. 193).

For 8 people

1.25 kg/3 lb pork, chopped	freshly ground black pepper
8 tsp thyme	2 tsp sage
2 bay leaves, crushed	16 to 24 slices smoked streaky
salt	bacon

Preheat the oven to 190°C/375°F/Gas Mark 5.

Mix the pork, herbs and spices. Shape the mixture into 8 large flat patties. Wrap each patty in bacon slices and place it on a square of oiled kitchen foil. Fold carefully and bake for 35–40 minutes.

Daube d'Agneau

A lamb stew

A tasty stew to serve with a *Purée de Choux* (p. 188) and home-made noodles (p. 194) or *Purée de Haricots Blancs* (p. 189).

For 8 people

1 large shoulder of lamb, cut in 5-cm/2-in. cubes	1 onion, peeled and sliced
	40 g/1½ oz lard
680 ml/1⅕ pt red wine	1 onion, peeled and chopped
3 garlic cloves, peeled and crushed	salt
thyme	freshly ground black pepper
bay leaves	2 garlic cloves
parsley	3 tbsp finely chopped parsley
1 carrot, peeled and sliced	15 g/½ oz unsalted butter

Marinate the cubes of lamb in wine with the garlic, herbs, carrot and sliced onion for a few hours.

Heat the lard in a thick-bottomed pan. Add the chopped onion. Dry the meat well and sauté it on all sides. Pour in the marinade and bring it to a boil. Season with salt and pepper, cover and lower the heat. Cook for 2 hours. Discard the bay leaves.

Sauté the garlic and parsley in butter for 1 minute and sprinkle on the dish just before serving.

Epaule d'Agneau Farcie
Stuffed shoulder of lamb

For 8 people

4 large onions, peeled and chopped	1 whole egg, beaten
55 g/2 oz unsalted butter	salt
2 tbsp vegetable oil	freshly ground black pepper
225 g/8 oz ham (or lean salt pork), chopped fine	1 garlic clove, peeled and chopped
2 slices of bread, dipped in 115 ml/4 fl oz milk	1 1.8-kg/4-lb shoulder of lamb, boned
1 tbsp rosemary	25 g/1 oz lard
4 tbsp thyme	6 carrots, peeled and chopped
	3 turnips, peeled and chopped

Sauté half the chopped onions in half of the butter and half of the oil, then mix with the ham and moistened bread. Add the rosemary, 1 tablespoon of thyme, egg, salt, pepper and garlic and spread on the boned shoulder of lamb. Roll it lengthways as tightly as you can, and tie it with a long piece of string.

Preheat the oven to 180°C/350°F/Gas Mark 4.

Heat the lard in a large pan. Add the lamb and brown on all sides. Sprinkle with some of the remaining thyme and cover with kitchen foil or a lid. Bake for 1 hour. Turn it twice.

Heat the remaining butter and oil in a heavy frying-pan and cook the carrots, turnips and the remaining onions until tender. Sprinkle with salt, pepper and the rest of the thyme and place around the lamb for its last 20 minutes of cooking time to soak in some of the roasting juices.

Sprinkle with salt and pepper before serving.

Foie de Porc Bourguignon

Marinated pork liver seasoned with sage, wrapped in bacon and cooked in white wine

In Burgundy each family celebrated the killing of the pig with a large meal and offered the pork liver to the neighbours as a ritual present.

This is a wonderful dish for a buffet or a summer meal, but pork liver can also be delicious simply sliced and sautéd with onions, then sprinkled with vinegar and sage.

For 8 people

900 g/2 lb pork liver
dry white wine, enough to cover
6 sage leaves, fresh or dried
salt

freshly ground black pepper
slices of streaky bacon, enough to
  wrap around the liver

Place the pork liver in a bowl, cover it with the wine and add the sage. Let it stand overnight in the refrigerator.

Remove the liver and let it dry. Sprinkle it with salt and pepper, place the sage leaves around it and wrap it with the bacon slices.

Reduce the marinade over high heat for 30 minutes and then place the wrapped liver in the pan. Lower the heat and simmer, half covered, for 30 minutes.

Remove the liver from the pan. Let it cool. Remove the slices of bacon.

Place the cooking liquid in the refrigerator to thicken and congeal a little and then put the liver in it. Cover with cling film and refrigerate for a few hours.

Unmould and serve, sliced, on lettuce leaves, as a first course or a lunch main course with a salad. You may want to spread the congealed liquid on the lettuce and place the slices of liver on it.

Fricot d'Oie

Goose or duck fricassee with turnips

Because young fowl was unusually good and profitable in Burgundy, the peasants kept the tough birds for themselves. They devised endless ways to prepare them, so *fricots* and fricassees have more imaginative recipes than roasted poultry in the Burgundy cuisine's repertory.

For 8 people

225 g/8 oz lean salt pork (or streaky bacon), diced
3 large onions, peeled and sliced
1 tbsp vegetable oil
25 g/1 oz unsalted butter
1 goose or duck, cut into serving pieces
2 tbsp flour
3 garlic cloves, peeled
1 bunch parsley
2 bay leaves
salt
freshly ground black pepper
900 g/2 lb small pink turnips, peeled

Sauté the salt pork and onions in the oil and butter for a few minutes, stirring. Set aside.

Add the pieces of fowl to the pan. Sauté on all sides. When golden, sprinkle flour over each piece and cook for a few minutes. Add the salt pork and onions, 115 ml/4 oz of water, garlic cloves, parsley, bay leaves, salt and pepper and cook for 45 minutes over medium heat. Add the turnips, cover and cook over low heat for 1 hour. Serve the pieces of goose surrounded by the turnips.

Gigot Boulangère

A baked leg of lamb cooked with onions and potatoes and seasoned with thyme and wine

This is called 'a baker's roast' because in every village housewives would bring some of their dishes to the neighbourhood baker on festive days. After his last batch of bread had been baked, and while the oven was still hot, he would cook the legs of lamb, geese and casseroles they had prepared.

For about 8 people

1 leg of lamb	8 potatoes, peeled and thinly sliced
225 g/8 oz unsalted butter	salt
1 tbsp thyme	freshly ground black pepper
2 garlic cloves, cut in slivers	2 bay leaves, crumbled
3 tbsp dry white wine	parsley
4 large onions, peeled and sliced	

Preheat the oven to 230°C/450°F/Gas Mark 8.

Rub the lamb with 25 g/1 oz of the butter and the thyme. Insert the garlic slivers into various parts of the lamb. Bake for 30 minutes, then add the wine, scraping the coagulated juices.

Meanwhile, sauté the onions in the remaining butter for 5 minutes, stirring. Pour into a large ovenproof dish. Add the potatoes. Season with salt, pepper and the bay leaves. Place the leg of lamb on top and pour the cooking juices over it. Sprinkle with salt and pepper and bake for about 30 minutes.

Serve in a warm serving dish with the sliced lamb on one side, the onions and potatoes on the other and little bunches of parsley in the centre.

Jambon au Torchon et au Foin
Ham boiled with herbs and spices

The flavour of ham depends on the diet of the pig – whether it is fed on sugar beets, chestnuts, cheese or acorns – and on the preparation of the meat. Ham is cured in so many ways and cooked in so many ways in Burgundy that there is no monotony in using it often.

Rubbed with salt, it is kept in deep boxes full of ashes, then wrapped in canvas rags and hung on a bar across a fireplace for two hours a day for about three to four weeks while sage, juniper and green hardwood branches provide a fragrant smoke. It can also be covered with salt and hung to dry in the mountain air for six months, rubbed with pepper and eaten raw; it acquires a tangy flavour and a deep rusty colour. For a less refined but quicker treatment, it can be kept in brine, then cooked with vegetables.

The following is an old-fashioned way to prepare ham, using the butt portion that is uncured and must be cooked before eating.

The original recipe calls for a handful of hay to be spread on the bottom of the cooking pot as a bed for the ham. But since hay is unlikely to be found in the average kitchen, you could use dried herbs of any kind as a substitute – or, because the ingredient isn't essential, omit it altogether.

For 8 people

1 4.5–9-kg/10–20-lb uncooked ham	2 tbsp rosemary
a handful of dried herbs (optional)	10 peppercorns
5 bay leaves	salt
3 tbsp thyme	dry white wine
	140 g/5 oz breadcrumbs

Wash the ham and leave it in cold water for 6 hours. Wrap it in a large piece of clean cloth and tie it with a string. Scatter a handful of dried herbs on the bottom of a large pan. Place the wrapped ham on top of the herbs and cover with cold water.

Add the other herbs, peppercorns and salt and bring to a boil. Simmer for 4 hours. Add the wine (about one-third of the amount of water in the pot) and simmer for 1 hour.

Let the ham cool in its cooking liquid overnight.

Remove from the liquid, cut the cloth and remove the skin and part of the fat. Rub with breadcrumbs, pressing down with the palm of your hand. Eat the ham warm or cold.

Jambon à la Saulieu
Slices of ham cooked with shallot, wine, cream and tomato sauce, sprinkled with cheese and grilled

With its delicate yet tangy sauce, this easy dish embodies all the flavours of Burgundy. Serve with home-made noodles (p. 194), *Purée de Fenouil* (p. 188), *Gâteau de Pommes de Terre* (p. 167) or *Gâteau au Céleri* (p. 166).

For 8 people

680 g/1½ lb mushrooms, sliced
2 tbsp vegetable oil
25 g/1 oz unsalted butter
225 ml/8 fl oz dry white wine
6 tbsp finely chopped shallots (or spring onions)
680 ml/1⅕ pt double cream
3 tomatoes, peeled, seeded and chopped
salt

freshly ground black pepper
25 g/1 oz unsalted butter mixed with 2 tbsp flour to make a *beurre manié*
10 slices cooked ham (about 85 g/3 oz per slice)
freshly ground coriander
70 g/2½ oz grated Gruyère or Parmesan cheese

Sauté the mushrooms in the oil and half of the butter for 5 minutes. Set aside. Reduce the wine and shallots in a saucepan for 5 minutes. Add the cream, tomatoes, salt and pepper and simmer for another 5 minutes. Add the *beurre manié* and remove from the heat, stirring. Cover and keep warm.

Butter a deep ovenproof dish. Cover the bottom with the ham slices. Sprinkle with pepper and coriander. Cover with the mushrooms and coat with the wine sauce. Sprinkle the grated cheese on top, dot with the remaining butter and place under a hot grill for a few minutes. It shouldn't boil, so don't put it too close to the heat.

Jambon Chaud Chablisienne
Spinach and ham baked in a wine, cream and herb sauce

Easy to prepare all year round, this is a wonderful dish you can make ahead of time. Perfect for a children's meal, too.

For 8 people

2.75 kg/6 lb spinach
1 large onion, peeled and chopped
15 g/½ oz unsalted butter
2 tbsp flour
225 ml/8 fl oz white wine
170 ml/6 fl oz chicken stock (or water)
1 tsp tomato purée

salt
freshly ground black pepper
4 tbsp tarragon
freshly ground nutmeg
4 tbsp single cream
8 slices (450 g/1 lb) cooked ham, shredded
3 tbsp grated Gruyère cheese

Blanch the fresh spinach in salted water for 10 minutes. Drain and chop.

. Sauté the onion in butter. Sprinkle with flour and cook over low heat for a few minutes. Add the wine, stock (or water) and tomato purée and stir. Sprinkle with salt and pepper. Add the tarragon, spinach, nutmeg and cream and cook for 5 minutes.

Preheat the oven to 180°C/350°F/Gas Mark 4.

Butter an ovenproof dish and spread with half of the spinach mixture. Cover with the ham, sprinkle with nutmeg and pepper and cover with the rest of the spinach mixture. Sprinkle with cheese, dot with butter and bake for 15 minutes. Serve hot.

Jambon Grand-Mère
Fresh ham rubbed with herbs and baked slowly

There is nothing better than this fresh ham baked for 5 hours with herbs and garlic and served with a *Paillasson* (p. 181), *Crépinette aux Marrons* (p. 29) and *Purée de Choux* (p. 188). The cold left-overs can be used in a variety of dishes.

For 20 people

5 garlic cloves, peeled and sliced	5 tbsp thyme and sage (or as much
1 5.5–6.5-kg/12–14-lb fresh ham	as needed)
or leg of pork, trimmed of	salt
some of its fat	freshly ground black pepper
	5 tbsp dry white wine

Preheat the oven to 180°C/350°F/Gas Mark 4.

Insert the garlic slices in the ham in various places. Rub the herbs, salt and pepper all over the surface of the meat, pressing with your hands.

Bake, fat side up, for 3 hours. Sprinkle more herbs on the surface. Turn it over and pat more herbs on it. Cover with kitchen foil and bake for 2 hours.

Remove the ham to a large dish. Add the wine to the coagulated juices in the pan, scraping the bottom vigorously. Slice the meat and pour the juice over it.

Lièvre de Pâques

Hare (or turkey) marinated, then cooked with cream and grapes

A traditional Easter dish – feudal lords let the people shoot on their land on that special holiday in order to have a festive meal. It has to be prepared two days in advance and can be made with turkey as well as hare.

For 8 people

1 saddle of hare or 1 large breast of turkey	1 tbsp thyme
	freshly ground pepper
115 ml/4 fl oz brandy	salt
8 shallots, peeled and chopped	55 g/2 oz unsalted butter
55 g/2 oz chopped celery	225 ml/8 fl oz cream
2 bay leaves	170 g/6 oz fresh grapes

Marinate the hare or turkey in a bowl with the brandy, shallots, celery, bay leaves, thyme and pepper for 2 days on a low shelf in the refrigerator or in a cool place. Turn the meat a few times.

Preheat the oven to 180°C/350°F/Gas Mark 4.

Drain the meat and place it in an ovenproof dish. Spread the top with salt, pepper and butter. Cover with a sheet of kitchen foil and bake for 30 minutes. Turn the meat over with tongs, pour the marinade over the top, cover and cook for 30 minutes longer.

Remove the bay leaves. Add the cream and grapes to the sauce and cook for 5 minutes.

Check the seasoning and serve with *Pouti* (p. 186) or *Gratin de Chou* (p. 171) or *Gratin Forestière* (p. 174).

Meurette de Poulet

A chicken cooked with wine, vegetables and herbs

Meurette, or stew, is, with snails, one of the cornerstones of Burgundy cooking. Its main ingredient can be eel, pike, carp or poached eggs. With chicken it is lighter than *coq au vin* and is often prepared with white wine instead of red.

For 8 people

20 very small pickling onions, peeled
70 g/2½ oz unsalted butter
salt
freshly ground black pepper
1 tsp sugar
225 g/8 oz streaky bacon, diced (12-mm/½-in. pieces)
225 g/8 oz mushrooms, quartered
1 tbsp vegetable oil
slices of bread, cut into triangles
4 yellow onions, peeled and finely chopped
2 1.8-kg/4-lb chickens, each cut into 8 pieces
3 spring onions, peeled and finely chopped
5 garlic cloves, peeled and finely chopped
3 tbsp flour
680 ml/1⅕ pt red wine
salt
freshly ground black pepper
2 bay leaves
thyme
1 garlic clove, peeled and left whole
finely chopped parsley

Place the pickling onions, 1 tablespoon of water, 25 g/1 oz butter, salt, pepper and sugar in a saucepan and cook, covered, for 10 minutes. Remove the cover, cook for 3 minutes and set aside, covered.

Heat 25 g/1 oz of butter in a frying-pan and sauté the diced bacon for a few minutes. Remove and set aside.

Add the mushrooms to the fat and sauté on all sides until cooked. Remove to another bowl and keep covered.

Add the oil to the pan and fry the triangles of bread on both sides. Place the bread on a baking sheet and keep warm in the oven on the lowest setting until ready to serve.

Add the remaining butter to the pan and sauté the minced yellow onions for 5 minutes, then add the chicken. Sauté on all sides, turning each piece with a pair of tongs, for 10 minutes. Add the spring onions and minced garlic, sprinkle with flour and stir. Cook for 5 minutes, then add the wine, salt, pepper, bay leaves and thyme. Cover and simmer for 50 minutes. Add the pickling onions, bacon and mushrooms. Pour the mixture into a warm serving dish and surround with the *croûtons* rubbed with the clove of garlic. Sprinkle with parsley.

Oie à la Moutarde

Braised goose with mustard and wine

Braised goose is more tender and has more flavour and less fat than roasted goose. Enhanced by a lively sauce, this is a truly festive dinner. The recipe can also be made with a duck (cook only 90 minutes). Serve with braised lettuce, a celery purée, *Pouti* (p. 186) or *Pommes de Terre aux Herbes* (p. 184).

For 8 people

2 onions, peeled and finely chopped	225 ml/8 fl oz dry white wine
2 tbsp vegetable oil	chicken stock to cover the meat
15 g/½ oz unsalted butter	2 bay leaves
1 large goose, cut into serving pieces	2 sprigs of thyme
salt	340 ml/12 fl oz single cream
freshly ground black pepper	3 tbsp Dijon-style mustard
	3 tbsp finely chopped tarragon (or any other fresh herb)

Sauté the onions in the oil and butter for 5 minutes. Add the pieces of goose, skin side down. Sprinkle with salt and pepper. Cook over low heat for 5 minutes, turning each piece on all sides. Add the wine, enough chicken stock to cover the meat, the bay leaves and the thyme. Cover and simmer for at least 2½ hours, or until the meat can be easily pierced with a fork and its juices run clear.

Place the pieces of goose in a warm serving dish, cover with a sheet of kitchen foil and keep in the oven on the lowest setting until ready to serve.

Spoon out as much fat as possible from the cooking juice. Scrape up the brown coagulated juices with a fork. Stir in the cream. Reduce by stirring constantly over medium heat for a few minutes. Remove from the heat, add the mustard and check the seasoning.

Spoon the sauce over the pieces of goose. Sprinkle with fresh herbs.

Porc au Vermouth

A loin of pork cooked with vegetables and seasoned with orange and lemon juice and vermouth

In Burgundy this dish is usually prepared with a sweet 'cooked' wine (to which sugar and brandy have been added). I have tried sweet dessert wine but have found that the best thing is to use a good-quality sweet vermouth and ignite the meat with brandy. It can be served with *Purée de Choux* (p. 188), braised chicory, *Purée de Fenouil* (p. 188) or *Terrine de Navets* (p. 190).

For 8 people

3 tsp thyme	6 onions, thinly sliced
6 tsp sage	3 carrots, thinly sliced
salt	3 tbsp brandy (cognac, preferably)
freshly ground pepper	juice and grated skin of 1 orange
1 2.25-kg/5-lb centre-cut loin of pork (bone in)	juice of 1 lemon
70 g/2½ oz unsalted butter	225 ml/8 fl oz good sweet vermouth

Sprinkle the thyme, sage, salt and pepper all over the piece of pork and press them down.

Heat 40 g/1½ oz of the butter in a heavy-bottomed pan and add the onions and carrots. Stir, then add the pork. Sauté for 25 minutes over low heat, uncovered.

Add the brandy and ignite. Add the orange juice, lemon juice, half of the vermouth and 2 tablespoons of water. Scrape the bottom of the pan and turn the meat. Cover and simmer for 1½ hours.

Put the meat on a dish and cover with kitchen foil to keep warm. Pour the rest of the vermouth into the hot pan and scrape with a fork. Add the orange skin and cook for 5 minutes, uncovered. Add the remaining butter, cover and turn off the heat.

Meanwhile, slice the meat and arrange it on a warm serving dish. Sprinkle with salt and pepper. Pour the hot sauce over the slices of meat and serve at once.

Porc aux Haricots Rouges

Pork spareribs cooked with onions, red wine, herbs and red kidney beans

The herbs, wine and garlic give this dish its rich distinctive flavour, and the red kidney beans are the right complement for it. A good accompaniment is a tossed dandelion-green salad (pp. 50, 51).

For 8 people

900 g/2 lb dried kidney beans
1 whole onion, peeled and stuck
    with 1 clove
1 garlic clove, peeled and left
    whole
2 bay leaves
sprigs of thyme
1.8 kg/4 lb spareribs, cut in large
    serving pieces

1 pig's ear (or pig's knuckle or
    large piece of pork rind)
40 g/1½ oz unsalted butter
225 g/8 oz lean salt pork, diced
3 onions, peeled and chopped
1 tbsp flour
450 ml/16 fl oz hearty red wine
freshly ground black pepper
3 tbsp finely chopped parsley

Soak the beans in cold water overnight. On the day of cooking, rinse them well and place them in a large saucepan, covered with the water they have soaked in. Boil for 10 minutes. Lower the heat and add the onion with the clove, the garlic, bay leaves and thyme. Cover and simmer for 1½ hours, or until tender.

Place the spareribs and the pig's ear (or pig's knuckle or rind) in a large saucepan of boiling water. Boil for 5 minutes. Drain.

Heat the butter and sauté the salt pork and chopped onions. Stir until the onions turn golden. Sprinkle with the flour. Stir while adding the wine, then add the spareribs and the ear. Bring to a boil and cook for 1 hour.

Drain the beans and add them to the pork. Season with pepper, cover and simmer for 15 minutes.

Just before serving, cut the pig's ear (or knuckle or rind) into thin strips and mix with the red beans. Discard the bay leaves and the onion with the clove. Put the beans in a warm serving dish, place the spareribs around them, and sprinkle with parsley. Serve very warm.

Porc Dijonnaise
Pork with vegetables and a shallot, cream and mustard sauce

You may use part of a whole ham; the butt portion is more flavourful, leaner and also more expensive (3 kg/7 lb will serve 10 people). A smoked shoulder of pork is less expensive but less flavourful with more waste (you need about 450 g/1 lb per person). This highly seasoned dish is superb with a celery purée, *Purée de Fenouil* (p. 188) or *Purée de Choux* (p. 188).

For 10 people

2 tbsp oil
55 g/2 oz unsalted butter
3 leeks (white part only) or 3
   onions, peeled and chopped
4 carrots, peeled and chopped
900 ml/1⅗ pt dry white wine
2 bay leaves
2 tsp thyme
1 3–4.5-kg/7–10-lb smoked
   shoulder of pork (or a ham butt)

stock (or water), enough to cover
   the meat
5 shallots, peeled and finely
   chopped
5 tbsp single cream
2 tbsp Dijon-style mustard
salt
freshly ground black pepper

Heat the oil and half the butter, and sauté the leeks (or onions) and the carrots until soft but not brown. Add the wine, bay leaves and thyme. Cook for 15 minutes, uncovered.

Place the pork on top of this vegetable mixture. Add enough stock (or water) to cover the meat and cook for about 2 hours, or until very tender.

Meanwhile, cook the shallots in the remaining butter. Add a few tablespoons of the cooking juices. Reduce the liquid by cooking, uncovered, for 5 minutes.

Drain the meat, place it on a warm serving dish and slice. Add the cream and mustard to the shallots, correct the seasoning with salt and pepper and spoon the sauce over the slices of pork. Serve at once.

Poule-au-Pot Bourguignonne
Stuffed chickens boiled with vegetables and herbs

Each region in France claims to own the genuine *poule-au-pot* recipe. Henry IV may have spoken about it in the Pyrenees; the dukes of Burgundy were fond of it and gave it its 'letters of nobility'. Then various chefs embellished the dish with such necessary ingredients as goose livers, but it was the housewives of Burgundy who brought to it a perfect balance of flavours.

Since large flavourful hens are hard to find, the secret here is to cook an extra chicken at the same time to make a *very* concentrated broth. Keep the extra fowl for making a salad. Serve with plain rice.

This must be prepared one day in advance for the best results.

For 8 people

············ *Court bouillon* ············

3 large chickens (including gizzards, feet and necks)
2 carrots, peeled
2 onions, peeled
2 turnips, peeled
freshly ground black pepper

salt
1 bay leaf
1 sprig of thyme
1 garlic clove, peeled
1 celery stalk

··············· Stuffing ···············

2 slices bread, soaked in 115 ml/4 fl oz milk
2 thick slices country ham, chopped
3 onions, chopped and sautéd in butter

4 chicken livers, chopped
2 garlic cloves, finely chopped
1 tbs finely chopped parsley
2 eggs, beaten
salt
freshly ground black pepper

············ Vegetables ············

4 carrots, peeled
4 turnips, peeled
1 celery stalk

4 onions, peeled
2 garlic cloves, peeled

Put all the ingredients for the *court bouillon* in a large cooking vessel, cover with water and cook for 1½ hours. Let it cool. Remove the chickens.

Remove all fat from the stock. (When it is cold, the fat will congeal at the top and should be easy to remove. It is better to make the broth a day in advance.) Discard the vegetables.

Prepare the stuffing. Mix all the ingredients well and season.

Stuff two of the chickens (save the third chicken for another use). Sew the openings. Place the chickens in the degreased stock and bring it to a boil. Simmer, covered, for 1 hour. Skim often.

Add the carrots, turnips, celery, onions and garlic and cook for 30 minutes.

Place the stuffed chickens on a large warm dish and cut them into serving pieces. Put the stuffing in the centre of the plate and surround it with the vegetables. Pour a ladle of hot stock over everything, sprinkle with salt and pepper and serve.

Serve the rest of the stock separately at the beginning of the meal, or, on another day, over buttered toasted slices of whole-wheat bread spread lightly with mustard.

Poulet à la Crème Charollaise

Chicken cooked in sweet white wine with herbs and enriched with cream, egg yolks and lemon

A succulent dish served with rice or home-made noodles and mushrooms. It can be prepared either with sweet white wine or with sweet sherry.

For 8 people

2 tbsp vegetable oil
70 g/2½ oz unsalted butter
2 1.8-kg/4-lb chickens, each cut
   into 8 pieces
salt
freshly ground white pepper
nutmeg
1 garlic clove, peeled
2 bay leaves

thyme
340 ml/12 fl oz white dessert wine
   (or sweet sherry)
680 ml/1⅕ pt single cream
4 egg yolks
juice of 2 lemons
cayenne pepper
salt

Heat the oil and butter in a heavy pan and sauté the pieces of chicken on all sides for 15 minutes, turning with a pair of tongs. Sprinkle with salt, pepper and nutmeg. Cook for 5 minutes, then add the garlic clove, bay leaves, thyme and wine. Cook, covered, for 30–40 minutes, until tender. Remove the chicken to an oven-proof serving dish, cover with a sheet of kitchen foil, and keep it in the oven at 120°C/250°F/Gas Mark ½.

Add the cream to the wine sauce, scrape up the coagulated juices and cook for 10 minutes, uncovered. Beat the egg yolks in a bowl. Gradually add the sauce to the yolks, stirring constantly. Stir in the lemon juice, cayenne and salt and pour over the chicken. The sauce should be smooth and thick enough to coat the pieces of chicken. Keep the chicken in the oven for 5–10 minutes, then serve.

Poulet à la Moutarde

Grilled chicken spread with onion, mustard and breadcrumbs, and served with a shallot, wine and herb sauce

A superb Lyon treat, this must be made with young, plump chickens and is best served with a dry white wine, *Estouffade de Carottes* (p. 162), *Galette aux Pommes de Terre* (p. 165) or *Gratin Forestière* (p. 174).

For 8 people

4 plump tender chickens
salt
freshly ground black pepper
170–225 g/6–8 oz unsalted butter, melted
2 tbsp vegetable oil
5 onions, minced
3 tbsp Dijon-style mustard
140 g/5 oz breadcrumbs

8 shallots, finely chopped
140 ml/5 fl oz red wine vinegar
salt
10 peppercorns, crushed
6 tbsp fresh herbs (tarragon, chervil, chives), cut with scissors
watercress

Split the chickens down the back. Flatten them with the side of a cleaver or a mallet. Sprinkle both sides with salt, pepper and about 8 tablespoons of the melted butter. Cook the chickens, skin side up, under a grill for 15 minutes, basting them with more butter.

Meanwhile, cook the onions in 1 tablespoon melted butter and the oil until soft and mushy. Place them in a bowl and mix them with the mustard.

Preheat oven to 180°C/350°F/Gas Mark 4.

Spread the onion–mustard purée on the chickens, then sprinkle the breadcrumbs all over them, pressing with your hands so that they hold well. Bake for 35 minutes.

Cook the shallots with the vinegar, uncovered, over high heat. Reduce the sauce slightly. Add salt, peppercorns and fresh herbs, serve the chicken surrounded with watercress, and pass the sauce in a separate bowl.

Poulet au Fromage
Chicken baked with a wine, mustard and cheese sauce

A classic in Burgundy gastronomy. Serve with a chilled white or good rosé wine. Superb with *Gâteau de Pommes de Terre* (p. 167), *Paillasson* (p. 181) or *Purée de Fenouil* (p. 188). It can be prepared ahead of time and reheated.

For 8 people

3 chickens, each cut into 6–8 pieces
3 tbsp vegetable oil
70 g/2½ oz unsalted butter
salt
freshly ground black pepper
cayenne pepper
370 g/13 oz grated Gruyère cheese

225 ml/8 fl oz dry white wine
2 tbsp Dijon-style mustard
225 ml/8 fl oz single cream
1 5-cm/2-in. piece fresh ginger, grated (optional)
pinch of nutmeg
breadcrumbs

Sauté the pieces of chicken on all sides for 5 minutes in the oil and 55 g/2 oz of the butter in a large frying-pan. Sprinkle with salt, pepper and cayenne and cook, uncovered, over low heat for 45 minutes.

Preheat the oven to 190°C/375°F/Gas Mark 5.

Place the pieces of chicken in an ovenproof dish. Stir 340 g/12 oz of the cheese into the cooking juices in the frying-pan and add the wine, mustard and cream (and ginger, if desired). Heat gently, stirring, while adding salt, pepper, nutmeg, breadcrumbs and then the remaining cheese. Dot with the remaining butter and bake for 15 minutes. Serve golden and sumptuous in its baking dish.

Note: After the pieces of chicken are sautéd, you may want to cook 4 leeks (white part only) in 40 g/1½ oz of unsalted butter until soft, and add them to the sauce around the chicken before baking. It thickens the sauce, and I find the dish becomes truly superb that way.

Poulet au Vinaigre
Sautéd chicken seasoned with vinegar, garlic, wine, mustard and cream

One of Burgundy's oldest treats, when sweet-and-sour flavouring was commonly used and wild boar was cooked with a honey sauce.

For 8 people

85 g/3 oz unsalted butter
1 tbsp vegetable oil
3 chickens, each cut into 8 pieces
salt
freshly ground pepper
10 garlic cloves, unpeeled
115–140 ml/4–5 fl oz red wine
   vinegar

225 ml/8 fl oz dry white wine
5 tsp Dijon-style mustard
2 tbsp tomato purée
3 tbsp double cream
2 tbsp cognac
2 tbsp fresh herbs (chives, parsley
   or dill), finely chopped

Preheat the oven to 140°C/275°F/Gas Mark 1.

Heat 25 g/1 oz of the butter and oil in a heavy-bottomed pan. Dry the chicken pieces with a tea-towel and add them to the pan. Sauté on all sides, turning with tongs, for about 10 minutes, or until each piece is golden. Add salt and pepper and the garlic cloves, cover, lower the heat and cook for 25 minutes. Remove from the heat, discard the cooking fat and reserve the garlic cloves. Keep the pieces of chicken, covered, in the oven.

Pour the vinegar into the pan and scrape up the coagulated juices from the bottom with a fork. Add the wine, mustard and tomato purée to the pan, stirring with the fork, and cook over medium heat for 3 minutes – no longer. Add the cream, the remaining butter and cognac, stirring all the time. Peel the garlic cloves and mash them into the sauce. Add the chicken and reheat for 3–5 minutes, stirring from time to time. Check the seasoning. Sprinkle with fresh herbs and serve on a warm shallow dish.

Poulet aux Crevettes

Sautéd chicken cooked with shallots, carrots, wine, cream and large prawns

I found large prawns to be a perfectly acceptable substitute for the crayfish traditionally used in Burgundy with chicken. This is a dressy, festive dish and should be served accompanied by a tossed green salad only.

For 8 people

2 bay leaves
thyme
24 large raw prawns
85 g/3 oz unsalted butter
2 tbsp vegetable oil
2 1.8-kg/4-lb chickens, each cut
    into 8 pieces
salt
freshly ground black pepper
3 shallots, peeled and finely
    chopped
2 carrots, peeled and diced

2 onions, peeled and finely
    chopped
2 tbsp cognac
140 ml/5 fl oz dry white wine
5 tbsp tomato purée
1 tsp saffron
2 garlic cloves, peeled
6 tbsp double cream
2 tbsp tarragon (or other fresh
    herbs), chopped or whole
cayenne pepper (if needed)

Put a large pot of salted water over high heat and add the bay leaves and thyme. Add the prawns as soon as the water reaches the boiling point. Cook for 2 minutes. Let them cool in the stock, then peel them.

Meanwhile, heat 40 g/1½ oz of the butter and the oil in a heavy frying-pan or *doufeu* pan and sauté the pieces of chicken in three batches. Season with salt and pepper and cook each piece on all sides by turning with kitchen tongs. Remove and set aside.

Add the remaining butter, the shallots, carrots and onions to the pan. Cook over low heat for 15 minutes. Add the cognac and wine and scrape the bottom of the pan vigorously. Add the tomato purée, saffron, garlic cloves and pieces of chicken. Cover and cook over medium heat for 30 minutes.

Add the prawns and the cream and stir vigorously. Add half of the chopped herbs and cook, uncovered, for 5–10 minutes.

Check the seasoning and add more salt and pepper if necessary. (This dish should be highly seasoned.) Add cayenne if needed.

Transfer to a warm shallow dish. Sprinkle with the remaining chopped herbs and serve with plain rice.

Poulet aux Noix

Sautéd chicken cooked with mushrooms, shallots, garlic, walnuts and vermouth

This tasty dish is usually made with fresh walnuts in the eastern part of Burgundy. It is equally interesting prepared with dry walnuts or pecans, and served with *Purée de Fenouil* (p. 188), a green bean purée, *Gratin Trois* (p. 176) or *Gâteau au Céleri* (p. 166).

For 8 people

2 tsp walnut or peanut oil
340 g/12 oz smoked lean salt pork, diced (12-mm/½-in. pieces)
2 1.8-kg/4-lb chickens, each cut into 8 pieces
salt
freshly ground black pepper
4 tbsp brandy
thyme
1.25 kg/3 lb mushrooms, washed, dried, and cut in half

2 tbsp vegetable oil
25 g/1 oz unsalted butter
225 g/8 oz shelled, halved walnuts
4 shallots, peeled and finely chopped
6 garlic cloves, peeled and finely chopped
20 g/¾ oz finely chopped parsley
340 ml/12 fl oz dry white vermouth

Heat the walnut or peanut oil in a heavy-bottomed pan and sauté the pork for 5 minutes, tossing. Remove the pork and set aside. Add the chicken pieces. Sprinkle them with salt and pepper and cook them on all sides for 10 minutes. Add the brandy and ignite, sprinkle with thyme, cover and cook over medium heat for 40 minutes.

Sauté the mushrooms in the vegetable oil and butter in another pan, season them and add them along with the walnut halves, pork, shallots, garlic and parsley to the chicken. Check the seasoning. Add the vermouth and cook for 15 minutes.

Spoon the chicken into a large, warm, shallow dish. Scrape the bottom of the pan with a fork, reduce the sauce over very high heat and pour it over the chicken. Serve at once.

Poulet aux Pruneaux
Chicken cooked with prunes and wine

This superb dish comes from the north of Burgundy. It must be prepared a day in advance. The unctuous wine-and-prune sauce is rich in flavour yet lean (since you have time to degrease it thoroughly). An easy dish to serve. Reheat it over low heat just before the meal. It will need very little accompaniment: a crisp watercress or dandelion-green tossed salad and a hearty red wine.

For 4 people

1 tbsp peanut or olive oil
115 ml/4 fl oz red wine (hearty Burgundy type)
2 tbsp red wine vinegar
2 onions, sliced
2 garlic cloves, crushed and peeled
2 bay leaves
about 12 black peppercorns
2 tsp thyme
1 1.8-kg/4-lb chicken, cut into 8 serving pieces
salt
freshly ground black pepper

2 tsp savory or marjoram
1 tbsp peanut oil
85 g/3 oz diced lean salt pork
3 large onions, thinly sliced
1 tsp flour
225 ml/8 fl oz red wine (hearty Burgundy type)
1 bay leaf
12 prunes
4 slices of bread
40 g/1½ oz unsalted butter
1 garlic clove, peeled, whole
2 tbsp chopped parsley

Prepare a marinade by mixing together the first 8 ingredients. Pour it over the chicken. Sprinkle with salt and pepper, cover and leave in the refrigerator overnight, turning the meat once.

The next morning, lift the pieces of chicken from the marinade, dry them with kitchen towels and sprinkle them with savory.

Heat the oil in a large heavy frying-pan or a heavy-bottomed saucepan and sauté the pork over moderate heat. Add the chicken and sauté for about 10 minutes, turning each piece once with tongs. Transfer the chicken to a plate and add the finely sliced onions to the pan. Sauté for 10 minutes, then add the chicken to the onions, sprinkle with flour, and let the chicken pieces brown for about 5 minutes, turning them once. Add the wine and the strained marinade. Cook, uncovered, over medium heat for 10 minutes, then add the bay leaf and the onions and herbs from the marinade and cook, uncovered, for 30 minutes.

Meanwhile, soak the prunes in tea or water for about 30 minutes and remove the pits. Add them to the chicken and cook for 15 minutes. Remove from the heat and let cool. Remove the pieces of chicken from the sauce. Skim the fat from top of the pan. Remove the skin of the chicken. Pass the sauce through a Moulinex mill or a blender.

The dish is now ready to be served whenever you need it. It can be kept in the refrigerator and will improve with reheating.

When ready to serve, place the pieces of chicken in a heavy-bottomed pan, taste the sauce and add salt, pepper, thyme or savory if needed and pour over the chicken. Cover and cook over low heat for 20–25 minutes.

Prepare the *croûtons* by frying the slices of bread in the butter or drying them in a hot oven. Rub them with a garlic clove. Place the chicken in a shallow dish, pour the sauce over it and place the golden *croûtons* all round. Sprinkle with chopped parsley.

Poulet aux Raisins

Marinated chicken cooked with cream and grapes

A lovely autumn dish, this chicken served with grapes must be marinated overnight for a richer flavour. Serve with *Gâteau de Pommes de Terre* (p. 167), *Gratin de Verdure* (p. 173), *Paillasson* (p. 181) or *Riz aux Herbes* (p. 195).

For 8 people

225 ml/8 fl oz dry white wine
1 tbsp brandy
2 shallots, finely chopped
2 garlic cloves, peeled
3 tsp thyme
2 bay leaves
10 peppercorns
2 chickens, each cut into 8 pieces

55 g/2 oz unsalted butter
1 tbsp vegetable oil
salt
freshly ground black pepper
225 ml/8 fl oz cream
170 g/6 oz grapes (white or red),
    peeled with a sharp knife

Prepare the marinade by mixing together the first 7 ingredients. Simmer it for a few minutes, then cool. Marinate the pieces of chicken overnight (or at least a few hours) on a low shelf of the refrigerator.

When you are ready to prepare the dish, heat the butter and oil in a heavy-bottomed pan and sauté each piece of carefully dried chicken on all sides for 30 minutes. Sprinkle with salt and pepper and cover with a large sheet of kitchen foil to keep warm. Meanwhile, simmer the marinade, uncovered, in a saucepan for 20 minutes. Add the cream and simmer 5 minutes longer to make a sauce.

Preheat the oven to 190°C/375°F/Gas Mark 5. Place the pieces of chicken in an ovenproof dish, add the peeled grapes and pour the sauce over it. Heat in the oven for 10–15 minutes and serve.

Poulet Surprise
Chicken breasts baked with onions, tomatoes, herbs, sherry and cream under a crisp crust of cheese

Easy to prepare, this is delicious with home-made noodles (p. 194) or chicory gratin or *Tomates au Fromage* (p. 191).

For 8 people

2 tbsp vegetable oil
55 g/2 oz unsalted butter
450 g/1 lb onions, peeled and finely chopped
680 g/1½ lb tomatoes, skinned and seeded
2 chicken livers, chopped

3 tsp thyme
3 tbsp sherry
salt
freshly ground black pepper
4 chicken breasts, split in half
225 ml/8 fl oz single cream
5 tbsp grated Gruyère cheese

Heat the oil and half the butter and cook the onions slowly until soft, then add the tomatoes, the chicken livers, thyme and sherry and simmer over very low heat for 1 hour. It will have the consistency of a purée. Add salt and pepper.

Sauté the chicken breasts on all sides for 1 or 2 minutes in the remaining butter. Place them in an ovenproof dish and cover with the purée. Pour the cream over the top and sprinkle with the grated cheese.

Place under the grill until the cheese turns crisp, and serve piping hot.

Rôti de Porc de Beaune
Marinated pork roasted with spices, mustard and wine, and served with mushrooms and cranberry sauce

This splendid dish includes such a variety of flavours and textures that it is better to serve it with little accompaniment – perhaps only sliced apples sautéd in butter or *Purée de Choux* (p. 188) or home-made noodles (p. 194). The chicken livers add texture to the sauce, but you may prefer to use simply a flour-and-butter paste. The pork must be marinated for 24 hours.

For 8 people

1 2.25-kg/5-lb boneless roast of
  pork
salt
450 ml/16 fl oz red wine
225 ml/8 fl oz port (or good sweet
  red vermouth)
5 peppercorns
5 juniper berries
1 clove
1 bay leaf
peel of 1 orange, finely chopped
peel of ½ lemon, finely chopped

3 tbsp Dijon-style mustard
10 chicken livers (or a mixture of
  2 tbsp flour and 25 g/1 oz
  butter)
85 g/3 oz unsalted butter
2 tbsp vegetable oil
450 g/1 lb mushrooms, trimmed
  and sliced
pepper
4 tbsp cranberry sauce
1 tsp cinnamon

Rub the pork with salt. Mix all the marinade ingredients (salt, wine, port, peppercorns, juniper berries, clove, bay leaf and orange and lemon peel) and pour over the pork. Cover and keep in a cool place for 24 hours, basting the pork at least five times.

Preheat the oven to 190°C/375°F/Gas Mark 5.

Remove the pork from the marinade and place it in a shallow roasting pan. Spread the mustard over the entire surface of the meat. Pour the marinade into the bottom of the pan. Roast for 2 hours, uncovered, basting from time to time.

When the meat is almost done, sauté the chicken livers in half the butter in a frying-pan for a few minutes. Crush them with a fork and set aside. Heat the remaining butter, add the oil and sauté the mushrooms, stirring with a wooden spoon. Add the marinade in the roasting pan (discard the bay leaf and the orange and lemon peel), the chicken livers, salt, pepper, the cranberry sauce and the cinnamon. Stir well. Cook over low heat for 2 minutes, or until smooth.

Place the pork on a warm serving dish. Slice it and season with salt and pepper. Pour some of the sauce over the slices and pass the rest of the sauce in a bowl.

Le Steak à la Moutarde
T-bone steak with a mustard, sherry and cream sauce

Any good T-bone prepared this way will acquire a Dijon accent and taste like Charollais.

This is splendid served with a *Gratin Dauphinois* (pp. 169–70), a *Gâteau de Pommes de Terre* (p. 167), *Haricots Verts à la Crème* (p. 179) or *Petits Légumes* (p. 182).

For each person

1 tbsp coarsely crushed black peppercorns	salt
1 good-size T-bone steak (about 2.5 cm/1 in. thick)	2 tbsp sherry
	2 tbsp double cream
vegetable oil	1 tbsp Dijon-style mustard

About 2 hours before cooking, press the peppercorns into both sides of the meat.

Preheat the oven to 150°C/300°F/Gas Mark 2.

Heat just enough oil in a frying-pan to coat the bottom and sear the meat on both sides over rather high heat. Turn the oven off, put the steak on a platter and place it in the oven to keep warm.

Add salt and sherry to the coagulated juices in the pan. Add the cream and mustard and scrape and stir vigorously. Bring to a boil while stirring and lower the heat. Cook for 5 minutes. Check the seasoning and pour the sauce over the steak.

Tarte Bourguignonne
A meat, vegetable and herb pie

A tasty dish served on most festive occasions in Burgundy. Serve it with a large bowl of strongly seasoned green salad and a hearty red wine. It is better cold on the third day than it is on the first – a perfect picnic or buffet dish, but it is lighter when served warm.

For 8 people

··· Pastry (a 25-cm/10-in. shell) ···
285 g/10 oz plain flour
pinch of salt
130 g/4½ oz unsalted butter
40 g/1½ oz lard

·················· Filling ··················

450 g/1 lb lean salt pork (or
   country ham), diced
450 g/1 lb boneless veal shoulder,
   diced
225 ml/8 fl oz dry white wine
4 onions, peeled and thinly sliced
4 garlic cloves, peeled and finely
   chopped
115 ml/4 fl oz brandy (cognac, if
   possible)

3 tbsp thyme
2 bay leaves
8 tbsp finely chopped parsley
salt
freshly ground pepper
1 egg yolk, beaten together with
   1 tbsp water

The night before

Prepare the pastry in a food processor or place the flour, salt, butter
and lard in a large bowl and rub them together between the tips of
your fingers very lightly and quickly. Add 6 tablespoons (or less)
cold water and blend well. Place the dough on a table and press
with the heel of your hand away from you three or four times.
Gather the dough with a spatula, place it in a bowl, cover with a
tea-towel and store in the refrigerator overnight.

Marinate the pork and veal in the wine with the onions, garlic,
brandy, thyme and bay leaves overnight in a large covered bowl.

Two hours before the meal

Roll out the dough as thin as possible (6 mm/¼ in.). Cover the
bottom and sides of a buttered pie dish with half of the pastry.

Preheat the oven to 200°C/400°F/Gas Mark 6.

Drain the contents of the marinade and set aside. Discard the bay
leaves. Pass the meat and onions briefly through a grinder or a food
processor. (The mixture should not be too thin.) Add the chopped
parsley and salt and pepper and place in heaping tablespoonfuls on

the pastry shell approximately 6 mm/¼ in. apart. Cover with the remaining pastry and close the edges of the pastry with moistened fingers.

With a pair of kitchen scissors, open a hole about 5 cm/2 in. wide in the centre of the top crust and place a little chimney made of greaseproof paper about 5–7.5 cm/2–3 in. high into it, so the steam will escape during cooking.

Brush the pastry surface with the egg yolk mixture and bake for 10 minutes. Reduce the heat to 180°C/350°F/Gas Mark 4 and bake for 40 minutes more.

Meanwhile, bring the marinade to a boil and reduce it to about 55 ml/2 fl oz. Pour this into the little chimney after the pie has been in the oven for 20 minutes.

Remove the chimney and serve the pie warm.

Travers de Porc aux Herbes
Spareribs with fresh herbs

A lively way to prepare spareribs – they will be delicately crisp and fragrant. Serve with a tossed salad and a purée of celery, cabbage or turnip and potatoes, a *Gratin Dauphinois* (pp. 169–70) or a *Galette aux Pommes de Terre* (p. 165).

For 8 people

3.5 kg/8 lb of spareribs (preferably the country-style back ribs, which are meatier), cut into bite-sized pieces with a pair of scissors
salt
freshly ground pepper

2 tbsp lemon verbena, fresh or dried (or lemon pepper)
2 tbsp thyme
2 tbsp finely chopped fresh coriander
3 tbsp finely chopped fresh herbs

Preheat the oven to 200°C/400°F/Gas Mark 6.

Place the spareribs in a shallow roasting pan and pierce all over with a fork. Cover with a sheet of kitchen foil and bake for 35 minutes. Remove the foil; skim and discard all fat. Reduce the oven heat to 190°C/375°F/Gas Mark 5. The ribs should be crisp. While they are steaming hot, sprinkle with salt, pepper, lemon verbena (or lemon pepper), thyme and coriander and press them into the meat with the back of a spoon. Continue to bake, uncovered, until crispy brown and well done – about 45 minutes. Place the ribs on a warm serving dish, sprinkle with herbs and serve at once.

Veau à la Moutarde
Veal sautéd with shallots, wine and mustard

A sharp and fragrant dish, quick to prepare and easy to serve, it can be accompanied by steamed rice, sprinkled with melted butter and a few drops of lemon juice, and a tossed green salad.

For 8 people

8 thin slices of veal cut from the leg (8-mm/⅓-in. thick or escalopes or cutlets cut in 5-cm/2-in. strips)
salt
freshly ground black pepper
25 g/1 oz unsalted butter
3 tbsp vegetable oil

8 shallots, peeled and finely chopped
225 ml/8 fl oz dry white wine
340 ml/12 fl oz double cream
2 tbsp (or more) Dijon-style mustard
juice of 1 lemon

Sprinkle the veal escalopes with salt and pepper and sauté them on both sides in butter and oil. Remove them and set aside. Add the shallots and then the wine to the frying-pan and cook until the shallots are soft. Add the cream and cook, stirring, until the cream is heated through. Remove the pan from the heat and add the mustard. Stir well and add the veal to the pan. Continue stirring and heat for 2 minutes. Pour into a warm shallow serving dish. Sprinkle with lemon juice and serve at once.

Veau Meurette

Sautéd veal cooked with herbs, onions and red wine

A delectable version of an old Burgundy favourite. It is high in flavour, yet light. It can be served with home-made noodles (p. 194), braised chicory or celery purée.

For 8 people

1.25 kg/3 lb veal breast, boned and cut into 4-cm/1½-in. pieces
2.25 kg/5 lb veal shoulder, cut into large pieces
salt
freshly ground black pepper
25 g/1 oz unsalted butter
2 tbsp vegetable oil
255 g/9 oz diced lean salt pork

2 garlic cloves, peeled and crushed
2 bay leaves
2 tsp thyme
1.1 l/2 pt hearty red wine
12 small, whole white onions, peeled (or 4 big onions, sliced)
3 tbsp finely chopped fresh herbs (chives, parsley, tarragon)

Preheat the oven to 180°C/350°F/Gas Mark 4. Sprinkle the veal with salt and pepper. Heat the butter and oil in a large frying-pan and brown the veal on all sides for 5 minutes. Set the veal aside. Sauté the diced pork and garlic. Put the veal, pork and garlic into a large casserole, add the bay leaves, thyme, wine and onions. Cover and bake for about 2 hours. Remove the veal and keep it warm in a serving dish.

Carefully remove the fat. Reduce the sauce, and if you wish, pass it through a sieve. Correct the seasoning. Pour the sauce over the veal. Sprinkle with herbs and serve at once.

Viande aux Baies

Marinated poultry cooked with white wine, vegetables and herbs

This can be prepared with chicken, turkey or rabbit. Serve with home-made noodles (p. 194), chestnuts or sautéd mushrooms, *Gratin d'Oignons* (p. 171) or *Gratin Rouge* (p. 175).

For 8 people

3 chickens, cut into 8 serving
    pieces each (or an equal amount
    of rabbit or turkey)
680 ml/1⅕ pt white wine
2 carrots, peeled and chopped
2 onions, peeled and chopped
2 tsp thyme
2 bay leaves
10 peppercorns
3 tbsp vegetable oil

255 g/9 oz streaky bacon, cut in
    small dice
salt
freshly ground black pepper
340 g/12 oz blackberry (or
    raspberry) jam
juice of 1 lemon
55 g/2 oz ripe blackberries (or any
    berries available)

Marinate the pieces of chicken (or rabbit or turkey) in the wine with the carrots, onions, thyme, bay leaves and peppercorns overnight.

Heat the oil in a large frying-pan, add the bacon and, after a few minutes, sauté the pieces of chicken on all sides for about 10 minutes, or until golden. Add the vegetables, then the marinade. Season with salt and pepper and cook for 1 hour, or until the meat is done. Remove the meat and keep it warm in a low oven.

Remove the bay leaves and pass the marinade through a sieve, crushing the vegetables with a wooden spoon, into a saucepan. Bring to a boil and let it reduce, uncovered. Stir in the jam, lemon juice and berries. Put the meat back into the sauce and pour into a warm serving dish at once.

If you can't find the fresh berries, omit them. The dish is interesting enough without them.

Les Légumes

Vegetables

The sample of vegetable recipes I have discovered in Burgundy dating from the Middle Ages to today is wide and rich. Vegetables have always been used with imagination and ingenuity. They are not the centre of a meal as they are in Provence, but they enhance or complement every meat, fish or poultry dish.

There is a quaint *fricot*, a medieval dish made with pears and potatoes sautéd in butter to accompany blood sausage. There are chestnuts and onions cooked with red wine to serve with pork or wild boar.

Sorrel purée thickened with eggs and cream does wonders with fish, in omelettes, as soup. There are twenty-two ways of preparing potatoes – at least one for every occasion, although to my taste, *gratin dauphinois* can be served with meat, fish and fowl with equal success.

Vegetables also mingle to enhance their individual taste. There is *ganèfle*, a gratin of grated potatoes, flour and eggs, covered with onions, cheese and truffles, cooked in butter, mixed with chestnuts, goose liver, brandy, cream and Madeira wine.

But there are also simpler dishes – cardoons (the top stalks have a delicious flavour) prepared with cream or beef marrow and cheese, and for New Year's Eve cooked with onions and anchovies; stews of butter beans, sorrel, spinach and Swiss chard; gratins of courgettes with Gruyère cheese, cream, eggs and garlic; white onions cooked unpeeled, then puréed with cream and mustard; dandelion greens cooked with lard; pumpkin prepared in all kinds of ways; and finally, mushrooms.

In Burgundy mushrooms come in all colours, tastes and sizes. There are sautéd *mousserons* seasoned with herbs and lemon juice or cooked with dry white wine and enriched with cream. There are *cèpes* and *bolets* mixed with garlic, parsley and diced country ham and cooked under the ashes for five hours. There are *chanterelles*, *girolles* and *morilles* (morels), mushrooms sautéd with shallots and enriched with cream. There are marinated mushrooms kept in walnut oil and herbs, stuffed with shallots and garlic, and a curious dish made of cooked leeks and *morilles*, bacon, shallots, thyme and red wine. The mushroom dishes I have selected can all be prepared with the white variety easily available fresh in all supermarkets and greengrocers, since canned mushrooms have never proven satisfactory. Make sure the mushrooms are firm and creamy, and use them the very day you buy them. Freshness is always important and, ideally, all vegetables should be prepared within a few hours of the time you pick or buy them. Select them carefully and give proper attention to their colour and texture.

The following are some of the vegetables most commonly used in Burgundy.

Artichokes *(les artichauts)*
It is mainly the globe variety that is used in Burgundy. They must be eaten fresh or the choke will be too large and the leaves too leathery. Fresh firm artichokes squeak when you squeeze them. Artichokes are stuffed with artichoke bottoms, country ham, sorrel, mushrooms and cream, then cooked in butter. Wine tastes awful with artichokes, so serve only cold water or cold beer with them.

Asparagus *(les asperges)*
Whether they are white, green or purple, they must have closed tips and firm stalks. They are served parboiled, seasoned with cream that has been reduced with herbs and pepper, or in a thick custard garnished with a bowl of cream seasoned with lemon and herbs.

Cabbage *(le chou)*
Head cabbage or Savoy varieties are used in purée with pork, in soups and stuffed. They must not be overcooked.

Cardoons (*les cardons*)
Only the tender stalks of the cardoons are eaten. Trim the strings as for celery. They are parboiled, then cooked with butter and anchovies or used in soups, sautéd with shallots and white wine and enriched with slices of courgette and chopped parsley.

Celery (*le céleri*)
Use it in soups, raw in salad, braised with pork or puréed.

Chestnuts (*les châtaignes; les marrons*)
They are used in soups, in *crépinettes*, sautéd with truffles and goose livers or with diced potatoes, and in pastry.

Chicory (*les endives*)
They must be as small as possible and should be blanched in a large amount of salted water. Cooked, they accompany fish as well as pork or poultry. Raw, they make crisp, lively salads.

Dandelion greens (*les pissenlits*)
Crisp and fresh, they make a delicious tossed salad seasoned with warm vinegar and crisp dices of streaky bacon.

Dried beans (*les haricots secs*)
The white beans are used in purées with milk and butter, warm in salads, with tomatoes and pork; the red are often cooked with red wine. Dried kidney beans must be boiled for at least 10 minutes to remove all toxins.

Garlic (*l'ail*)
Garlic has been used in both cooking and medicine since the Chinese, the Egyptians and the Hebrews discovered it. It must be firm and fresh. Do not use a clove of garlic that is yellow and soft and has a green sprout in the centre. Buy garlic in a wreath or a rope and hang it in a dry place.

Burgundy cooking uses a lot of garlic, mostly cooked. Whereas raw garlic is potent, cooked garlic tastes sweet and light.

Green beans (*les haricots verts*)

They snap between your fingers when they are fresh. The flat green beans are used in soups; the round plump ones and the yellow ones, in warm salads with cream or in gratins. The best way to cook them is simply to steam them until just tender. You can do this in specially designed steamers or by using a vegetable steamer (widely available) that fits into most saucepans. Otherwise, cook the beans by putting them into a pan with a large amount of salted boiling water; bring to a second boil, uncover and simmer until tender.

Leeks (*les poireaux*)

They are called 'the asparagus of the poor'. Delicious in soups; with crisp diced ham; in gratins with herbs, nutmeg and cream; in *flamiche*, a pie enriched with cream and eggs; or slowly cooked and puréed to thicken fish or meat dishes; or served as a side dish.

Mushrooms (*les champignons*)

There is a wide choice of mushrooms in Burgundy. Morels grow in the spring, chanterelles in the summer, and *cèpes* later, but there are endless varieties. They can be sautéd with garlic and parsley; creamed with dry white wine, herbs and cream; deep-fried and sprinkled with herbs; stuffed with country ham and grilled; stuffed with snails; sautéd with chestnuts; or cooked in a gratin with potatoes.

The cultivated variety will be delicious in the following recipes, but you must choose firm, plump mushrooms with a smooth creamy cap and cook them the day you buy them. You can always reheat them later. Never use canned or frozen mushrooms.

Onions (*les oignons*)

Onions are the basis of Lyon cooking and are also widely used in Burgundy. Yellow onions are for omelettes and tarts; little white onions, for *meurette* sauce and with fresh vegetables as garnish; red Spanish onions, for *court bouillon* and marinade. Onions are used in purée to thicken meat or fish sauces or in stews.

Potatoes (*les pommes de terre*)
These were indeed brought to Europe from America for the benefit of the poor, but they have come a long way in Burgundy and are now the basis of many sumptuous dishes. A *paillasson* is as elegant as it is delicious. Stuffed with ham, shallots and herbs and cooked in a rich beef broth, or sliced with onions and sautéd in butter in the Lyonnaise way, potatoes become truly refined treats.

The *rapée*, a rich mixture of grated potatoes, fresh cheese, cream and brandy, cooked in walnut oil, and the various *gratin dauphinois* and *savoyard* have given superior status to this vegetable.

Pumpkin (*la citrouille, le potiron*)
Used in the famous Lyon soup, in gratins with cream and eggs, puréed with garlic, in cake, in custard, in preserves, pumpkin is one of the staples of Burgundy cooking. Acorn hubbard or butternut squash can be used in the following recipes, but remember they all need a lot of salt.

Shallots (*les échalotes*)
Not always available everywhere, but they are well worth looking for. They keep well and are truly compulsory if you want to cook *bourguignon*. They have a pungent light flavour, and are used in practically every dish.

Spinach (*les épinards*)
One of the few vegetables you can buy frozen without regretting it. Spinach can be used in soups, omelettes and stuffing.

Turnips (*les navets*)
The little purple or pink ones are blanched, then cooked with cream, herbs and a pinch of sugar and are used in many gratins and soups.

Bonnet de Chou

Baked cabbage leaves with sausages, apples and sage

A perfect treat for a cold winter night.

For 8 people

2 large heads of cabbage
225 g/8 oz sliced streaky bacon
8 country sausages (French, Polish
  or Italian, highly seasoned),
  sliced

3 large Granny Smith apples,
  peeled, cored and quartered
2 tsp sage
40 g/1½ oz lard
1 spicy dried sausage, sliced

Preheat the oven to 170°C/325°F/Gas Mark 3.

Cook the cabbage in a pot of boiling salted water for 20 minutes. Drain well.

Cover the bottom of a large mould or a large ovenproof bowl with the sliced bacon, then spread with half of the cabbage leaves. Cover with the sausages and apples, then with the other half of the cabbage leaves. Sprinkle with sage and dot with lard. Bake for about 4 hours. Unmould and serve surrounded by sliced sausage.

Champignons de Dijon

Mushrooms in a Dijon sauce

A sumptuous dish to serve with a good smoked ham sliced paper-thin or with a roast, it can also be an elegant hors-d'oeuvre.

For 8 people

900 g/2 lb small whole white
  mushrooms, trimmed, washed
  and dried (or simply well
  cleaned)
juice of 2 lemons
salt
freshly ground black pepper
115 g/4 oz unsalted butter

2 tbsp vegetable oil
4 shallots, peeled and finely
  chopped
2 egg yolks
225 ml/8 fl oz single cream
2 tbsp Dijon-style mustard
115 ml/4 fl oz dry white wine
3 tbsp finely chopped parsley

Prepare the mushrooms and sprinkle them with the lemon juice, salt and pepper.

Heat 100 g/3½ oz of the butter and the oil in a large, heavy-bottomed frying-pan and add the mushrooms over medium heat. Cook for 5–6 minutes. Remove them and their liquid and set aside.

Add the minced shallots to the pan, with the remaining butter. Cook for 5–6 minutes over low heat.

Mix the egg yolks, cream and mustard in a bowl. Stir in the wine and the mushroom liquid and pour this mixture over the shallots. Add the mushrooms and cook over medium heat, stirring, for about 5 minutes. Pour into a warm shallow dish, sprinkle with parsley and serve at once.

Chou Farci

Cabbage stuffed with apples, prunes and herbs and cooked with wine and sausages

A light and sophisticated Burgundy version of the traditional stuffed cabbage. Serve with *Purée de Choux* (p. 188) and a chilled white wine.

For 8 people

1 large head of cabbage, trimmed	3 tsp thyme
225 g/8 oz cooked ham, chopped	1 tsp freshly grated nutmeg
225 g/8 oz lean salt pork or streaky bacon, chopped	salt
	8 slices thickly cut streaky bacon
70 g/2½ oz cooked rice	(or pork fat)
2 garlic cloves, peeled and crushed	8 whole prunes, pitted
2 Granny Smith apples, peeled and chopped	450 ml/16 fl oz dry white wine
	2 large, highly seasoned sausages
1 whole egg, beaten	(preferably French or Polish)
freshly ground black pepper	3 tbsp chopped parsley
6 prunes, pitted and chopped	

Put the cabbage in a large saucepan of boiling salted water and cook for 20 minutes. Drain.

Remove the tough core with a small sharp knife and discard it. Cut out the centre of the cabbage. Chop it and place it in a large bowl. Add the chopped meats, rice, garlic, apples, egg, pepper, chopped prunes, thyme and nutmeg. Stir carefully and check the seasoning before adding the salt. (This mixture is the stuffing.) Set aside the outer portion of the cabbage.

Preheat oven to 190°C/375°F/Gas Mark 5.

Place four 50-cm/20-in. long pieces of string flat on a table in a cross(#)pattern. Cover them with the strips of streaky bacon. Place the outer portion of the cabbage in the centre. Open the leaves (at the bottom) with your fingers. Spoon most of the stuffing mixture into the centre and the rest between the leaves of the cabbage, pushing with your fingers. Close the cabbage leaves and tie the string around it. It should be a neat package. (The bacon strips will prevent the strings from cutting through the leaves.)

Place the cabbage, tied end up, in a deep narrow ovenproof container barely wider than the cabbage. Place the whole prunes around it and cover with the wine. Cover the pan with a lid or sheet of heavy kitchen foil and bake for 1½ hours. Add the sausages and cook for 30 minutes longer.

Holding the string, lift the cabbage from the container, and place it on a warm serving dish. Remove and discard the strings and bacon strips. Slice the sausages. Cut the cabbage into wedges like a pie and serve it surrounded with prunes and sausages. Pour 3 tablespoons of the cooking juice over it. Sprinkle with pepper and parsley and serve with a separate bowl of cabbage purée.

Estouffade de Carottes
Carrots seasoned with mustard and butter

A lovely accompaniment to roasted meat or grilled chicken.

For 8 people

2.25 kg/5 lb small carrots, peeled and thinly sliced
200 g/7 oz unsalted butter
1 tbsp vegetable oil
salt
1 tsp sugar

4 slices home-made bread
2 tbsp flour
2 tbsp Dijon-style mustard
3 tbsp stock (or meat or chicken juices)
3 tbsp finely chopped parsley

Bring a large saucepan of salted water to the boil. Add the carrots and cook for 4–6 minutes. Drain.

Heat 170 g/6 oz of the butter and the oil in a heavy frying-pan. Add the carrots, salt and sugar and stir with a wooden spoon. Cook slowly for 10 minutes. Add 6 tablespoons of water and cook, uncovered, until all the water has evaporated.

Meanwhile, make the *croûtons*: fry the slices of bread on both sides in a frying-pan with half the remaining butter, then cut each into 4 triangles.

Mix the rest of the butter with the flour and add to the carrots. Add the mustard and stock. (Meat juices may be used here, previously obtained by scraping the bottom of a pan used for roasting a joint or chicken and adding 3 tablespoons of water or wine.) Stir with a wooden spoon and cook for 3 minutes.

Pour into a warm serving dish. Sprinkle with parsley, place the *croûtons* around, and serve.

Flan de Pommes de Terre à la Bourguignonne

Sautéd potatoes baked with crisp pork, onions, spices, cream and eggs

A true wonder.

For 8 people

125 g/4½ oz diced lean salt pork (or shredded slices of prosciutto or country ham)	8 or 9 potatoes, peeled, sliced, rinsed in cold water and dried
3 tbsp vegetable oil	salt
8 or 9 onions, peeled and thinly sliced	freshly ground white pepper
	pinch of nutmeg
55 g/2 oz unsalted butter	2 tsp ground coriander
	450 ml/16 fl oz single cream
	4 eggs, well beaten

If you use salt pork, place it in a heavy frying-pan and sauté it over low heat for 5 minutes with 1 tablespoon of oil. If you use ham, sauté for 1 minute only. Add 2 tablespoons of oil and the onions and cook over low heat for 15 minutes. Then remove with a slotted spoon into a large bowl. Add the butter to the pan and sauté the potatoes over medium heat for about 30 minutes, tossing them from time to time. Remove with a slotted spoon into the bowl with the onions.

Preheat the oven to 200°C/400°F/Gas Mark 6.

Spread the salt pork or ham and the onions in an oiled ovenproof dish. Sprinkle with salt, pepper, nutmeg and coriander, then add the potatoes and sprinkle again with pepper, nutmeg and coriander. Beat the cream and the eggs together and pour over the onion–potato dish. Place it in the oven and cook for about 20 minutes. It should be golden crisp and smell delicious.

Frites à la Crème

French-fried potatoes and sautéd mushrooms seasoned with a garlic, egg, vinegar and cream sauce

Truly delicious. The original recipe calls for wild mushrooms, but ordinary mushrooms will do.

For 8 people

oil for deep-frying
9 potatoes, peeled and cut into
　sticks
900 g/2 lb fresh mushrooms,
　cleaned and sliced
40 g/1½ oz unsalted butter
1 tbsp vegetable oil

2 garlic cloves, peeled and finely
　chopped
2 eggs
1 tbsp wine vinegar
3 tbsp single cream
salt
freshly ground black pepper

Deep-fry the potatoes. Drain on kitchen towels and keep warm in a turned-off oven.

Meanwhile, sauté the mushrooms in the butter and tablespoon of oil. Mix the garlic, eggs, vinegar, cream, salt and pepper in a bowl.

Place the potatoes in a shallow dish. Add the mushrooms and pour the sauce over them. Toss gently and serve. This dish must be served very warm.

Galette aux Pommes de Terre
A crisp potato and salt pork cake seasoned with fresh herbs

Golden and crisp outside, moist inside, this makes a glorious winter meal served by itself or as an accompaniment.

For 8 people

4 onions, peeled and finely
   chopped
25 g/1 oz lard
900 g/2 lb potatoes, peeled and
   thickly sliced
salt
freshly ground white pepper
thyme

2 bay leaves
900 g/2 lb lean salt pork (or
   country ham), cut into small
   dice
55 g/2 oz unsalted butter (or lard)
3 tbsp chervil (or parsley or
   chives), finely chopped

Preheat the oven to 180°C/350°F/Gas Mark 4.

Sauté the onions in hot lard. Put them in a round ovenproof dish. Dry the potato slices thoroughly with kitchen towels and add half of them to the onions. Sprinkle with salt, pepper and thyme and place the bay leaves on top.

Sauté the salt pork for a few minutes and put on top of the potatoes. Add the remainder of the potatoes and sprinkle with pepper only. Press down hard with your hands and dot with butter (or lard).

Bake for 1 hour. Run a knife around the inside edge of the dish to loosen and unmould on a warm round serving dish. Sprinkle with herbs and serve very warm.

Gâteau au Céleri

A celery, parsley and egg gratin

Light and delicate, this is a lovely first course, and also a splendid accompaniment to pork, chicken or beef. The celery leaves add colour and flavour to the dish – don't discard them!

For 8 people

2 celery hearts (about 450 g/1 lb each) with leaves
3 tbsp finely chopped parsley
4 eggs, separated

170 g/6 oz grated Gruyère cheese
salt
freshly ground pepper
freshly grated nutmeg

Cook the celery hearts in a large saucepan of salted water for 20 minutes. Drain and purée them in a food processor or a Moulinex mill. Add the parsley, egg yolks, cheese, salt, pepper and nutmeg.
Preheat oven to 190°C/375°F/Gas Mark 5.
Whip the egg whites and fold them gently into the celery-and-egg-yolk mixture. Pour into a buttered ovenproof dish and bake for 20 minutes. The crust should be firm.
Serve with a tomato sauce (p. 58), a Béchamel sauce or by itself.

Gâteau de Carottes

A carrot cake with mushroom, shallots, cheese and herbs

A superb first course for a light meal, or a colourful accompaniment to any meat dish.

For 8 people

900 g/2 lb carrots, peeled and quartered
115 g/4 oz mushrooms, diced
2 shallots, peeled and finely chopped
55 g/2 oz unsalted butter
1 tbsp vegetable oil

4–5 eggs, beaten
3 tbsp single cream
55 g/2 oz grated Gruyère cheese
2 tbsp finely chopped chervil
salt
freshly ground black pepper
freshly grated nutmeg

················· Garnish ·················

cabbage or spinach leaves,
    blanched
2 tbsp finely chopped parsley

Cook the carrots for about 20 minutes in a saucepan of boiling, salted water. Drain.

Meanwhile, sauté the mushrooms and shallots for 5 minutes in half the butter and 1 tablespoon of oil in a large frying-pan.

Purée the carrots, mushrooms and shallots in a blender, a food processor or a Moulinex mill (for a less mushy consistency).

Add the eggs, cream, cheese and chervil to the purée; add salt, pepper and nutmeg to taste. It must be highly seasoned.

Preheat the oven to 180°C/350°F/Gas Mark 4.

Pour the mixture into a buttered ovenproof dish, dot with the remaining butter and bake for 20 minutes.

Let cool until lukewarm and then unmould on to the centre of a serving plate covered with cabbage leaves or spinach leaves for a colourful effect. Sprinkle with parsley and serve.

Note: For a lighter cake, the egg whites can be whipped separately and 3 tablespoons of cream added to the mixture. This should not be unmoulded but served in the baking dish.

Gâteau de Pommes de Terre

A crisp potato cake seasoned with herbs and cheese

Wonderful-looking, this is a splendid accompaniment to any roasted meat or fowl dish.

For 8 people

115 ml/4 fl oz vegetable oil
70 g/2½ oz unsalted butter
10 large boiling potatoes, peeled
    and cut into 12-mm/½-in. slices
225 g/8 oz Gruyère cheese, grated
salt

freshly ground pepper
nutmeg
3 bay leaves
3 tbsp finely chopped fresh herbs
1 garlic clove, peeled and minced

Preheat the oven to 180°C/350°F/Gas Mark 4.

Melt one-third of the oil and 40 g/1½ oz of the butter in a large frying-pan and sauté one-third of the well-dried potatoes for 15 minutes. Scrape the bottom of the pan from time to time with a spatula. Put the potatoes in a well-buttered ovenproof dish and cover with one-third of the cheese, salt, pepper, nutmeg and a bay leaf.

Add one-third of the oil to the frying-pan and sauté the second third of the potatoes for 15 minutes. Add to the ovenproof dish, covering with another layer of cheese, salt, pepper, nutmeg and 1 bay leaf. Do the same with the last batch of potatoes. Cover the dish with kitchen foil and bake for 35 minutes.

Unmould on to a warm serving dish. Dot with the remaining butter, sprinkle with fresh herbs, garlic and pepper, and serve at once.

Grapiau

A grated potato, onion, egg and cheese pancake

A perfect main course for a children's meal and a beautiful accompaniment to almost any meat or fish dish. Sometimes instead of one *grapiau* for four people, small individual ones are made. Serve with a garlicky, bitter tossed green salad.

For 8 people

8–10 potatoes, peeled and grated
    by hand or in a food processor
2 eggs, beaten
2 onions, peeled and grated, either
    raw or sautéd in 25 g/1 oz
    unsalted butter
2 tbsp flour
salt
1 tbsp good brandy

pinch of freshly crushed coriander
115 g/4 oz grated Gruyère
    cheese
freshly ground pepper
4 tbsp oil (preferably walnut)
3 shallots, peeled and finely
    chopped
2 tbsp finely chopped parsley

Rinse the potatoes and dry them thoroughly with a tea-towel. Put them in a large bowl and add the eggs, onions, flour, salt, brandy, coriander, cheese and pepper.

Heat the oil in one or two large frying-pans and cook the mixture for 15 minutes, then place about 20 cm/8 in. below the grill flame for 10 minutes. The pancake should be very crunchy on both sides yet moist in the centre.

Sprinkle with the shallots and parsley and serve warm.

Gratin Dauphinois I

Potato gratin enriched with nutmeg, egg and cheese

The only vegetable to grow in the Dauphiné and Savoy, the potato is the main ingredient of two of the most delicious dishes: *gratin savoyard* and *gratin dauphinois*.

Dauphinois and Savoyard were not kissing cousins and neither are the gratins. The first is more delicate, the second more rustic. Both are superb accompaniments to fish and meat preparations and should be served with a dry white wine.

The variations on this dish are simply endless. Here are two of my favourites.

For 8 people

9 large potatoes (about 1.25 kg/3 lb)	1 egg, beaten
450 ml/16 fl oz milk	1 garlic clove, peeled
salt	170 g/6 oz grated Gruyère cheese
freshly ground white pepper	(or half Gruyère and half
freshly grated nutmeg	Parmesan)
	40 g/1½ oz unsalted butter

Peel and cut the potatoes into thin slices (don't rinse them) and dry thoroughly with a tea-towel.

Preheat the oven to 170°C/325°F/Gas Mark 3.

Bring the milk to a boil, add the salt, pepper, nutmeg and potatoes. Cook for 10 minutes, stirring frequently to prevent sticking. Stir in the beaten egg.

Rub an ovenproof dish with a garlic clove, then with a little butter. Spread half of the potato-and-milk mixture in the dish, and sprinkle with half of the cheese. Add the rest of the potatoes, sprinkle with the rest of the cheese and dot with butter. Bake for 1 hour. The dish must be creamy, and golden crisp on the top. To prevent it from drying out (if the meal is delayed), place a sheet of kitchen foil over the top and turn off the oven. This will keep it warm and soft.

Note: Often two turnips are added to the potatoes for that extra touch.

Gratin Dauphinois II

A delicious, prettier version, but without cheese. The best accompaniment for roast beef, chicken or even fish.

For 8 people

285 ml/10 fl oz milk
10 potatoes (about 1.5 kg/3½ lb), peeled and thinly sliced
1 garlic clove, peeled
55 g/2 oz unsalted butter
salt
freshly ground white pepper

freshly ground nutmeg
1 garlic clove, peeled and finely chopped
3 shallots, finely chopped
2 eggs, beaten
115 ml/4 fl oz single cream

Preheat the oven to 180°C/350°F/Gas Mark 4.

Heat the milk to the boiling point and let it cool to lukewarm. Prepare the potatoes, drying them carefully with a tea-towel.

Rub an ovenproof dish with a garlic clove, then sprinkle with salt and rub with half of the butter. Pour the potatoes into the dish. Sprinkle with salt, pepper, nutmeg, garlic and shallots. Stir thoroughly with your hands to coat the potatoes evenly with the seasonings.

Beat the eggs in a bowl, add the lukewarm milk and the cream and pour over the potatoes. Dot with the remaining butter and bake for 40–50 minutes. Serve warm.

Gratin de Chou
A cabbage, apple, ham, meat, shallot, cream and cheese gratin

A vegetable treat that is unusual yet very easy to prepare, since the ingredients are always available. It is a wonderful way to use meat left-overs.

For 8 people

225 g/8 oz boiled beef, pork or chicken (or any left-over meat)

115 g/4 oz boiled ham (or country ham)

115 g/4 oz lean salt pork (or bacon)

1 large head of Savoy cabbage

3 Granny Smith or firm tart apples, sliced

3 shallots, peeled and finely chopped

1 garlic clove, peeled and finely chopped

3 tbsp minced parsley

freshly ground black pepper

225 ml/8 fl oz single cream

2 tbsp grated Gruyère cheese

15 g/½ oz unsalted butter

Chop the left-over meat, ham and salt pork and mix them well.

Preheat the oven to 180°C/350°F/Gas Mark 4.

Cook the cabbage in boiling salted water for 20 minutes. Drain and chop finely.

Butter an ovenproof dish. Add a layer of one-third each of the cabbage, apples and meat mixture and sprinkle with one-third each of the shallots, garlic, parsley and pepper. Repeat this procedure twice.

Pour the cream over the whole dish and sprinkle with the grated cheese and butter. Bake for 20 minutes.

Gratin d'Oignons
Onion gratin

A luscious dish from Lyon, perfect for serving with a roasted meat or a pork stew.

For 8 people

1.8 kg/4 lb onions	freshly ground black pepper
40 g/1½ oz unsalted butter	nutmeg
2 tbsp oil	3 tbsp double cream
salt	4 tbsp grated Gruyère cheese

Preheat the oven to 180°C/350°F/Gas Mark 4.

Mince the onions by hand or in a food processor and cook them slowly in 25 g/1 oz of the butter and the oil on top of the cooker for 10 minutes, stirring, until soft.

Add the salt, pepper, nutmeg and cream. Check the seasonings and pour the mixture into a buttered ovenproof dish. Sprinkle with cheese, dot with the remaining butter and bake for 30 minutes.

Serve in its baking dish.

Gratin de Potiron
A highly seasoned pumpkin gratin

Pumpkin was used by the Romans with honey. In Burgundy there are many versions of luscious pumpkin soups. The *nouvelle cuisine* chefs sometimes turn it into elegant sherbet.

This traditional gratin is a true delight served as an accompaniment or by itself. You may substitute the tasty butternut squash for pumpkin.

For 8 people

about 1.8 kg/4 lb pumpkin (or butternut squash), peeled and cut into large pieces	salt
	freshly ground white pepper
	pinch of freshly grated nutmeg
2 tbsp vegetable oil	2 tbsp breadcrumbs (preferably home-made)
4 onions, peeled and finely chopped	115 g/4 oz freshly grated Gruyère cheese
12 thick slices of streaky bacon (each piece cut in half)	15 g/½ oz unsalted butter
4 eggs, beaten	

Place the prepared pumpkin (or squash) in a large saucepan of boiling, salted water. Cook for 20 minutes.

Heat the oil and sauté the onions for 5–10 minutes. Remove and set aside. Add the bacon to the pan and fry until crisp on both sides. Set aside. Pass the cooked pumpkin through a sieve or a Moulinex mill. Let it drain to get rid of as much water as possible, pressing down with your hands.

Preheat the oven to 190°C/375°F/Gas Mark 5.

Place the pumpkin purée in a large bowl. Add the eggs, salt, pepper and nutmeg and stir. Check the seasoning. Add the bacon and pour into a buttered ovenproof dish. Sprinkle with breadcrumbs and cheese. Dot with butter. Bake for 30 minutes. Serve in its cooking dish.

Gratin de Verdure
A spinach, egg and herb gratin

A delectable dish, easy to prepare ahead of time, that goes well with a baked ham, a leg of lamb or poultry.

For 8 people

1.8 kg/4 lb fresh spinach (and/or watercress), or 1.1 kg/2½ lb frozen spinach
2 onions, peeled and chopped
1 tbsp vegetable oil
155 g/5½ oz unsalted butter
450 ml/16 fl oz milk
1 bay leaf
6 tbsp flour
4 eggs, separated
nutmeg
salt
freshly ground black pepper
8 tbsp grated cheese (preferably Parmesan or Romano)

Cook the spinach rapidly. Drain well, squeezing with your hand.

Sauté the onions in the oil and 40 g/1½ oz of the butter until soft, then add the spinach. Shake the frying-pan until no water is left. Remove from the heat.

Preheat the oven to 190°C/375°F/Gas Mark 5.

Heat the milk with the bay leaf. Knead the remaining butter and flour and heat this mixture in a heavy-bottomed saucepan. Stir in the milk. When the sauce is quite thick, add the egg yolks, stirring briskly, and pour it on the spinach. Season with nutmeg, salt and pepper. It must be lightly flavoured.

Beat the egg whites until they are stiff, then fold them into the mixture and pour it into a buttered ovenproof dish. Sprinkle with cheese and bake for 30 minutes.

Gratin Forestière

A potato, mushroom and onion gratin

From Savoy comes this lovely fragrant gratin, which can be served as a first course or an accompaniment to meat or grilled poultry. It can be prepared ahead of time.

For 8 people

100 g/3½ oz unsalted butter	8 potatoes (about 1.25 kg/3 lb),
2 tbsp vegetable oil	peeled and thinly sliced
680 g/1½ lb firm white mushrooms,	salt
cleaned, dried and sliced	freshly ground white pepper
2 onions (or 8 shallots), peeled and	5 tbsp finely chopped parsley
sliced	225 ml/8 fl oz single cream
1 garlic clove, peeled and lightly	
crushed	

Heat 55 g/2 oz of the butter and the oil in a frying-pan and sauté the mushrooms for a few minutes. Remove from the pan. Sauté the onions for a few minutes and remove from the heat.

Preheat the oven to 180°C/350°F/Gas Mark 4.

Rub an ovenproof dish with the garlic clove, then butter it carefully. Place the first layer of half of the well-dried potato slices in the bottom of the dish. Sprinkle with salt and pepper and dot with half of the remaining butter. Add the mushrooms and sprinkle with salt, pepper and parsley. Add the onions and then the rest of the potatoes. Sprinkle with salt and pepper and dot with the remaining butter.

Bake for 15 minutes. Pour the cream all over the top, letting it go through evenly. Continue baking for 20 minutes. The gratin should be crisp and golden on top.

Note: One version of this asks for grated cheese (about 3 table-spoons) on top of the gratin.

Gratin Rouge
An onion, vinegar and wine gratin

Another medieval recipe that has been constantly improved; the latest version even includes grenadine.

For 8 persons

40 g/1½ oz unsalted butter
1 tbsp oil
2 kg/4½ lb onions, finely chopped
6 tbsp sugar
2 tbsp wine vinegar

salt
freshly ground black pepper
nutmeg
4½ tbsp red Burgundy wine
1 tbsp grenadine (optional)

Heat the butter and oil in a heavy frying-pan. Sauté the onions for about 10 minutes. Add the sugar, vinegar, salt, pepper and nutmeg; cover and simmer for 30 minutes, stirring from time to time.

Add the wine and cook, uncovered, for 30 minutes more. Check the seasonings and serve. (You may add 1 tablespoon grenadine during the last 5 minutes of cooking.)

Gratin Savoyard
A potato gratin seasoned with onions and garlic, and baked under a cheese crust

This poor cousin of the more elaborate gratins is superb with a leg of lamb, a pork roast or a plain chicken.

For 8 people

10 potatoes (about 1.5 kg/3½ lb),
   peeled and thinly sliced
4 onions (or shallots) peeled and
   either finely chopped or thickly
   sliced
225 ml/8 fl oz milk
225 ml/8 fl oz stock

salt
freshly ground white pepper
freshly ground nutmeg
1 garlic clove, peeled
salt
unsalted butter
170 g/6 oz grated Gruyère cheese

Preheat the oven to 190°C/375°F/Gas Mark 5.

Prepare the potatoes and onions, drying the potatoes well. Heat together the milk, stock, salt, pepper and nutmeg. Rub an oven-proof dish with garlic, then salt, then butter. Add one layer of sliced potatoes, one layer of onions and half of the milk–stock mixture. Sprinkle with half of the cheese.

Add the rest of the potatoes, onions, milk–stock mixture, and sprinkle with the rest of the cheese. Bring to a boil on top of the cooker, dot with butter and bake for 30 minutes uncovered.

Gratin Trois

A potato gratin

This classic potato gratin is sheer perfection in its simplicity. You can prepare it ahead of time and reheat for 20 minutes before serving.

For 8 people

450 ml/16 fl oz single cream
340 ml/12 fl oz milk
salt
freshly ground black pepper
freshly grated nutmeg

10 large potatoes (about 2.8 kg/6
   lb), peeled and thinly sliced
1 garlic clove, peeled
55 g/2 oz unsalted butter

Bring the cream, milk, salt, pepper and nutmeg to a boil in a saucepan. Add the carefully dried potatoes and cook until tender (about 15 minutes).

Preheat the oven to 180°C/350°F/Gas Mark 4.

Rub a very large ovenproof dish with the garlic clove, then butter it and pour in the potatoes and cream. (There should not be more than one or two layers of potatoes in the dish.) Dot with butter and bake for about 30 minutes.

Haricots Blancs au Vin Rouge

White beans with a wine and shallot sauce

If you use fresh white beans, serve them as a separate course and eat them with a spoon. If dried beans are used, this is a good accompaniment to pork and lamb.

For 8 people

1.25 kg/3 lb fresh white beans (or 680 g/1½ lb dried white beans)
1 onion stuck with 1 clove
1 carrot, peeled and chopped
2 onions, peeled and chopped
6 shallots, peeled and finely chopped
55 g/2 oz unsalted butter

2 tbsp vegetable oil
5 tbsp red wine
1 garlic clove, peeled and finely chopped
2 tbsp finely chopped parsley
salt
freshly ground black pepper

If you use dried beans, let them stand in lukewarm water as directed on the package. If you use fresh ones, shell them only.

Bring the beans, onion with a clove, carrots and onions to a boil in a large pot of salted water and cook until the beans are tender. (See cooking time on package if using dried beans.)

Meanwhile, cook the shallots in half of the butter and the oil until soft. Add the wine and let the liquid reduce, uncovered, for a few minutes.

Drain the beans and pour them into a warm bowl. Add the wine and shallots, the garlic, the remaining butter, parsley, salt and pepper. Stir and serve.

Haricots Rouges

Red kidney beans cooked with wine and spices

This can be served as a vegetable dish or as an accompaniment to grilled meat. A cheek and an ear of pig were traditionally added to the beans for extra flavour as they cooked, but they are not essential. For a smoother dish, you may pass the beans through a Moulinex mill or food processor and add the crisp pork on top just before serving.

For 8 people

680 g/1½ lb dried red kidney beans
1 carrot, peeled
1 large onion studded with 1 clove
1 garlic clove, peeled
bouquet garni
225-g/8-oz piece lean salt pork or
    streaky bacon

450 ml/16 fl oz red Burgundy-type
    wine
1 onion
40 g/1½ oz unsalted butter
salt
freshly ground pepper

Soak the beans in cold water overnight. The next day, put them in a saucepan with the carrot, onion with a clove, garlic clove, bouquet garni, pork, half of the wine and water to cover. Boil for 10 minutes and then simmer for about 2 hours. (Check the bean-package directions for cooking time.)

When the beans are tender, remove the carrot, onion, bouquet garni and pork and drain the beans.

Chop a fresh onion and sauté it in 25 g/1 oz of the butter. Dice the pork and add it to the onion. Sauté for a few minutes on all sides, then add the remaining wine and let it reduce for 5 minutes. Add the beans and simmer for 3 minutes. Add salt, the remaining pepper and butter and serve at once.

Haricots Verts à la Crème
Green beans with a light cream sauce

When green beans are in season and tender, they are delicious cooked this way. This dish can be served as a separate course, but it can, of course, be a good accompaniment to any roasted meat or poultry.

For 8 people

1.25 kg/3 lb green beans, trimmed
25 g/1 oz unsalted butter
1 tbsp flour
70 ml/2½ fl oz hot milk
2 egg yolks
2 tbsp single cream

salt
freshly ground black pepper
1 garlic clove, finely chopped
  (optional)
2 tbsp finely chopped parsley

Blanch the green beans in a large saucepan of salted water until cooked but slightly crunchy. Drain.

Over medium heat, melt the butter in a thick-bottomed pan. Stir in the flour and then the milk. Add the beans to this white sauce.

In a separate bowl, beat the egg yolks and the cream and pour over the beans, stirring gently. Season with salt, pepper, garlic and parsley and serve lukewarm or warm.

Matelote de Pommes de Terre
Potatoes and onions cooked with herbs and red wine

Serve this sprinkled with chives, because, despite its splendid flavour, the colour is not appealing.

For 8 people

25 g/1 oz unsalted butter
2 tbsp vegetable oil
450 ml/16 fl oz red wine,
  Burgundy type
salt
freshly ground black pepper

2 bay leaves
2 tsp thyme
2 onions, peeled and thinly sliced
8 potatoes, peeled and thickly
  sliced
2 tbsp chopped chives

Melt the butter and oil in a frying-pan. Add the red wine, salt, pepper, bay leaves, thyme, onions and potatoes. Bring to a boil, then simmer, uncovered, for 1 hour. Sprinkle with chopped chives and serve at once.

Oignons aux Épinards

Yellow onions stuffed with spinach, cream, cheese, eggs and spices

This takes rather long to prepare, but it is pretty and very well worth it. It can also be served cold with a little olive oil dribbled over it.

For 8 people

8 large yellow onions, peeled	nutmeg
65 g/2¼ oz unsalted butter	freshly ground black pepper
salt	3 eggs, beaten
680 g/1½ lb spinach	16 bay leaves
115 ml/4 fl oz single cream	4 carrots, thinly sliced
55 g/2 oz grated Gruyère cheese	

Preheat the oven to 190°C/375°F/Gas Mark 5.

Cut the onions into halves and remove the centres, keeping only three layers on each onion.

Melt 25 g/1 oz of the butter in a large frying-pan over medium heat. Add the shells of the onions in two or three batches. They should become slightly brown after 10 minutes. Gently remove them with a spatula and set aside. Mince the onion centres, sprinkle them with salt and cook them in the frying-pan over low heat for 10 minutes.

Cook the spinach and dry it thoroughly in a tea-towel. Place it in a bowl and add the cream, cheese, the minced onion centres, salt, nutmeg, pepper and the eggs. Stir carefully and check the seasoning. Add more cream if the mixture is too dry.

Fill each onion shell with the mixture. Place 2 bay leaves on each side of the shell and a slice of carrot on top. Tie a piece of string around each shell and across the bay leaves, and dot each shell with a knob of the remaining butter. Wrap individually in kitchen foil and bake in an oiled ovenproof dish for 30 minutes.

Le Paillasson
A crisp potato patty

These crisp little 'mats' (*paillassons*) of golden potatoes are served throughout Burgundy and in Lyon. They must be small, and the two secrets of success in making them are to use several frying-pans (and prepare a *paillasson* only for two or three people at the most) and to sprinkle on the garlic and parsley at the last moment. Make as many batches as you have guests and keep them warm in a turned-off oven.

Paillassons are a good accompaniment to beef, poultry, pork and lamb and are a child's idea of the absolute treat.

For 2 people

4 large potatoes	2 tbsp vegetable oil
salt	2 garlic cloves, peeled and finely
freshly ground black pepper	chopped
70 g/2½ oz unsalted butter	2 tbsp finely chopped parsley

Peel and dry the potatoes and cut them into matchstick-sized pieces. Sprinkle them with salt and pepper. Heat 55 g/2 oz of the butter and the oil in two small frying-pans (each about 13 cm/5 in. wide). When they are frothy, add the potatoes, half in each pan. The potatoes will spread and be about 5 cm/2 in. thick. Cook over medium heat for 5 minutes, pressing down with a fork.

After 5 minutes, turn the *paillassons* over. (Add a little butter and lower the heat if necessary to prevent burning.) They should be ready in about 15 minutes.

Mix together the garlic, parsley and remaining butter.

Place the *paillassons* on a warm dish and spread with the garlic mixture just before serving.

Petits Légumes

An assortment of turnips, carrots, broad beans, mushrooms and cucumbers cooked with herbs, cream and lemon juice

This can be served with any meat, but it is also an unusually light and fresh first course.

For 8 people

16 small pink turnips, peeled and halved lengthways

16 small carrots (or 8 large ones), peeled and cut into 25 x 12-mm/2 x 1-in. sticks

85 g/3 oz broad beans

2 small cucumbers, peeled and cut in 25 x 12-mm/2 x 1-in. sticks

450 g/1 lb white mushrooms, halved

85 g/3 oz unsalted butter

4 tsp thyme

salt

freshly ground pepper

6 tbsp single cream

3 tbsp finely chopped fresh herbs (chives, parsley, mint)

juice of 1 lemon

Blanch the turnips in a large pot of boiling salted water for 5 minutes, then add the carrots, beans and cucumbers and cook for 10 minutes. Drain.

Sauté the mushrooms in 55 g/2 oz of the butter for 5 minutes in a large frying-pan. Add the remaining butter and the vegetables to the frying-pan, sprinkle with thyme, salt and pepper and cook, uncovered, for 5 minutes, stirring frequently.

Add the cream and fresh herbs and cook 5 minutes longer. Sprinkle with lemon juice, check and correct the seasoning and serve at once.

Petits Navets en Ragoût

Turnips, onions, herbs and garlic simmered in stock

For 8 people

2 tbsp vegetable oil
4 big onions, peeled and thinly
    sliced
85 g/3 oz streaky bacon, cut in
    small dice
1.5 kg/3½ lb small pink turnips,
    peeled and quartered

2 bay leaves
thyme
1 garlic clove, peeled and crushed
about 225 ml/8 fl oz stock
salt
freshly ground black pepper

Heat the oil in a heavy-bottomed pan and sauté the onions and bacon for 3 minutes. Add the turnips, bay leaves, thyme and garlic and cover with stock. Sprinkle with salt and pepper and bring to a boil. Simmer, covered, for 20 minutes and then, uncovered, for 30 minutes more. Check the seasoning before serving.

Petits Oignons à la Bourguignonne

Little onions braised with raisins, herbs and wine

An absolutely marvellous accompaniment, served warm or cold.

For 8 people

425 g/15 oz small white pickling
    onions
70 g/2½ oz raisins
225 ml/8 fl oz vegetable oil
115 ml/4 fl oz wine vinegar
3 tbsp tomato purée
6 garlic cloves, peeled and crushed
2 bay leaves

1 sprig of thyme (or 1 tsp dried
    thyme)
1 tsp savory
1 tsp sage
salt
freshly ground pepper
dry white wine (enough to cover
    everything)

Peel the onions and, with a knife, mark an 'x' in the stem end to keep the layers from separating during cooking. Put all the ingredients in a saucepan. Bring to a boil. Cover and simmer for 45 minutes. Let cool, uncovered. Check the seasoning and serve.

Poireaux à la Savoyarde
Leeks coated with breadcrumbs, cheese and spices

For 8 people

1.25 kg/3 lb leeks (white part
  only), sliced
100 g/3½ oz unsalted butter
70 g/2½ oz breadcrumbs
  (preferably home-made)

1 garlic clove, peeled
115 g/4 oz grated Gruyère cheese
salt
freshly ground black pepper
freshly grated nutmeg

Cook the leeks in a large pan of salted water for 15 minutes. Drain.
Melt 55 g/2 oz of the butter in a frying-pan and add the breadcrumbs,
stirring over medium heat until golden.

Butter an ovenproof dish and rub it with the garlic clove. Spread
a layer of leeks, sprinkle with breadcrumbs, cheese, salt, pepper and
nutmeg and continue to layer until all ingredients are used.

Heat the remaining butter until it is foamy, then pour it on top
of the leek dish and grill for about 10 minutes. Serve in its cooking
dish.

Pommes de Terre aux Herbes
Sautéd potatoes with fresh herbs coated with a light cream and egg yolk
sauce

A splendid accompaniment to any roasted meat or to serve in
spring with new potatoes and fragrant herbs as a first course.

For 8 people

16 medium potatoes, peeled and
  diced (do not peel new
  potatoes)
85 g/3 oz unsalted butter
2 tbsp vegetable oil
5 shallots, peeled and finely
  chopped

salt
freshly ground black pepper
7 tbsp fresh herbs (chives,
  tarragon, mint), finely chopped
225 ml/8 fl oz single cream
4 egg yolks

Prepare the potatoes and dry them thoroughly. Heat the butter and oil and sauté the shallots for a few minutes. Remove and set aside. In the same frying-pan, sauté the potatoes over high heat. You may do them in two or three batches so that all the potatoes will turn crisp and golden. Remove the potatoes to a warm serving dish. Add salt and pepper, the herbs and the shallots and stir. Cover with a sheet of kitchen foil and keep warm.

Mix the cream and egg yolks together well and, with the heat turned off, add the mixture to the frying-pan, stirring rapidly. Return to the heat for 1 minute, until the mixture thickens a little, then pour it over the potatoes, stir gently, and serve at once.

Potée aux Lentilles

Cooked lentils served with toast, spread with pâté and bacon and seasoned with fresh cream

This is a most unusual variation of *potée*, since *potée* in Burgundy is usually a cabbage soup with various additions and this has no cabbage. It comes from Dijon and makes for a wonderfully hearty dinner.

For 8 people

340 g/12 oz lentils	8 slices stale or toasted wholewheat
225-g/8-oz piece of streaky bacon	bread, each cut in 4 triangles
(or lean salt pork)	25 g/1 oz unsalted butter
1 large onion, stuck with 2 cloves	225 g/8 oz good pâté, preferably
1 carrot, peeled	home-made country pâté or
3 tsp thyme	liver pâté
salt	6 tbsp single cream
peppercorns	

Wash and put the lentils in a saucepan, add 1.8 l/3⅕ pt cold water and cook, according to the instructions on the package, with the bacon, onion, carrot, thyme, salt and peppercorns.

Meanwhile, either toast the slices of bread or sauté them in the butter. Set aside.

Spread the pâté on the bottom of a warm tureen or, if it is firm, dice it. Place the toast over it.

Remove the bacon from the pan and dice it. Discard the cloves stuck in the onion. Add the cream and bacon to the pan. Stir well and pour over the bread and pâté. Check the seasoning and serve.

Pouti
A potato and chestnut purée with milk or wine

A traditional winter dish from Savoy that goes splendidly with pork or game.

For 8 people

9 potatoes, unpeeled
900 g/2 lb chestnuts, unpeeled (or
    canned)
salt
freshly ground black pepper
340 ml/12 fl oz milk (or white
    wine)

Cook the potatoes and chestnuts in separate saucepans of salted water.

Peel the potatoes while hot, holding them with a tea-towel or oven mitts as you peel. Purée the potatoes and keep them warm.

Peel the chestnuts, purée them and add them to the potato purée. Whip and season to taste. Continue whipping as you add the milk until you have a light, fluffy mixture.

Pommes de Terre Lyonnaise
A sautéd onion and potato accompaniment

For 8 people

10 potatoes (1.25–1.5 kg/3–3½ lb),
    unpeeled
4 onions, peeled and thinly sliced
4 tbsp vegetable oil
85 g/3 oz unsalted butter

salt
freshly ground black pepper
freshly grated nutmeg
3 tbsp finely chopped parsley

Boil the potatoes in a large saucepan of salted water. Cook for 30 minutes, or until soft.

Meanwhile, prepare the onions and sauté them in the oil and 70 g/2½ oz of the butter over rather low heat for 10 minutes; season with salt. Remove from the pan and set aside.

Peel the potatoes, holding them with a tea-towel. Slice them 12 mm/½ in. thick. Reheat the butter and oil and sauté the sliced potatoes for 3 minutes. Add the onions, salt, pepper and nutmeg and cook for 2 minutes, shaking the pan.

Add the remaining butter and the parsley before serving.

Pommes Sautées

Sautéd onions and potatoes seasoned with vinegar and fresh herbs

For 8 people

170 g/6 oz diced lean salt pork (or streaky bacon)	salt
20 g/¾ oz unsalted butter	freshly ground black pepper
12 small white onions, peeled	thyme
1 tsp flour	1 bay leaf
450–680 ml/16–24 fl oz stock (beef or chicken)	8 potatoes (small boiling type), peeled and quartered
2 tbsp wine vinegar	2 tbsp finely chopped fresh herbs (tarragon, savory, mint)

Sauté the diced pork in 15 g/½ oz of the butter for 2 minutes in a heavy-bottomed pan. Add the onions and sauté for 5 minutes. Soften the remaining butter. Mix it with the flour and stir it into the pan. Cook for a few minutes, then add the stock and vinegar. Add salt, pepper, thyme and bay leaf. Add the potatoes, cover tightly and cook over medium heat for 45–60 minutes. Discard the bay leaf.

Sprinkle with the fresh herbs and serve.

Purée de Choux
A cabbage purée

Superb with pork and prepared in a jiffy, this reheats well.

For 8 people

> 2 heads of cabbage, cores removed
> and cut into quarters
> 25 g/1 oz unsalted butter
> salt
> freshly ground black pepper

Blanch the cabbage in a saucepan of salted boiling water until tender, about 15 minutes. Drain. Pass through a sieve, a blender or a food processor. Add butter, salt and pepper, stir carefully and serve.

Purée de Fenouil
Fennel purée

For 8 people

5 fennel bulbs
2 potatoes, peeled and sliced
salt
freshly ground black pepper
2 tbsp single cream
1 tbsp chopped fennel leaves

Cut off the base and tops and any tough, fibrous parts of the outer layer of the fennel. Quarter the bulbs. Place them and the potatoes in a saucepan of hot salted water and cook for 20 minutes. Drain.

Purée the potatoes and fennel in a Moulinex mill, a food processor or a blender. Stir in the salt, pepper and cream.

This may be reheated over low heat. Sprinkle with the fresh fennel leaves, and serve with pork or fish.

Purée de Haricots Blancs
A white bean purée seasoned with garlic, onions and cream

A superb accompaniment for roasts but mostly for pork. This has a wonderful nutty flavour but must be highly seasoned.

For 8 people

900 g/2 lb dried white beans
1 whole bulb of garlic, unpeeled
bouquet garni
3 potatoes, peeled and cut in half

1 large onion, peeled and stuck
   with 1 clove
3 tbsp single cream
70 g/2½ oz unsalted butter
freshly ground white pepper

Cook the beans with the garlic and the bouquet garni in a large pot of salted water for about 2 hours – or according to the instructions on the package. Add the potatoes and the onion for the last 20 minutes. Remove the garlic, peel it, then return the flesh to the beans. Remove and discard the bouquet garni and the clove stuck in the onion. Pass everything else through a Moulinex mill or a food processor. Beat lightly. Add the cream, butter and pepper and serve very warm with a few little pieces of butter on top.

Tarte aux Légumes
A tomato, onion and courgette pie seasoned with herbs

The most fragrant, the freshest, the lightest of summer dishes. It is better warm, but can be served cold with a tossed salad.

For 8 people

155 g/5½ oz unsalted butter
1 egg, beaten
salt
225 g/8 oz flour
1 tbsp vegetable oil
2 onions, peeled and thinly sliced
4 tomatoes, each cut into 3 or 4
   thick slices

4 courgettes (or 4 cucumbers),
   unpeeled and thinly sliced
thyme
salt
freshly ground pepper
5 tbsp finely chopped basil (or
   chives) and parsley
vegetable oil

Make the pastry for the pie crust, adding 115 g/4 oz of the butter, egg and salt to the flour and mixing quickly with your fingertips. Make a ball of the dough, cover it with a tea-towel, and let it rest for at least 1 hour.

Prepare the filling. Heat 15 g/½ oz of the butter and the oil in a frying-pan and sauté the onions until soft. Remove them into a bowl. Add half the remaining butter to the pan, then add the tomatoes, cut side down. Cook for five minutes over low heat. Remove to a bowl, pouring off the liquid. Add the remaining butter to the pan and cook the courgettes until soft.

Preheat the oven to 190°C/375°F/Gas Mark 5.

Flatten the dough ball; roll it and fold it three times. Roll it again. It should be smooth and soft. Spread it on a buttered 25-cm/10-in. pie plate, prick it with a fork and place a few dried beans or pebbles on it to keep it from puffing up. Bake for 20 minutes.

Let the crust cool, then spread the onions on it and sprinkle with thyme, salt and pepper. Spread the courgettes over the onions and sprinkle again with thyme, salt and pepper. Cover with the tomatoes, cut side up and close together. Sprinkle with the basil and parsley (or chives), salt, pepper and a few drops of oil. Bake for 15 minutes and serve warm.

Terrine de Navets

A turnip, herb, ham, cream and cheese gratin

A very tasty dish, easy to prepare ahead of time.

For 8 people

900 g/2 lb tender pink and purple turnips, peeled and very thinly sliced
dried savory (or thyme)
salt
freshly ground black pepper
170 g/6 oz sliced and shredded ham (country ham or prosciutto)

225 ml/8 fl oz double cream
170 g/6 oz grated cheese (Romano, Gruyère or Parmesan)
70 g/2½ oz breadcrumbs, preferably home-made
25 g/1 oz unsalted butter

Preheat the oven to 190°C/375°F/Gas Mark 5.

Blanch the turnips in a large pan of boiling salted water for 5 minutes. Drain.

Place one-third of the turnips in a buttered deep ovenproof dish. Sprinkle with savory, salt and pepper, then add a layer of one-third of the ham and one-third of the cream. Continue layering, and seasoning each layer, until all the turnips, ham and cream are used up. Cover with the cheese and breadcrumbs. Dot with butter and bake for 45–60 minutes. Serve in the baking dish.

Tomates au Fromage
Baked tomatoes stuffed with cheese and shallots

This is a good buffet dish that is also a splendid accompaniment to many meat and fish dishes.

For 8 people

5 tbsp finely chopped shallots	8 tomatoes
4 tbsp finely chopped parsley	2 tbsp vegetable oil
salt	3 tbsp breadcrumbs
freshly ground black pepper	40 g/1½ oz unsalted butter
3 tbsp grated Gruyère cheese	

Place the shallots, parsley, salt, pepper and cheese in a bowl and mix well.

Cut the tomatoes in half and squeeze gently to remove the seeds. Heat the oil in a large frying-pan and cook the tomatoes (cut side down) for 3–5 minutes, depending on their ripeness.

With a spatula, remove the tomatoes and place them cut side up in an ovenproof dish. Fill them with the shallot-and-cheese mixture. Sprinkle with breadcrumbs, dot with butter and grill for about 5 minutes.

Farineux

Pasta and Grain Dishes

As hunters became shepherds, then farmers, cereals were for a long time the staple of most people's diets. Oats, rye, wheat and corn were prepared in many ways. The Romans enjoyed their *poulte*, which became the Italian *polenta* and, later, *gaudes* in Burgundy.

The Chinese and then the Italians created the raviolis that were to become goat cheese *ravioles* in Savoy.

Matafam (literally hunger-killer), a large pancake of flour and vegetables, was popular; so was *farcement*, a cake of grated potato, raisins, prunes and flour. *Rambollet*, a cake made with potato and egg, was a favourite dish. *Fricot*, a purée of pears and potatoes, was served with game.

For centuries starchy dishes were widely enjoyed in the poor regions of Burgundy and Savoy. Most of them were heavy, dull, true 'Christian chokers', as they were later nicknamed. So in spite of the memories they may evoke – a grandmother's speciality, a cheerful meal shared during a village festival – few of those dishes appeal to our taste, which requires intensity of flavour and lightness. I have chosen the dishes that travelled well in time and space. And I have added new creations, such as home-made pasta served with tender crayfish or thinly sliced fish and herbs.

Crousets
Dough sticks

Crousets were served in Savoy and Dauphiné on Christmas Eve. They are delicious with a roast joint or a turkey.

For 8 people

450 g/1 lb plain flour	4 tbsp milk
4 eggs, beaten	4 tbsp single cream
salt	25 g/1 oz unsalted butter
225 g/8 oz grated Gruyère cheese	6 walnuts, chopped

Place the flour in a bowl and form a well in the centre. Add the eggs, salt and 3 tablespoons of water and knead lightly until you have a soft, firm dough.

On a table dusted with flour, spread the dough to a 6-mm/¼-in. thickness. Cut it in strips 2.5 cm/1 in. wide. Roll each strip into a cylinder 12 mm/½ in. in diameter and cut it into sticks 2.5 cm/1 in. long.

Preheat oven to 180°C/350°F/Gas Mark 4.

Put the sticks of dough in a large pot of salted boiling water. Let them simmer for 15 minutes. Drain.

Carefully place the *crousets* in a large buttered ovenproof dish. Sprinkle with the cheese. Add the milk and cream and dot with butter. Bake for 15 to 20 minutes. Sprinkle with the chopped walnuts and serve.

Crozets
Potato and flour sticks seasoned with cheese

For 6–8 people

3 large potatoes, boiled in their skins	salt
	freshly ground black pepper
450 g/1 lb plain flour	115 g/4 oz crumbled blue cheese
4 eggs	170 g/6 oz grated Gruyère cheese
1 tbsp walnut oil	15 g/½ oz lard

Peel the potatoes and mash them along with the flour, eggs, walnut oil, salt and pepper and 3 tablespoons of water. (It must be a rather dry mixture.) Stir vigorously. Divide it into small balls and roll them in the shape of short pencils. Cut them into 2.5-cm/1-in. pieces and bend them so they look like plump commas. Preheat the oven to 190°C/375°F/Gas Mark 5.

Bring a large pot of salted water to a boil and poach the *crozets* in three batches (so they have enough room) for 10 minutes each. Drain them.

Place a layer of *crozets* in a buttered ovenproof dish and sprinkle with the blue and Gruyère cheeses. Heat the lard to the boiling point and sprinkle it on top of the dish. Heat the *crozets* in the oven until lightly browned.

Pâtes Fraîches
Home-made noodles

This clearly comes from the South by way of Lyon, and has become a favourite in *nouvelle cuisine*.

It can be served for dinner with rich classical dishes, such as *Boeuf Bourguignon* (p. 198) or *Travers de Porc aux Herbes* (p. 151), or with sautéd vegetables, fillets of fish or tender crayfish, or as a main lunch dish.

For 8 people

450 g/1 lb plain flour	2 tbsp olive oil
6 eggs, lightly beaten	1 tbsp peanut oil
1 tbsp salt	unsalted butter

Put the flour in a large bowl and make a well in the centre. Put into the well the eggs, salt, 2 tablespoons of water and olive oil, and, with your fingers, work it gradually into the flour. Place the dough on a floured counter or table and knead it for 15–20 minutes. Flouring your hands and the counter or table often, push the dough away from you with the heel of your hand, then gather it back into a mass and repeat until the dough is smooth and elastic. Let it rest, covered with a towel, for 1–2 hours.

Divide the ball into eight parts (each the size of a fist). Roll each part through a pasta machine into thin layers, starting on setting No. 1, then 2, then skipping to 4 and finally 5 or – if you like thin noodles – 6. Sprinkle a little flour on the machine every time you put in a new layer of dough so it will not stick to the metal. In using No. 6, be sure to reach underneath and pull out the thin strip as it is being rolled. If allowed to pile up under the machine, the strips will stick together. If you do not have a pasta machine, you can roll out the dough by hand, dusting it with flour as you roll it repeatedly to make it as thin as you like. Sprinkle flour on all the trays you have (use counters and tables also) and let the sheets of thin pasta dry on them for 30 minutes. Then cut the sheets into thin or wide strips, as you prefer. Dust lightly with more flour and let them fall loosely on to the floured surfaces.

Bring a large saucepan of salted water to a boil. Add the peanut oil and drop the noodles into the pot. Cook, stirring twice, for 5–10 minutes over medium heat. Drain in a colander and pour into a shallow dish. Add desired amount of butter at once.

Riz aux Herbes
Rice with herbs

For 8 people

300 g/10½ oz raw rice	25 g/1 oz unsalted butter
3 bay leaves	freshly ground pepper
2 tsp thyme	2 tbsp chopped herbs (tarragon,
2 tbsp olive oil	chives, fresh thyme)

In a very large saucepan, bring 6.5 l/11 pt of salted water to a boil and add the rice while slowly stirring with a fork. Add the bay leaves and thyme and boil, uncovered, for 20 minutes.

Rinse the rice under cold water and drain in a colander. Transfer it to a smaller saucepan, add the olive oil and butter and fluff the rice with two forks.

Reheat, stirring lightly with two forks a few times, for 5 minutes just before serving. Sprinkle with pepper and the fresh herbs.

Ravioles
Cheese-filled pasta

This is a delicious Savoy and Dauphiné version of the Chinese and
Italian dish. A pasta machine is a great help.

For 8 people

285 g/10 oz flour
2 tbsp olive oil
2 eggs, beaten
2 tsp salt
55 g/2 oz goat cheese
2 eggs

225 g/8 oz grated Gruyère cheese
salt
5 tbsp chopped parsley
55 g/2 oz unsalted butter
stock (or water)
3 tbsp grated Gruyère cheese

Sift the flour into a large bowl. Make a well in the centre and pour
in 1 tablespoon of the olive oil, the beaten eggs, salt, and 6
tablespoons of water. Mix with a fork until all the flour is absorbed,
adding another tablespoon of water if necessary. Knead for 10
minutes, either in the bowl or on a floured counter, until the dough
becomes smooth and elastic. Form a ball of the dough, place it in
an oiled bowl, cover with a clean cloth and let it rest for 1 hour.

Place the pasta machine on the table and flour it. Divide the
dough into four balls the size of small oranges. Roll each ball
through No. 1, then 3, then 5, then on the highest setting. Reach
underneath and pull out the thin strip as it is being rolled. If
allowed to pile up under the machine, the strips will stick together.
Lay the paper-thin sheets of dough on a floured tray or table to dry
for 10 minutes.

If you do not have a pasta machine, roll each small ball of dough
on a floured board as thinly as you can.

Prepare the stuffing. Crush the goat cheese, eggs, Gruyère cheese
and salt with a fork or a blender. Sauté the chopped parsley in half
of the butter and add to the mixture.

Place a sheet of dough on a floured surface, put a teaspoon of
filling every 5 cm/2 in. along the entire sheet, making 2 long rows.
Place another sheet of dough on top of the mounds and carefully
press around each little heap with your fingers, sealing the two
layers together. With a pastry wheel, cut around each heap so that

you have neat little squares that look like plump cushions. If the pasta strips have become too dry to adhere to one another, dip the pastry wheel into warm water and work them together. When all the squares are cut, sprinkle them with a little flour and allow them to rest for 1 hour before cooking.

Bring a large container of stock or salted water to boil. Add the remaining olive oil. Lower the heat and gently slide the *ravioles* in. Simmer gently for 10 minutes. When they rise to the surface they are ready. Take them out with a slotted spoon and drain them in a colander.

Arrange the *ravioles* in a warm dish, dot with the remaining butter, sprinkle with grated cheese and serve at once.

Les Plats de Festin
Festive Dishes

Boeuf Bourguignon, Fondue Bourguignonne, Fondue Savoyarde, Gratinée Lyonnaise, La Pauchouse, Pot-au-Feu Bourguignon, Potée Bourguignonne and the two versions of *Saupiquet* are the sumptuous party dishes presented here.

A crisp salad or a few light appetizers can precede these splendid dishes and a light fruit dessert or a single good cheese conclude the meal. Nothing more is required for a hearty feast.

They can be prepared ahead of time and you can gather as many guests as you wish – nothing will go wrong or need your attention at the last minute. You will truly be able to share the feast.

And because these dishes are exuberant, highly flavoured and generous, they can be the core of all your celebrations.

Boeuf Bourguignon
Beef stew of Burgundy

There are so many variations of this dish that the definitive one cannot be determined. It can be made with beef heart or beef cheek or any good eye of round or round steak. It is better prepared in advance, degreased and reheated, and is best served with a plain potato or pasta accompaniment and a sharp celery or fennel purée (p. 188) or with boiled chestnuts.

For 8 people

1.25 kg/3 lb round steak, rump
  joint, eye of round or chuck,
  cut into 5-cm/2-in. cubes
3 tbsp brandy
900 ml/1⅗ pt good red wine
5 yellow onions
2 bay leaves
5 whole peppercorns
1 sprig of thyme
1 tbsp vegetable oil
40 g/1½ oz lard (or 40 g/1½ oz
  unsalted butter and vegetable
  oil)

225 g/8 oz streaky bacon (or lean
  salt pork) cut into small cubes
2 tbsp flour
3 carrots, sliced
20 pearl onions (or 10 yellow
  onions, cut in half)
3 whole garlic cloves, peeled
grated nutmeg to taste
680 g/1½ lb mushrooms, thickly
  sliced
1 tbsp butter
2 tbsp finely chopped parsley

Place the beef cubes in a large bowl with the brandy, wine, 1 yellow onion (peeled and quartered), bay leaves, peppercorns, thyme and oil. Cover and store on the lowest shelf of the refrigerator for 48 hours.

Heat the lard in a heavy-bottomed pan and sauté the bacon on all sides. Remove and keep for later use. Add the drained meat cubes to the pan and sauté on all sides for 10 minutes. Sprinkle flour over them and stir with a wooden spoon. (The flour will form a light crust on each piece.)

Bring the marinade to a boil and pour half of it over the meat. Cook the meat, uncovered, for 30 minutes. Peel and chop the remaining yellow onions. Add the rest of the marinade, the onions and the reserved bacon to the meat. Cover and cook gently for 2½–3 hours. Add the carrots, pearl onions, garlic and nutmeg. Check the seasoning and cook for 30 minutes. Let cool. Remove the bay leaves, peppercorns and the sprig of thyme, cover and refrigerate overnight.

The next day, remove as much fat from the top of the pan as possible. Reheat and check the seasoning. Sauté the mushrooms in the butter until they are browned and add to the pan. Cover and cook for 10 minutes. Serve in a warm dish, sprinkled with parsley.

Fondue Bourguignonne
Cubes of beef cooked in oil and served with a variety of sauces

A newcomer to the Burgundy repertory, this is an easy dish to prepare and a festive experience to share with friends.

Serve with a hearty red wine and a large bowl of tossed green salad.

To serve this communal dish, you will need a table-top brazier (a butane-fired one is best), and a long-handled fork as well as a standard fork for each guest.

For 8 people

2.25 kg/5 lb very tender fillet or sirloin of beef, diced 5 x 5-cm/ 2 x 2-in. cubes
900 ml/1⅗ pt peanut oil
1 bowl of home-made mayonnaise flavoured with lemon
1 bowl of home-made mayonnaise flavoured with curry
1 bowl of home-made mayonnaise flavoured with Spanish saffron
1 bowl of spicy tomato sauce
1 bowl of tiny onions
1 bowl of cornichons
1 bowl of capers

Place the oil in a heavy-bottomed enamel or copper pan over a lit brazier in the middle of the table. Heat it to just the boiling point and then adjust the heat to maintain the temperature. Pass the various bowls of sauce to each guest.

Each guest will cook his or her meat for a few seconds, changing forks for dipping so as not to burn the lips or to cloud the oil with the sauces, then dip the meat in one of the sauces and nibble capers, cornichons or onions with it.

La Fondue Savoyarde
Fondue of cheese, wine and brandy

This is a mountain dish usually eaten in autumn and winter when the sheep are brought down from the mountains and shepherds and villagers celebrate. It is also eaten during the *veillées*, when village people meet to speak and sing and shell walnuts (for making walnut oil) and entertain each other in large groups.

This is a lovely dish to share with friends. Don't serve too much wine. Better to drink water instead, and a little kirsch.

You will need a table-top brazier (preferably fired by butane) and both a long-handled fork and a standard fork for each guest.

For each person

1 garlic clove
25 g/1 oz unsalted butter
170 g/6 oz grated or Gruyère
    cheese
7 tbsp dry white wine
½ tsp cornflour, stirred in 2 tbsp
    water

115 ml/4 fl oz kirsch
freshly ground black pepper
freshly grated nutmeg
1 bowl of diced bread
1–2 egg yolks

Put a heavy-bottomed enamel or copper pan over a lit brazier and rub it with the clove of garlic, then add the butter. Add the cheese and wine and cook over a low flame, stirring with a wooden spoon until you have a smooth mixture. When it reaches the boiling point, add the cornflour and water and stir in the kirsch. Keep stirring. Add pepper and nutmeg. If you think the fondue is too thick, add a little more wine and check the seasoning again.

Each guest will use a long-stemmed fork to spear a piece of bread, then coat it in the hot fondue cooking in the centre of the table. The bread should be transferred to a standard fork to avoid burning the lips.

When most of the fondue has been consumed, add one or two egg yolks and the rest of the diced bread to the pot and stir until golden.

Note: There are many variations on this recipe. Some marinate diced pieces of cheese in milk, then stir it with egg yolks over a low flame and sprinkle it with truffles, but the recipe above is the classic one.

Gratinée Lyonnaise

A superb version of onion soup enriched with eggs, cheese and Madeira wine

Whether it is at dawn after the theatre or in the evening for a large family dinner, onion soup is always a treat. It should be followed by a plate of highly seasoned country ham and sausages or, better, by a plate of raw oysters and a good beer. It should be accompanied by an old brandy or Calvados, the fine apple brandy.

For 8–10 people

1.8 kg/4 lb yellow onions, peeled and thinly sliced
225 g/8 oz unsalted butter
3 tbsp flour
1.8 l/3⅕ pt chicken stock (or beef stock or water)
salt

freshly ground white pepper
10 slices of stale bread, lightly toasted
4 tbsp Madeira
680 g/1½ lb grated Gruyère cheese
2 eggs
1 onion, finely grated (optional)

Sauté the sliced onions in 170 g/6 oz of the butter in a large covered frying-pan until they turn golden. Sprinkle them with flour and stir with a wooden spoon for a few minutes. Meanwhile, heat the stock and blend it little by little with the onions. Add salt and pepper and simmer for 30 minutes, uncovered, skimming the froth off the top from time to time.

Preheat oven to 200°C/400°F/Gas Mark 6.

Sauté the slices of bread in the remaining butter until crisp on both sides (or simply toast and butter them). Pour 3 tablespoons of the Madeira into an ovenproof dish, or, if you prefer, into small individual ovenproof bowls. Add a layer of the bread and sprinkle with half of the grated cheese.

Beat the eggs with the remaining Madeira and pour the mixture into the broth, stirring constantly. Pour the broth over the bread and cheese, sprinkle with the remaining cheese and bake for about 20 minutes. Just before serving, a nice touch is to lift the cheese crust slightly and beat 1 tablespoon of grated onion into each bowl.

Variation

You may wish to add 115 ml/4 fl oz of wine to the stock while preparing the soup, then 4 tablespoons of good brandy just before serving.

La Pauchouse

A fish stew prepared with white wine, onions, garlic and cream

The name comes from *poche*, the fisherman's bag where he puts his catch, and it can be spelled either *pauchouse* or *pochouse*. It is a sort of Burgundy bouillabaisse, a fragrant fish stew, with a rich sauce.

The mixture of four kinds of fish – pike, perch, eel and carp – and dry white wine is the essence of the dish, but each restaurant and each family has its own tricks to personalize its *pauchouse*. It is a cousin of the *meurette*, which is made with red wine.

The recipe we have comes from medieval sources. Serve with white wine of the kind used in the preparation of the dish.

For 8 people

2 tbsp vegetable oil
20 garlic cloves, peeled and crushed
4 shallots, peeled and chopped
10 pickling onions (or 4 quartered yellow onions)
2 bay leaves
1 sprig of thyme
10 peppercorns
1.4 l/2⅖ pt dry white wine
900 g/2 lb pike, chopped in 5-cm/2-in. pieces
900 g/2 lb carp, chopped in 5-cm/2-in. pieces

450 g/1 lb eel, skinned and chopped in 5-cm/2-in. pieces
450 g/1 lb perch, chopped in 5-cm/2-in. pieces
salt
freshly ground black pepper
4 tbsp flour
55 g/2 oz unsalted butter
6 tbsp single cream
8 slices of bread fried in butter and rubbed with garlic to make *croûtons*

Put the oil in a heavy-bottomed pan and add the garlic, shallots, onions, bay leaves, thyme and peppercorns. Pour the wine into the pan and cook over medium heat, covered, for 10 minutes, stirring from time to time. Add the pieces of fish, sprinkle with salt and pepper, cover and simmer for 15 minutes.

Knead the flour and butter into a paste. Add to the sauce and simmer for 10 minutes. Remove from the heat and add the cream. Check and correct the seasoning.

Place crisp *croûtons* and pieces of fish on each plate and pour some of the broth on top through a sieve.

Le Pot-au-Feu Bourguignon
Burgundy's version of the boiled dinner

Every province boasts its own version of this wonderful boiled dinner, but it is in Burgundy that it becomes a truly superb creation. It is, of course, never boiled, but gently simmered. In this harmonious dish composed of many ingredients, the meat remains moist and tasty, the vegetables crunchy and full of flavour, and the broth heady yet lean. It is, in fact, such a treat that in the old days the broth used to be kept for new mothers, old people and lovesick teenagers. At springtime a branch of the boxwood tree dipped in the broth scared away bad spirits, snakes and ill omens for a whole year.

Pot-au-feu is a glorious meal in itself, and only a crisp tossed green salad and a robust red wine are needed to accompany it. The secret of a great *pot-au-feu* is to prepare it a day in advance and degrease it completely before you add the vegetables. The bones, the vegetables and the meat must be fresh and well trimmed. Remember that the dish has to be highly seasoned to be genuinely *bourguignon*, so taste the broth before serving it and prepare two or three sauces to accompany the meat. Since everything can be prepared ahead of time, you, too, can relax and enjoy the feast.

For about 10 people

1 large onion studded with 2 cloves
1 tbsp vegetable oil
2 large beef bones (about 450 g/1 lb)
1.25 kg/3 lb brisket of beef, tied with a string

1.25 kg/3 lb rump roast (or sirloin tip or boneless chuck), tied with a string to keep its shape
900 g/2 lb short ribs
1 oxtail, cut in 4 pieces
4.5 l/8 pt chicken stock (or cold water)

11 carrots, peeled
1 celery stalk
1 garlic bulb (with about 7 cloves),
  unpeeled
3 bay leaves
2 sprigs thyme
10 peppercorns
salt
1 1.8-kg/4-lb stewing hen
70 g/2½ oz chicken livers
15 g/½ oz unsalted butter
1 onion, finely chopped
170 g/6 oz lean streaky bacon (or
  lean salt pork)
3 tsp thyme
freshly ground pepper
1 egg, beaten

140 g/5 oz cooked rice
1 garlic clove, chopped
20 g/¾ oz finely chopped parsley
2 onions, peeled
4 large Polish sausages (or any
  similar sausage)
1 celery heart
10 potatoes, peeled
10 turnips, peeled
1 small head of green cabbage
10 slices of bread, each cut into 2
  triangles and fried in butter
55 g/2 oz grated Gruyère cheese
kosher salt
2 large marrow bones, cut into 10
  2.5-cm/1-in. pieces by the
  butcher

········ Accompaniments ········

tomato sauce (p. 58)
vinaigrette
1 bowl of kosher salt
1 bowl of pickled gherkins
  (cornichons)

Brown the clove-studded onion in oil in a heavy frying-pan for 2 minutes. (You will add it to your broth to give it a pretty caramel colour.)

Place the beef bones in the bottom of a very large container, add
all the meat on top, and cover with chicken stock (or cold water).
Bring to a boil and cook for 5 minutes, skimming the froth off the
surface. Add the clove-studded onion, 1 carrot, celery, garlic bulb,
bay leaves, thyme, peppercorns and salt. Bring to a boil and skim
off once more. Partially cover and simmer for 2 hours.

Meanwhile, prepare the stuffing for the hen. Cut the chicken
livers with scissors. Heat the butter in a frying-pan and sauté the
chopped onion, cooking over low heat for 3 minutes. Add the
bacon (or lean salt pork) and the chicken livers and cook for 2
more minutes, tossing. Remove from the heat; add the thyme,

pepper, egg, rice, chopped garlic and parsley. Check the seasonings, and then stuff, sew the chicken closed.

Add the stuffed chicken to the bones and meat and cook for 1½ hours. Remove from the heat, cover and refrigerate overnight.

The next day, carefully remove all the fat on the surface of the broth, the clove-studded onion, the bay leaves, thyme and garlic bulb. Bring the broth with the bones, meat and chicken to a boil. Add the whole onions and 10 carrots and cook for 15 minutes, then add the sausages, celery heart, potatoes and turnips. Simmer for 30 minutes. Check the seasoning.

Boil the cabbage separately in a saucepan of salted water for 15–20 minutes. Meanwhile, prepare the *croûtons*, the grated cheese, the sauces you want to serve, the bowls of kosher salt and pickled gherkins.

Press a teaspoon of kosher salt on both openings of each marrow bone to prevent the marrow from melting away, and add the bones to the cabbage and cook for 10 minutes.

Preheat the oven to 150°C/300°F/Gas Mark 2.

When you are ready to serve, place the beef on a warm ovenproof serving platter. Remove the strings and slice the meat. Season with salt and pepper and pour a tablespoon of broth over it. Cover with kitchen foil and place in the oven. Remove the chicken from the broth. Scoop out the stuffing, slice it and place it in the centre of a warm ovenproof platter, surrounded by the pieces of chicken. Pour a little broth over everything, cover with kitchen foil and put in the oven.

Arrange the vegetables on a warm ovenproof serving dish and place the thickly sliced sausages and marrow bones in the centre. Cover with kitchen foil and place in the oven to keep warm.

Serve the broth in soup bowls with *croûtons*, sprinkled with cheese. You may also want to add – as old Burgundy gourmets do – 1 tablespoon of red wine to each bowl of soup or 1 tablespoon of cream and 1 tablespoon of sherry, stirring well.

Then comes the second course, served on three platters: beef, chicken, and sausage, marrow bones and vegetables. Be sure to serve small teaspoons or butter knives with the marrow bones so that each guest can scoop out the marrow and spread it on the warm potatoes.

Pass the sauces, kosher salt and gherkins.

Note: You can use the left-over broth two days later by adding to each bowl of hot broth 1 egg yolk mixed with 1 tablespoon of cream and 1 tablespoon of chervil and stirring vigorously.

You can use the left-over meat or chicken in croquettes, shepherd's pie, or in a cold salad with sliced potatoes, shallots soaked in a spicy vinaigrette sauce, or in a *Boeuf à la Mâcon* (p. 101) cooked with sliced onions and vinegar.

Potée Bourguignonne
Burgundy boiled dinner with shoulder of pork, spareribs, sausages, ham and a variety of vegetables

This hearty and invigorating dinner slowly simmered in the Burgundy way celebrates the perfect harmony between the region's garden and its pork. It is good reheated, so you had better make an abundant *potée*. In some part of Burgundy, white or green beans are added.

For about 16 people

1 head of green cabbage, trimmed and quartered	4 garlic cloves, peeled
1 shoulder (or butt) of pork	3 onions, peeled and each studded with 1 clove
450-g/1-lb piece of lean salt pork	bouquet garni
half of a precooked ham – about 1.8 kg/4 lb	10 peppercorns
1 pig's knuckle	4 smoked sausages
450 g/1 lb spareribs	2 large Polish cooking-type sausages, such as kielbasa
kosher salt	10 large potatoes, peeled
6 leeks, trimmed	salt
10 whole carrots, peeled	freshly ground black pepper
8 whole turnips, peeled	Dijon-style mustard

Blanch the cabbage in a large saucepan of salted water for 5 minutes. Drain and set aside.

Place all the meat except the sausages in a large saucepan of cold water with salt. Bring it to a boil and cook for 1½ hours, removing the foam from time to time.

Add all the vegetables except the cabbage and potatoes; add the bouquet garni and the peppercorns. Cook for 20 minutes. Add the sausages, potatoes and cabbage and cook for 30 minutes. Degrease as much as you can.

Serve the broth with toasted bread. (The broth will be very tasty, but will be better kept for the next day, when you can degrease it more easily.)

Place all the meat and sausages in the centre of a large warm shallow dish. Slice the sausages. Pile the vegetables all around. Pour a ladle of broth over the dish, sprinkle with salt and pepper and serve with a bowl of mustard.

Saupiquet I

A whole ham baked with vegetables, spices, wine, cream and fresh herbs

This is a medieval dish, interpreted through the centuries in so many ways that I had to be very, very selective in my choice. The following two versions are piquant yet mellow in some subtle way and will be wonderful for a festive meal. Serve with *Champignons de Dijon* (p. 160), *Crépinette aux Marrons* (p. 29) or a tossed salad.

For 8 people

1 precooked 2.75–3.5-kg/6–8-lb smoked ham
3 carrots, peeled and sliced
3 onions, peeled and sliced
115 g/4 oz unsalted butter
2 garlic cloves, peeled
2 tsp thyme
2 bay leaves, crushed
5 juniper berries, crushed
freshly ground pepper
680 ml/1⅕ pt white wine

900 ml/1⅗ pt stock (preferably beef)
900 g/2 lb mushrooms, cleaned and sliced
2 tbsp vegetable oil
salt
freshly ground pepper
juice of 1 lemon
450 ml/16 fl oz single cream
fresh tarragon (or any other fresh herb), finely chopped

Cover the ham with cold water and simmer it, covered, according to the directions given by the butcher or written on the package, until very tender.

Remove the ham from the liquid. Peel off the skin and discard most of the fat.

Sauté the carrots and onions in half the butter for 5 minutes. Scatter them in the bottom of a very deep pan and put the ham on top. Add the garlic, thyme, bay leaves, juniper berries and pepper. Pour the wine and stock into the pan, cover and bring to a boil. Simmer for 1 hour.

Meanwhile, sauté the mushrooms in the remaining butter and the oil for 10 minutes. Sprinkle with salt, pepper and lemon juice and set aside.

Preheat the oven to 150°C/300°F/Gas Mark 2.

Pour all the cooking juices from the ham into a saucepan. Degrease carefully and cook, uncovered, over high heat until the liquid is reduced to 450 ml/16 fl oz. Slice the ham and cover it with kitchen foil, keeping it warm in a turned-off oven.

Pour the reduced liquid over the mushrooms and reheat. Stir in the cream and check the seasoning.

Spoon this sauce over the ham, sprinkle with tarragon and serve the rest of the sauce in a bowl along with the sliced ham.

Saupiquet II

Ham cooked with garlic and herbs and served with a vinegar, shallot, juniper and cream sauce

A more pungent version.

For 8 people

1 3-kg/7-lb uncooked ham	salt
coarse salt	340 ml/12 fl oz wine vinegar
freshly ground pepper	10 shallots, peeled and finely
3 garlic cloves, peeled and cut into	chopped
6-mm/¼-in. slivers	5 juniper berries, crushed
3 bay leaves	680 ml/1⅕ pt single cream
2 tbsp thyme	tarragon, finely chopped
1 tsp sage	watercress ·
1 tsp savory	

Preheat the oven to 180°C/350°F/Gas Mark 4.

Remove the skin, the top part of the bone and part of the fat from the ham and rub with coarse salt. Let the ham sit for 2 hours.

Dry it with a clean cloth and rub it with pepper. Insert the garlic slivers with a sharp knife all over the ham.

Crush together the bay leaves, thyme, sage and savory and sprinkle the mixture all over the ham, pressing to make it stick; sprinkle with salt and pepper.

Place the ham in a deep baking dish and bake, uncovered, in the oven for 2–3 hours. Then cover with kitchen foil and cook for 1½ hours more.

During the last 30 minutes, prepare the sauce. Heat the vinegar and add the shallots and juniper berries. Boil for 20 minutes, or until most of the liquid is gone. Stir in the cream and check the seasoning.

Remove the ham from the oven and slice it. Put the slices of ham on a warm serving dish and spoon the sauce over them. Sprinkle with tarragon and serve surrounded with watercress.

Les Fromages

Cheeses

Cheese adds to the enjoyment of wine tasting and it's a true part of Burgundy's patrimony because it has been prepared by generations of attentive monks and patient farmers' wives.

When milk turns, it is usually put in an earthenware pot pierced with holes. As the cheese becomes firmer it is placed on a wooden tray covered with a layer of straw. Salted water is spread on the surface and, according to the season, the crust becomes pale gold or red. The cheese is ready after fifteen to thirty days and may be covered with ashes to help it dry. About 2.7 l/4¾ pt of milk are needed for an average cheese.

In Burgundy, making cheese is an endless activity because it has always been the main food for grape pickers and workers in the fields.

There is a wide variety of cheese made from cow's milk and from goat's milk. The rich pastures along the rivers are territory for dairy cattle, while goats graze near the vineyards on the rocky hills.

Cheese made from cow's milk is eaten fresh in desserts or whipped with fresh herbs (*claqueret*). It can be mixed with white wine, brandy, leeks and broth and then fermented, or dried and then marinated in oil or brine. The main soft fresh cheeses are Sainte Marie des Laumes and Sainte Reine d'Alise, along with many highly flavoured cheeses from Beaujolais. Then there are the soft cheeses with washed crusts, such as Epoisses, with its orange crust and sumptuous texture and flavour; Boule des Moines Pierre Qui Vire; Saint Forentine; and Soumaintrain. There are many

tommes; there is Emmenthal and Bresse Bleu, a blue cheese as smooth as Gorgonzola.

In Savoy, east of Burgundy, there is a rich kind of Emmenthal, a Reblochon and different *tommes*, flavoured with brandy, fennel and herbs.

Goat cheese can also be served fresh with thick cream. It tastes best from April to October, after the nanny-goats have produced their young. Goat cheeses are shaped like logs, cones or balls; are wrapped in plane, grape or chestnut leaves, and sprinkled with pepper, grape seeds, herbs or ashes. As they dry in straw the crusts turn pale blue. They always have evocative names; Bouton de Culotte (breeches button), Claquebiton, Chevreton, Plardon, Picodon.

Finally, there are home preparations. The *cancoillotte* is a creamy mixture of butter stirred with *meton* (the milk left after making Emmenthal). To ferment it, *cancoillotte* used to be kept under the family-bed eiderdown in farmers' houses in the past. It is served with garlic, salt, pepper and white wine.

Then there is the invigorating *fromage fort*, a tasty mixture of fresh cheese, white wine, walnut oil, brandy, salt and pepper that is fermented; it is used as a spread for warm toast.

There is also the *fromage pourri* (rotten cheese), made with goat cheese wrapped in leaves, sprinkled with brandy and kept in earthenware pots for three weeks.

Usually the wines served with the cheeses come from the same regions, and white wines are generally served with goat cheese, hearty red wine with strong cheese made from cow's milk, light red wine with mild cheese.

Baguettes
Deep-fried cheese sticks

These make good appetizers.

For 8 people

225 g/8 oz Gruyère cheese cut in
    sticks 12 mm/½ in. thick and
    5 cm/2 in. long
225 ml/8 fl oz milk
85 g/3 oz flour

2 eggs, beaten
100 g/3½ oz breadcrumbs
85 g/3 oz butter
parsley

Place the cheese sticks in the milk for 2 hours. Drain and roll them in the flour, then in the eggs and finally in the breadcrumbs.

Fry the cheese sticks in the butter for 2 minutes on each side and serve with fried parsley.

Délice de Fromages
A blend of various cheeses, wine and stock

A hearty mixture from Beaujolais, perfect for a robust dinner, a picnic or a buffet. Use the different cheeses available where you are.

For 8 people

3 tbsp goat cheese, grated or diced
3 tbsp freshly grated cow's-milk
    cheese of any kind
2 tbsp freshly grated Gruyère
    cheese
2 tbsp cottage cheese
115 ml/4 fl oz vegetable stock,
    made with leeks or celery

2 tbsp dry white wine
15 g/½ oz unsalted butter,
    softened
1 tsp freshly ground pepper or
    nutmeg (optional)

Mix all the cheeses in a large bowl and crush them with a fork. Stir in the stock, then the wine and the butter to make a thick soft mixture. Check the seasoning. You may want to add a little pepper or grated nutmeg.

Spread on the toasted bread and serve with a hearty red wine.

La Cervelle de Canut
A highly seasoned blending of fresh cheese, herbs and wine

A traditional Lyon dessert, also called *claqueret battu*. It is invigorating, and you can use whatever fresh herbs are available. It must be beaten vigorously, 'as if it were your wife' goes the saying. A *canut* is a worker in the silk factories of Lyon, the French silk capital.

For 8 people

450 g/1 lb *fromage frais* (or cottage
    cheese mixed with 3 tbsp
    soured cream)
salt
freshly ground black pepper
25 g/1 oz finely chopped chives,
    tarragon and dill

1 garlic clove, peeled and finely
    chopped
3 tbsp single cream
1 tbsp soured cream
2 tbsp dry white wine
1 tbsp good wine vinegar
2 tbsp vegetable oil

Whip the *fromage frais* (or cottage cheese and soured cream). Add the salt, pepper, herbs and garlic and continue whipping. Add the single cream, soured cream, wine, vinegar and oil and stir well. It will be smooth and creamy. Check the seasoning and chill. Spread on lightly toasted slices of wholewheat bread.

Chèvre Chaud
A tossed salad topped with a melted goat cheese

A lovely first course.

Prepare a mixed green salad. Season it with wine vinegar and olive oil or only walnut oil. Place a 2.5-mm-/1-in.-thick round of creamy goat cheese on a baking sheet and leave it for 2 minutes in the oven at 170°C/325°F/Gas Mark 3.

Spread a little salad on each individual plate and place a piece of the melting goat cheese on top. Serve at once.

Fromage Fort du Beaujolais
A cheese blend with white wine

For 8 people

40 g/1½ oz grated goat cheese
55 g/2 oz grated cow's-milk cheese
55 g/2 oz Gruyère cheese
55 g/2 oz *fromage frais*
55 g/2 oz grated Parmesan or Romano cheese

25 g/1 oz unsalted butter
55 ml/2 fl oz vegetable stock (preferably made with leek and celery)
55 ml/2 fl oz dry white wine

Mix all the ingredients by hand or in a blender or food processor and add the stock and wine to make a soft paste. Place in a tightly closed pot for 15 days.

Spread on toast or chicory leaves or eat as is with a spoon. Drink a Beaujolais wine with it, of course. This can be served as an hors-d'oeuvre or at the end of a meal.

Les Desserts

Desserts

The Greeks and the Romans used honey, spices and pepper in their pastry, and Burgundian cuisine has kept some of these curious pungent blends in some desserts. The famous *pain d'épice* follows the original medieval recipe, but many of the overly elaborate desserts – heavy fruit pancakes, creamy custards, chestnut or corn-flour confections – have been lightened and sharpened in taste in the past few years. Rich, bland desserts have no appeal to our palates, so the addition of fruits, spices, brandy and liqueurs, of tart fruit purées and bitter sauces has increased. A tray of cheese is also truly appealing when served with a beautifully arranged basket of pears, grapes, cherries or melon.

I looked for exciting desserts to complement any meal in selecting the following recipes.

Beignets à la Crème
Cream fritters

For 8 people

·············· Custard ··············

680 ml/1⅕ pt single cream
115 g/4 oz plain flour
6 egg yolks, beaten
300 g/10½ oz granulated sugar
peel of 2 lemons, grated

·················· Batter ··················

2 egg yolks, beaten
2 tbsp granulated sugar
85 g/3 oz plain flour
1 tsp salt
15 g/½ oz unsalted butter, softened
140 ml/5 fl oz water

oil for deep frying
sugar

Heat the cream in a heavy-bottomed pan. While stirring, slowly add the flour, beaten egg yolks, sugar and lemon peel. Continue stirring. When the mixture coats the spoon, remove from the heat. Let the custard cool until it sets. Cut into 5-cm/2-in. squares.

Prepare the batter by mixing together all the ingredients. Dip the cubes of custard into the light batter and deep-fry them until they turn golden. Drain on kitchen towels and sprinkle with sugar.

Beignets au Caillé
Delicate fritters made with cheese, flour and egg whites

There are endless varieties of fritters in Lyon and in Burgundy. They can be made of potato flour and grated cheese, and called *talmouzes*; of corn flour, egg whites, breadcrumbs; and of all kinds of fruit and blossoms.

These fritters are made with freshly made curds (*caillé*), but curds can be replaced by a mixture of soured cream and cheese, which are easier to find.

For 8 people

115 g/4 oz cottage cheese
115 ml/4 fl oz soured cream
115 g/4 oz plain flour
3 eggs, beaten
1 tsp salt

6 tbsp granulated sugar
2 tbsp orange-flower water or
    lemon juice
oil for deep frying
115 g/4 oz icing sugar

Mix the first seven ingredients in a bowl. The mixture should be smooth and thick. Heat the cooking oil and deep-fry 1 tablespoon of the mixture at a time until each fritter turns golden. Drain on kitchen towels and sprinkle with icing sugar while still warm.

Beignets de Compote
Applesauce fritters

This delicate dessert comes from Lyon and remains a favourite among fritter lovers.

For 8 people

2 eggs, separated	900 g/2 lb apples (Granny Smith
150 ml/5¼ fl oz sweet white wine	or any other tart apples),
4 tbsp granulated sugar	peeled, cored and grated
85 g/3 oz plain flour	1 lemon peel, grated
1 tsp salt	oil for deep-frying
15 g/½ oz unsalted butter,	icing sugar
softened	

Beat the egg yolks and blend them in the wine and half the sugar with a fork. Stir in the flour, salt and butter to form a smooth batter. Cover and leave in a warm place, such as a turned-off oven, until ready to use.

Cook the apples with the remaining sugar and lemon peel, uncovered, until soft.

Heat the oil in a frying-pan until it is very hot. Beat the egg whites until they are stiff but not dry, and delicately fold them into the batter (it should be very smooth). Take a tablespoon of the applesauce at a time, dip it in the batter for a second, then drop it into the hot oil. Fry the fritters until golden on all sides, turning them with a pair of tongs after about 3 minutes. Remove with a slotted spoon and drain on kitchen towels. Keep warm in a low or turned-off oven.

Line a large serving plate or a basket with a napkin, place the fritters on it, sprinkle with icing sugar and serve warm. Some people like to sprinkle a little brandy on the warm fritters just before serving.

Biscuit de Savoie

A light cake made with cornflour, flour, eggs and lemon

Prepared in Chambéry, Savoy, in the middle of the fourteenth century, and tested by generations of cooks, this is one of the most popular cakes. It is served either with a bowl of stewed fruit, or coated with a fruit *coulis* (p. 226), with tangerines in Armagnac (p. 238) or with a warm butter–chocolate sauce.

Potato flour, which is traditionally used, is replaced here by plain cornflour or arrowroot, which is easier to find and equally light.

For 6–8 people

370 g/13 oz granulated sugar	2 tsp grated lemon peel
6 eggs, separated	2 tbsp orange-flower water (or
115 g/4 oz plain flour	lemon juice)
125 g/4½ oz cornflour	2 tsp icing sugar

Butter a tall mould and dust it with flour. Whip 300 g/10½ oz of the sugar and the egg yolks until they form a pale yellow ribbon.

Preheat the oven to 180°C/350°F/Gas Mark 4.

Whip the egg whites and the remaining sugar until stiff. Combine the flour and cornflour. Fold the egg whites and flour alternately into the yolk mixture. Add the lemon peel and orange-flower water. Pour into the prepared mould. It should only be three-quarters filled.

Sprinkle the top with icing sugar and bake for 35–45 minutes, until cooked through. If the top begins to brown, place a sheet of wet paper on it.

Remove from the oven and let cool. Wrap in kitchen foil and keep fresh.

Biscuits au Citron
Light crisp lemon biscuits

65 g/2¼ oz icing sugar
115 g/4 oz plain flour
50 g/1¾ oz ground almonds
150 g/5¼ oz unsalted butter,
    softened

1 egg, well beaten
pinch of salt
peel of 2 lemons, grated

Mix the sugar, flour and the almonds. In another bowl, combine the butter, egg, salt and lemon peel and mix vigorously. Stir in the sugar mixture. Cover and refrigerate for a few hours.

Preheat the oven to 180°C/350°F/Gas Mark 4.

Roll out the dough as thin as you can and cut it in strips or circles. Place the pieces on a well-buttered baking sheet. Bake for 10 minutes, or until golden.

Bugnes Lyonnaises
Light fritters

For 8 people

115 g/4 oz unsalted butter,
    softened
200 g/7 oz granulated sugar
1 tsp salt
peel of 1 lemon, grated
3 egg yolks

2 tbsp rum
285 g/10 oz plain flour
1 tbsp vegetable oil
oil for deep-frying
icing sugar

Mix together the soft butter, sugar, salt and grated lemon peel until fluffy. Stir in the egg yolks, one at a time, then the rum. Add the flour and stir. Add the oil, cover with a towel, and let stand for 3 hours.

Shape the dough into walnut-size balls and flatten them until they are very thin. Cut in half and deep-fry in very hot oil for about 3 minutes on each side. Drain on kitchen towels and sprinkle with icing sugar.

Caramels

450 ml/16 fl oz single cream
25 g/1 oz unsweetened chocolate,
  cut in pieces

300 g/10½ oz granulated sugar
2 tbsp honey
25 g/1 oz unsalted butter

Bring to a boil half of the cream, the chocolate and the sugar. Add the rest of the cream little by little, stirring all the time with a wooden spoon. Add the honey, then the butter, about a fifth at a time, until you can clearly see the bottom of the pan. Remove from heat.

Pour into a buttered square mould and let cool for 2 hours. When it is no longer too soft, cut into squares and wrap individually in greaseproof paper.

Cassolettes Meringuées

Black cherries in red wine, covered with meringue and baked

An elegant dessert you can make with fresh or canned black cherries and serve with a sweet wine.

For 8 people

900 g/2 lb black cherries
150 g/5¼ oz granulated sugar
1 tsp cinnamon
225 ml/8 fl oz good red wine

6 egg whites
pinch of salt
55 g/2 oz icing sugar

Wash and pit the cherries. Place them in a heavy-bottomed saucepan with the sugar, cinnamon and wine. Simmer for 10 minutes, shaking from time to time.

Place the cherries in individual ovenproof dishes.

Preheat the oven to its lowest setting.

Whip the egg whites with the salt and gradually beat in 40 g/1½ oz icing sugar until stiff. Cover each little dish with the egg whites. Sprinkle with the remaining icing sugar and bake for about 40 minutes. Serve warm or lukewarm.

La Châtaigne
A chestnut pie

This delicate dessert is Burgundy's poor man's treat, since chestnuts have always been the cheapest commodity in the region. Colette, the writer, remembered her favourite dessert as a child: she would place a few boiled chestnuts in a clean handkerchief, sprinkle them with sugar and crush them to make a sweet warm purée.

For 8 people

900 g/2 lb chestnuts (fresh or canned)	115 g/4 oz unsalted butter, softened
2 tsp fennel seeds	3 eggs, separated
1 clove	70 g/2½ oz chopped almonds or hazelnuts
300 g/10½ oz granulated sugar	

Preheat the oven to 150°C/300°F/Gas Mark 2.

Boil the chestnuts in a large saucepan of salted water with the fennel seeds and the clove. Peel, crush and pass them through a sieve or a Moulinex mill. If you use canned blanched chestnuts, add ½ teaspoon of fennel seeds and a touch of powdered clove to your purée.

Stir in the sugar and butter. Beat the egg yolks then stir them in. Beat the egg whites until they are stiff, and carefully stir them in. Pour into a well-buttered ovenproof dish. Sprinkle with the nuts and bake for 40 minutes. It can be served lukewarm or cold with a bowl of double cream.

Clafoutis I
A fruit dessert

Clafoutis comes in many different guises. It can be prepared with red or black cherries, peaches, pears or apples, and sometimes it is baked in a pastry shell. I have chosen two versions. The first tends to be essentially a custard; the second, more of a cake.

For 8 people

900 g/2 lb black cherries, unpitted	40 g/1½ oz unsalted butter,
450 ml/16 fl oz milk	softened
3 eggs	170 g/6 oz plain flour
1 egg yolk	pinch of salt
255 g/9 oz granulated sugar	2 tbsp kirsch

Break a few cherry pits with a nutcracker and put them in the milk to add flavour to the custard. Bring the milk to a boil and cool. Mix the eggs, egg yolk and 155 g/5½ oz of the sugar vigorously. Add the butter, flour, salt and kirsch. Stir until smooth. Pass the milk through a sieve into the egg mixture, stirring.

Preheat the oven to 180°C/350°F/Gas Mark 4.

Prepare the caramel. Heat the remaining sugar and 1 tablespoon of water until browned and pour into a well-buttered ovenproof mould. Add the egg-and-milk mixture, then add the cherries, letting them sink in slowly.

Place the mould in a large pan containing 225 ml/8 fl oz of warm water and cook for 10 minutes on top of the cooker, then bake for 40 minutes. Remove from the oven, wait a few minutes, then unmould. Serve warm or cold.

Clafoutis II

For 8 people

900 g/2 lb cherries, unpitted	200 g/7 oz sugar
285 g/10 oz plain flour	4 eggs
225 g/8 oz unsalted butter	3 tbsp milk

Preheat the oven to 180°C/350°F/Gas Mark 4.

Mix together all the ingredients. Bake in a well-buttered dish for 30 minutes.

Coeurs à la Crème
Fresh cheese coated with fruit purée

The old Abbé Burjeud invented the 'triple cream dessert' to make anguished souls sleep peacefully. To make it, mix 225 ml/8 fl oz double cream, 1 teaspoon of lemon juice and 1 teaspoon of grated lemon peel. Let the mixture rest for 15 minutes. Add 55 ml/2 fl oz of orange-blossom water. Whip lightly and chill for 2 hours.

The recipe given below is for a simpler cream dessert. It can be prepared all year round, is light and fresh and will do beautifully for a buffet or at the end of a simple meal.

For 8 people

900 g/2 lb cream cheese	100 g/3½ oz sugar
pinch of salt	55–85 g/2–3 oz raspberries or
4 tbsp double cream	blackcurrants
450 ml/16 fl oz soured cream	3 tbsp kirsch

Beat the cream cheese, salt and double cream until light. Add the soured cream, stir well and pour into individual moulds. Cover with cling film and chill for a few hours.

Meanwhile, make the fruit purée: blend the sugar, fruit and kirsch in a Mouli mill or a blender. If blackcurrants are used, add more sugar to taste.

Either unmould the chilled cheese mixture onto a large serving dish and pass around a bowl of raspberry or blackcurrant purée, or unmould each individual mould on to separate plates and put a few teaspoons of purée over it. A few mint leaves placed on the serving plate would make the dish look even more refreshing.

Corniottes
Little dumplings filled with cheese and cream

These crisp little caps are sometimes filled with apple and honey only, but the following recipe is more interesting.

For 8 people

·············· Pastry ··················

285 g/10 oz plain flour
115 g/4 oz unsalted butter,
  softened

pinch of sugar
1 egg yolk, beaten
salt

·············· Filling ··················

5 tbsp grated cheese or cottage
  cheese
2 tbsp sugar
1 egg
2 tbsp soured cream
2 tbsp single cream

2 tbsp vanilla (or orange-blossom
  or rose water)
1 egg yolk
1 tbsp milk
115 g/4 oz grated Gruyère cheese

Mix together all the pastry ingredients and 1–2 tablespoons of water and make into a ball.

Preheat the oven to 190°C/375°F/Gas Mark 5.

Filling: mix the cheese or cottage cheese, sugar, egg, soured cream, single cream and vanilla (or orange-blossom or rose water) into a fluffy mixture.

Roll the dough to 6-mm/¼-in. thickness and cut into circles about 10 cm/4 in. in diameter.

Place 2 tablespoons of the cheese mixture in each circle of dough. Lift three sides of the circle and, with your fingers, pinch them to make a triangle. Brush with a well-beaten mixture of egg yolk and milk, sprinkle with cheese, place on a buttered baking sheet, and bake for 30 minutes.

Serve hot or cold.

Confiture au Potiron

A delicious pumpkin jam with lemon, carrot, wine and rum

This jam can also be made with pumpkin, apple juice and orange, but I love this version.

900 g/2 lb pumpkin, peeled, cut
    into large cubes
2 lemons or 1 orange, peeled and
    diced

1 carrot, peeled and diced
500 g/17½ oz sugar
1 tbsp dry white wine
1 tbsp dark rum (optional)

Toss the pumpkin, lemons and carrot in the sugar and leave overnight, stirring twice.

Simmer, uncovered, in a wide saucepan for 30 minutes. Add the wine and continue cooking for 10 minutes more. Cool. Stir in the rum and pour into a pot. Serve after 2 days.

Coulis de Fruits
A thick purée of fruits

You can use either fresh or canned fruit for this *coulis*. It can be stored for a week in the refrigerator or frozen. Put it in the blender for two minutes after you take it out of the freezer for a smooth consistency. It is delicious with Savoy cake, plain ice cream, poached pears or biscuits.

For 900 ml/1⅗ pt

900 g/2 lb of peaches or apricots
    or berries (redcurrants,
    blueberries, etc.)
3 tbsp lemon juice
500 g/17½ oz sugar (as needed)

Peel, pit and quarter the fruit if you are using peaches or apricots. Put it in a blender with the lemon juice and half of the sugar. Blend and continue adding sugar in small amounts until desired sweetness is obtained.

Note: Use only the drained fruit, not the syrup, if you use canned fruit.

Coupes aux Fruits
Fruit delight

An extravagant and luxurious fruit dessert.

For 8 people

juice of 8 large oranges
3 pink grapefruit (each section
   peeled of all membrane)
5 large prunes, soaked for 1 hour
   in warm tea or water
450 g/1 lb strawberries (cut in half
   if large)

225 g/8 oz raspberries (or
   blueberries)
7 egg yolks
6 tbsp sugar
3 tbsp orange brandy or cognac

Put the orange juice in a saucepan and bring it to a boil. Lower the heat and add the grapefruit sections, the drained prunes and the strawberries. Heat for 2 minutes, then remove the fruit, covering it with kitchen foil to keep it warm. Return the juice to the low heat.

Beat the egg yolks and sugar until frothy. Add to the warm juice, stirring constantly until the custard covers the spoon. Check the taste and add more sugar if needed, then the orange brandy.

Place some of the grapefruit, prunes, strawberries and raspberries in individual dessert bowls and pour the warm custard over them.

Serve lukewarm or at room temperature with thin wafers.

Crapiau de Pommes
Apple and rum pancakes served with cream

There are many names for this traditional country dessert: *crapiaux*, *grapiaux*, *sauciaux*. It is always made with tart apples and a thick pancake batter, and served with cream. The original recipe, *tartouillat* (*tartouillat* means 'to mix'), was made with pancake batter and quartered apples or cooked cherries spread on cabbage leaves and baked. This is a good treat for children or for Sunday-night supper. Not elegant, not very light either, but tasty and warm, it has been dear to generations of little Bourguignons.

For 8 people

1.25 kg/3 lb crisp apples
  (preferably Granny Smith),
  peeled, cored and thinly sliced
6 tbsp sugar
115 ml/4 fl oz good brandy or
  dark rum
340 g/12 oz plain flour

7 eggs, lightly beaten
225 ml/8 fl oz milk
pinch of salt
70 g/2½ oz unsalted butter
4 tbsp icing sugar
single cream

Sprinkle the apples with 2 tablespoons of the sugar and marinate in the brandy for 1–2 hours.

Mix the flour, eggs, remaining sugar, milk, and salt in a large bowl, stirring vigorously. Add the brandy from the marinade and stir well. Add the apples.

Heat the butter in a frying-pan and make small pancakes. Sprinkle them with icing sugar and serve with cream.

Crème aux Fruits

Light custard prepared with fruit juices and served with sections of fruits

A variation on the old Burgundy dessert *Pommes Sévigné* (p. 248). It can be made with apples, pears, pineapples and, of course, oranges and grapefruit, which are the key ingredients of this otherwise traditional custard.

For 8 people

4 apples *or* pears, peeled, cored and
  poached in syrup (or 1
  pineapple, peeled and sliced)
12 large oranges
4 grapefruit

10 egg yolks
300 g/10½ oz sugar
4 tbsp dark rum
225 ml/8 fl oz double cream,
  whipped

Prepare the apples (or pears or pineapple). Peel 10 of the oranges and 2 of the grapefruit and divide them into sections. Be careful to remove all of the white pith from the skin. Set aside.

Press the juice of the remaining oranges and grapefruit through a sieve into a saucepan. Bring to a boil and remove from the heat.

Mix the egg yolks and sugar and, stirring vigorously, add gradually to the fruit juice. Stir in the rum. Place over low heat and stir until thick enough to coat the spoon. Remove from the heat and pour into a bowl.

Preheat the oven to 180°C/350°F/Gas Mark 4.

Whip the cream and fold it into the lukewarm custard. Place the fruit sections in individual ovenproof dishes or one large dish and cover with the custard. Heat it in the oven for 3 minutes. Serve lukewarm. You may decorate the top with strawberries or raspberries just before serving.

Flamous

A creamy pumpkin pudding

Sometimes called *flamusse*, this is also made with sliced pears or apples sautéd in butter. The pumpkin version is the most delicate of autumn desserts.

For 8 people

1.8 kg/4 lb pumpkin, peeled, cooked and well drained	450 ml/16 fl oz single cream
4 eggs, separated	100 g/3½ oz sugar
55 g/2 oz unsalted butter	2 tbsp brandy
4 tbsp plain flour	peel of 1 lemon, grated
	2 tbsp crystallized sugar

Peel, cut and blanch the pumpkin in very little water for 20 minutes. Drain, and put it through a sieve.

Beat the egg yolks. Heat the butter in a thick-bottomed pan. Add the puréed pumpkin and stir with a wooden spoon over low heat. Add the flour, stirring, then the cream. Remove from the heat and quickly stir in the egg yolks, sugar, brandy and lemon peel.

Preheat oven to 170°C/325°F/Gas Mark 3.

Beat the egg whites until stiff and fold them delicately into the pumpkin mixture. Pour into a buttered ovenproof dish and bake for 25 minutes.

Cool for a few minutes and unmould. Sprinkle with crystallized sugar before serving.

La Flamusse aux Pommes
A warm apple dessert

Of the many different ways this dessert has been made, the most curious was to dip slices of apple in a crêpe-like batter, spread them on buttered cabbage leaves and bake them in an oven. The leaves would disappear, leaving a puzzling taste.

This is a rich, lovely dessert, easy to prepare and very tasty.

For 8 people

25 g/1 oz unsalted butter	450 ml/16 fl oz milk
8 large Granny Smith apples, peeled and cut into thick slices	3 tbsp sugar
	2 tbsp dark rum (or orange-flower water)
4 eggs, beaten	
1 tbsp plain flour	

Heat the butter in a frying-pan and cook the apple slices slowly.

Preheat the oven to 180°C/350°F/Gas Mark 4.

Beat the eggs, add the flour, milk, sugar and rum (or orange-flower water), stir well and add the cooked apples. Pour into a buttered ovenproof dish.

Bake for 30–45 minutes and serve warm in its baking dish.

Framboises à la Neige
Floating island prepared with raspberry purée

A light and lovely dessert to serve after an elaborate meal.

For 8 people

900 g/2 lb raspberries, fresh or frozen (or strawberries or redcurrants)	sugar to taste
	16 egg whites
	pinch of salt

Pass the berries through a blender, pour the purée through a sieve and add sugar to taste. Chill.

Beat the egg whites with the salt until stiff.

Heat about 1.75 l/3 pt of water in a wide pan. Using a ladle, scoop up the egg whites and dip each ladleful in the simmering water. Cook each ball for 30 seconds on each side, place on a layer of kitchen towels and set aside.

Just before serving, pile the white balls in a shallow dish and serve the raspberry purée in a separate bowl.

Fruits Caramélisés au Vin Rouge
Caramelized fruits cooked in red wine

A tart, lovely dessert. Prepare a day in advance for a richer flavour and serve with *Massepains* (p. 239).

For 8 people

450 g/1 lb large pitted prunes
1 orange, unpeeled, sliced
1 lemon, unpeeled, sliced
225 g/8 oz raisins, preferably the large black Spanish type
5 coriander seeds
5 bay leaves

350 g/12¼ oz sugar
900 ml/1⅗ pt red wine, enough to cover
2 oranges, peeled and very thinly sliced
2 lemons, peeled and very thinly sliced

Let the prunes stand in tea or water for 3 hours. Place them in a large saucepan with the unpeeled orange and lemon slices, raisins, coriander, bay leaves, 150 g/5¼ oz of the sugar and enough red wine to cover. Bring to a boil, uncovered, reduce the heat and cook for 20 minutes. Cool in the juice and let stand for a day.

A few hours before the meal, remove the prunes and raisins and set aside. Bring the wine, herbs and unpeeled orange and lemon slices to a boil and reduce by half until it becomes syrupy. Discard the unpeeled orange and lemon slices. Add the peeled orange and lemon slices and cook for 5 minutes. Let the mixture cool.

Place the prunes and raisins in a large glass bowl. Pour the liquid over them, placing the slices of lemon and orange all around the dish and the bay leaves in the centre.

Put the remaining sugar and 2 tablespoons of water in a thick-bottomed pan. (Always use the same pan for this purpose and keep it strictly for making caramel.) Place over high heat and boil about 5 minutes, until the syrup turns dark brown and is caramelized.

Trickle the caramel lightly over the fruit. Let the whole dish cool in the refrigerator and, just before serving, poke the top of the caramel layer with a fork to crack it so it will be easier to serve.

Fruits Cuits au Vin
Stewed fruit in white wine with spices

Poached in wine and spices, fruit can make the lightest and liveliest of desserts. Apricots, pears, quince, peaches can be stewed with white wine separately or together. This must be done a day in advance for greatest flavour.

For 8 people

900 ml/1⅗ pt sweet white wine
(Sauterne type or a dry Chablis
type of white wine)
400 g/14 oz sugar (or, better:
100 g/3½ oz sugar, 170 g/6 oz
honey)
1 whole lemon, sliced

1 whole orange, sliced
2 bay leaves
1 clove (or 3 coriander seeds)
1.25 kg/3 lb fruit, peeled, pitted
and sliced (quince should be
very thinly sliced)
mint leaves (optional)

Heat the wine, sugar, lemon, orange, bay leaves and clove (or coriander). Add the fruit when the liquid is hot but not boiling. Lower the heat and simmer for 15–20 minutes. Check to see if the fruit is tender. Place it in a large glass or china bowl, cool and let rest overnight in the refrigerator. Remove the bay leaves and clove and sprinkle with whole mint leaves if you have them. Serve cold.

Galette de Goumeau

A very plain, traditional country dessert.

For 8 people

·········· Pastry ··········

340 g/12 oz flour
140 g/5 oz unsalted butter
15 g/½ oz lard
1 egg
3 tbsp hot water

·········· Filling ··········

1 egg
3 tbsp single cream
salt
freshly ground black pepper
70 g/2½ oz raisins

Preheat the oven to 190°C/375°F/Gas Mark 5.

Knead all the pastry ingredients into a soft dough. Spread the dough in a quiche or tart pan.

Mix the ingredients for the filling and pour it into the pan over the dough. Bake for 20 minutes.

Galette Grand-mère

An apple cake

For 8 people

·········· Cake ··········

1½ tsp active dry yeast
1 tbsp sugar
1 small egg
salt
15 g/½ oz unsalted butter,
    softened
170 g/6 oz plain flour

················· Topping ················

25 g/1 oz approximately unsalted
    butter, softened
sugar
cinnamon
1 ripe apple (or pear), peeled,
    cored and thinly sliced

Dissolve the yeast in 55 ml/2 fl oz of lukewarm water with 1
tablespoon of sugar for 5 minutes. Beat the egg in a bowl and add
the salt, butter, and 115 g/4 oz of the flour. Mix quickly with your
fingertips. Add the yeast mixture and work quickly, adding as
much of the remaining flour as needed to make a firm, elastic
dough. Knead briefly, form into a ball and put in a greased bowl.
Cover with a tea-towel and put in a warm place (such as in an oven
with a pilot light) for 1–1½ hours, or until it has doubled in size.

Preheat the oven to 200°C/400°F/Gas Mark 6.

Knead the dough briefly and press it into a greased 25-cm/10-in.
quiche or tart pan. Smear with the butter and sprinkle with sugar
and cinnamon. Put the fruit slices on top of the butter in a circular
pattern, then sprinkle again with sugar and cinnamon. Leave at
room temperature for 20 minutes, then put on the top shelf of the
oven and bake for 15–18 minutes.

This can be frozen and reheated. It is delicious when sprinkled
with more sugar and caramelized under the grill.

Gâteau au Caramel

A rich, caramel-flavoured cake

For 8 people

················· Pastry ·················

115 g/4 oz unsalted butter
300 g/10½ oz granulated sugar
1 egg
510 g/18 oz plain flour
salt

·················· Filling ··················

100 g/3½ oz brown sugar
50 g/1¾ oz ground almonds
115 g/4 oz unsalted butter
3 tbsp cream
2 egg yolks

Mix the butter and sugar. Add the egg and beat until well mixed. Add the flour and salt. Pound and stretch the dough away from you with the heel of your hand to be sure all the ingredients are well blended. Shape the dough into a ball, cut it into four parts, place them one on top of the other, then mix them again vigorously into one ball. Repeat this process three times. Finally shape the dough into a ball, cover with a clean cloth and leave for 1 hour at room temperature.

Preheat the oven to 190°C/375°F/Gas Mark 5.

Spread the dough 6 mm/¼ in. thick on a well-buttered 30-cm/12-in. mould. Cover with a sheet of kitchen foil and weight it down with dried beans. Prick the foil and dough with a fork and bake for 30 minutes. Remove the beans.

Meanwhile, mix the brown sugar, ground almonds, butter, cream and egg yolks. Pour into the cooked pie shell. Reduce the oven heat to 180°C/350°F/Gas Mark 4 and bake for 15 minutes.

Gâteau aux Noix et au Rhum
A rich walnut, rum and apricot jam cake

A sumptuous dessert.

For 8–10 people

·················· Pastry ··················

25 g/1 oz unsalted butter, chilled
225 g/8 oz plain flour
2 tbsp vegetable oil

¼ tsp salt
2 tbsp sugar

·················· Filling ··················

9 tbsp apricot preserves	1 tbsp single cream
225 g/8 oz walnut meats, chopped (about 1½ cups)	4 eggs, separated
	4 tbsp icing sugar
225 g/8 oz granulated sugar	2 tbsp dark rum
115 g/4 oz unsalted butter, softened	24 large walnut halves

Mix the butter rapidly with the flour, oil, salt and sugar. Add 4 tablespoons of cold water. Knead rapidly with the heel of your hand into a thick dough. It should not be sticky. Wrap it in a piece of cling film and refrigerate for at least 1 hour.

Pass the apricot preserves through a sieve to make a purée.

Spread the chilled dough on a buttered 30-cm-/12-in.-wide tart mould. Cover with 6 tablespoons of the apricot purée.

Preheat the oven to 190°C/375°F/Gas Mark 5.

Mix the walnuts, granulated sugar, butter, cream and egg yolks thoroughly in a large bowl. Beat the egg whites and gently add them to the walnut mixture. Spread this mixture on the apricot purée in the pastry shell. Bake for 50 minutes. Cool on a rack and unmould on to a large platter.

Mix the icing sugar and the rum into a thick paste.

Spread the top and sides of the cooled cake with the remaining 3 tablespoons of apricot purée, top with the sugar-and-rum mixture and decorate with walnut halves.

Gaufrettes au Miel
Honey wafers

A light crisp waffle, fragrant with honey and orange-flower water.

570 g/1¼ lb flour	900 ml/1⅗ pt milk
225 g/8 oz honey	115 g/4 oz unsalted butter, melted
3 egg yolks	2 egg whites, stiffly beaten
2 tbsp orange-flower water (or brandy or grated lemon peel)	icing sugar

Mix all the ingredients. Cover and set aside for at least 4 hours.

Heat an oiled waffle iron. Cook and serve hot, sprinkled with icing sugar.

Gouerre au Cirage
A prune pie

There are all kinds of *gouerre*, fruitcake made with apples or pears. This one, because it is made with prunes, is called 'shoe-polish pie'.

For 8 people

············· Pastry ···············

225 g/8 oz plain flour
100 g/3½ oz unsalted butter
pinch of salt

············· Filling ···············

225 g/8 oz large prunes, pitted
3 tbsp apricot preserves
1 tbsp good plum brandy
3 tbsp icing sugar

Mix the flour and butter, kneading lightly. Add the salt and 115 ml/ 4 fl oz cold water briskly. Make into a ball. Cover with a towel and leave in the bottom part of the refrigerator for at least 1 hour.

Soak the prunes in cold water for 2 hours.

Preheat the oven to 200°C/400°F/Gas Mark 6.

Roll the dough 6 mm/¼ in. thick and spread it in a 25-cm-/10-in.- wide buttered mould. Prick it with a fork.

Crush the pitted prunes with a fork and mix them with the apricot preserves. Fill the pastry shell with this mixture. Bake for 40 minutes.

Remove the pie from the oven and place it on a rack to cool. Sprinkle with plum brandy and sugar and serve.

You may also, when it is cooled, sprinkle it with crystallized sugar and place it under the grill for a few minutes to caramelize the top. Place on a rack to cool and serve lukewarm or cold.

Lait de Poule
A light custard

This is the best of medicines against colds or just the melancholy of long winter evenings. Have a good book and a warm blanket handy.

For 1 person

225 ml/8 fl oz hot milk
2 tbsp granulated sugar
1 egg yolk, beaten
pinch of nutmeg
2 tsp cognac (or bourbon)

Heat the milk, add the sugar, egg yolk and nutmeg and stir over low heat for 5 minutes. Add the cognac and drink. Preferably served in a bowl or mug.

Mandarines à l'Armagnac
Small tangerines with brandy

This is a superb accompaniment to chocolate cake, Savoy cake, chocolate mousse, plain vanilla ice cream and *Rigodon* (p. 251). It must be kept about two months. Look for the smallest tangerines you can find – clementines, if possible – and use a good-quality Armagnac brandy.

1.8 kg/4 lb tangerines, peeled
900 ml/1⅗ pt brandy
400 g/14 oz granulated sugar

Peel the fruit very delicately by hand and make sure that all the white pith is removed and the skin is not broken.

Place the whole tangerines if they are small (or sliced, if they are larger) in a jar and add the sugar. Shake the jar twice. Then pour in the brandy and close tightly. Store the jar in a dark place for one month, turning it upside down every week. Add a little sugar and wait another month before testing.

If you want to use kumquats instead of tangerines, use 200 g/7 oz more sugar.

Massepains
Light almond and lemon wafers

Delicious, crisp, light biscuits made in different versions throughout Burgundy.

Makes about 60 biscuits

> 500 g/17½ oz granulated sugar
> 200 g/7 oz ground almonds
> 1 tbsp flour
> 4 egg whites, stiffly beaten
> rind of 2 lemons, grated

Mix the sugar, almonds and flour. Slowly fold in the beaten egg whites and the grated lemon peel.

Preheat the oven to 180°C/350°F/Gas Mark 4.

Drop by teaspoonfuls on a sheet of buttered kitchen foil on a baking sheet and flatten each mound slightly with the back of a spoon. Bake for 10 minutes.

Let the biscuits cool before removing them from the foil. Store in an airtight box.

Mousse au Chocolat
Chocolate mousse with orange peel

My very favourite of all chocolate mousses. It must be made at least eight hours before serving.

For 8 people

peel of 4 oranges, grated
450 g/1 lb unsalted butter,
  softened
115 ml/4 fl oz orange juice
450 g/1 lb semisweet chocolate bits
  or chopped pieces

9 eggs, separated
100 g/3½ oz granulated sugar
2 tbsp icing sugar (or grated black
  bitter chocolate)

Beat the grated orange peel with the butter until the butter becomes frothy.

Bring the orange juice and chocolate slowly to a boil in a saucepan, then remove from the heat and let cool.

Beating vigorously, slowly add the egg yolks, then the sugar to the chocolate and juice. The mixture has to be smooth. Stir in the orange peel–butter mixture. Beat the egg whites until they are stiff and gently fold them in. Pour into individual cups or a large bowl. Cover with cling film and refrigerate for at least 8 hours.

Sprinkle with icing sugar or grated black bitter chocolate just before serving. Pass a bowl of *Mandarines à l'Armagnac* (see p. 238) along with the chocolate mousse.

Mousse au Citron
A lemon and wine custard

A tart, invigorating dessert you can serve with *Massepains* (p. 239) or thinly sliced *Pain d'Épice* (p. 243). Don't worry if there is a fluff of egg white on top.

For 8 people

rind of 1 lemon, grated
12 tbsp granulated sugar (or more,
  according to taste)

juice of 4 lemons
570 ml/1 pt dry white wine
10 eggs, separated

Mix the grated lemon peel and sugar, and add the lemon juice. Pour into a heavy-bottomed saucepan and stir in the white wine over low heat. (You can use a double boiler instead of a pan.) Beat the egg yolks and add them, stirring constantly. When the custard is thick enough to coat the spoon, remove from the heat. Beat the egg whites until they are stiff. Add them to the custard and pour into a large glass bowl or individual dishes. Cover with cling film and refrigerate.

Noeuds d'Amour
Love-knot fritters

These crisp little bows are fritters made at Christmastime and served in large baskets lined with white napkins.

450 g/1 lb flour	1 tbsp orange-flower water
3 eggs, beaten	115 g/4 oz unsalted butter, melted
1 tsp salt	oil for frying
1 tsp good brandy or dark rum	icing sugar

Pour the flour on a table. Make a well in the centre and add the eggs, salt, brandy, orange-flower water and butter. Stir, then knead well. Make a ball. Cover it and let it stand for about 3 hours.

Roll out the dough 6 mm/¼ in. thick. Cut it into 2.5-cm-/1-in.-wide strips and then into 25-cm-/10-in.-long ribbons.

Heat the oil in a large pan until very hot. Fold each ribbon into a bow and fry in the oil, one at a time, for 3–5 minutes, turning each with tongs. Remove with a slotted spoon and drain on kitchen towels. Sprinkle with icing sugar. These can be eaten warm or cold.

Nonnettes
Little honey and almond cakes made with rye flour, flavoured with rum and stuffed with apricots or marmalade

These delicate little honey-and-spice cakes were prepared as early as the sixteenth century in convents, hence the name *nonnettes* (little nuns). They are sometimes covered with bitter chocolate and become *duchesses* because of their fancy look.

For 1 dozen cakes

340 g/12 oz honey, as fragrant as possible
100 g/3½ oz granulated sugar
¼ tsp salt
½ tsp bicarbonate of soda
225 g/8 oz rye flour
70 g/2½ oz chopped almonds with their skins

55 ml/2 fl oz dark rum
2 tsp anise powder (or anise seeds)
½ tsp cinnamon
½ tsp powdered cloves
70 g/2½ oz Malaga raisins or diced glacéd fruits
12 tbsp apricot purée or orange marmalade

Preheat the oven to 170°C/325°F/Gas Mark 3.

Heat the honey, 115 ml/4 fl oz of water and sugar in a large bowl. Turn off the heat; add the salt and soda and, little by little, vigorously stir in the flour. (You may use a food processor or a blender.) Add the almonds, rum, spices and raisins. Pour into buttered muffin tins, filling to only two-thirds of each mould. Bake for 25 minutes, or until a knife plunged into the centre of the cake comes out clean.

Remove the cakes from the oven. Let them cool in their moulds for 15 minutes before unmoulding on to a cake rack to finish cooling.

Meanwhile, pour the apricot purée (or marmalade) into a saucepan and heat over low heat.

Slice the cold cakes horizontally through the middle, pour some warm jam on the bottom half and replace the top half. Cover the top with more jam or sprinkle with icing sugar or with a light icing. Wrap individually in kitchen foil.

Omelette aux Pommes
A soufflé apple omelette flavoured with rum

Sweet omelettes are always exciting, whether they are filled with fruit, jam or ice cream. This light, tart omelette must be served with a bowl of cream, whipped with Calvados. You must use two frying-pans.

For 8 people

5 apples (Granny Smith or any
    other tart apple), peeled and
    sliced
225 ml/8 fl oz dark rum
130 g/4½ oz unsalted butter

10 eggs, separated
400 g/14 oz granulated sugar
icing sugar
1 bowl double cream
3 tbsp Calvados

Soak the sliced apples in rum for 1 hour. Remove them and cook them in 85 g/3 oz of the butter for 15 minutes over low heat.

Stir the egg yolks, sugar and rum marinade together until frothy. Beat the egg whites until they are stiff and gently fold in.

Over medium heat, heat the remaining butter in two frying-pans and pour half of the egg mixture into each. Cook for 5 minutes. Holding a plate over each frying-pan, invert the omelette on to the plate, then slide it back into the pan for 2 minutes more. Place the two omelettes on a warm serving dish. Spread the cooked apples in the centre and fold each omelette. Sprinkle the tops with icing sugar and serve at once with a bowl of whipped cream flavoured with brandy.

Pain d'Épice

The rich Burgundy version of gingerbread

It was the practice of Greek and Roman cooks to spread their pastry with honey. The Arabs mixed flour with the honey and brought the idea to Europe in the Middle Ages, during which time spices were added and Dijon became known for its honey-and-spice bread. As early as the fourteenth century, this type of bread was mentioned in chronicles as an aid to digestion, and it was served at all banquets. In the eighteenth century the standard version was finally established: it specified ten spices, egg yolks, rye flour and good honey.

This is the recipe I found to be the tastiest. *Pain d'épice* is best served in very thin slices, lightly buttered, with tea or coffee.

450 g/1 lb honey
570 g/1¼ lb light rye flour
1 tsp coriander
½ tsp cinnamon
1 tbsp aniseed
½ tsp powdered cloves
1 tsp grated nutmeg

5 drops lemon extract
2 tbsp lemon peel, cut in tiny dice
4 tbsp crystallized or fresh orange
    peel, cut in tiny dice
2 tsp bicarbonate of soda
2 egg yolks, beaten
1 tsp milk

Combine the honey and 115 ml/4 fl oz water and bring to a boil. Mix the flour, spices, lemon extract, peel of lemon and orange and add the honey and water, stirring vigorously. Cover and let stand 20–24 hours.

Mix the soda and egg yolks and add the batter, which should be very soft and smooth. (Add a little water to soften it if needed.) Stir well.

Preheat the oven to 150°C/300°F/Gas Mark 2.

Pour the batter into two well-buttered loaf pans. Bake for 1 hour. Brush the tops with milk and let cool.

Wrap in kitchen foil. The flavour will improve after three days. Always keep tightly wrapped.

Pâte de Cassis

1.8 kg/4 lb very ripe blackcurrants
900 g/2 lb granulated sugar
    (approximately)

Wash and put the blackcurrants in a large pan. Add 115 ml/4 fl oz of water and bring to a boil. When the fruit is soft, crush it and pass it through a Mouli mill or a sieve. Mix the purée with an amount of sugar equalling three-quarters of the purée's volume and boil for 5 minutes.

Pour into a dish 2.5 cm/1 in. deep. Leave it for a few days in a cool place. Cut into cubes and sprinkle on all sides with granulated sugar. Keep in a tin box.

Pogne

A cake flavoured with lemon and rum

When everyone in the Burgundy countryside used to make their own bread, they often kept a handful of dough (*une poignée*), added a little sugar and lemon, shaped it like a crown and made a *pogne*.

There are many variations of this simple cake made of bread dough. Some are cut in the shape of little fat boys and girls; some have fresh fruit in the summer and pumpkin in the autumn added to the dough. The recipe given here is what I have found to be the tastiest of the *pognes*. It must be prepared a day in advance.

15 g/½ oz fresh yeast or 1½ tsp dried yeast
1 tbsp lukewarm milk
400 g/14 oz plain flour
6 eggs, beaten
salt
200 g/7 oz granulated sugar

130 g/4½ oz unsalted butter, softened
½ tbsp rum
juice of 1 lemon
peel of 1 lemon, grated
1 egg yolk, beaten with 1 tbsp water

Mix the yeast and lukewarm milk and let stand for a few minutes, according to the package directions.

Put the flour in a mound on the table and make a well in the centre. Add the beaten eggs, salt, sugar and butter and knead well. Add the yeast–milk mixture and mix well. Knead until the dough is soft and elastic, then add the rum, lemon juice and grated lemon peel. Knead into a ball, cover and let rise overnight at room temperature.

Preheat the oven to 180°C/350°F/Gas Mark 4.

Butter a baking sheet. Using your hands and scissors, make two crowns with the ball of dough, paint their surfaces with the egg-yolk–water mixture and bake for 40 minutes.

Le Poirat

A pear pie

This pear pie is a medieval dessert that remains a favourite for many family meals in Burgundy. The dough must be very thin, and it must be served lukewarm. *Le Poirat* may be the French answer to England's apple pie brought to France during the Hundred Years War.

For 8 people

·················· Pastry ··················

500 g/1 lb 2 oz plain flour
225 g/8 oz unsalted butter
2 tbsp vegetable oil
1 tsp salt

·················· Filling ··················

8 ripe pears, peeled, cored and
    sliced (marinated in brandy or
    not)
4 tbsp single cream
3 tbsp granulated sugar

Mix the flour, butter, oil, salt and 2 tablespoons of water together. Knead for a few minutes then make a ball. Cover with a towel and let stand for 2 hours.

Preheat the oven to 180°C/350°F/Gas Mark 4.

Spread the dough as thinly as you can on a floured table. Place half of it in a well-buttered 25-cm/10-in. baking dish. Cover the dough with the sliced pears (be sure they are well drained if you have marinated them first), then cover with the rest of the dough, leaving a 5-cm/2-in. hole in the centre.

Prick the dough with a fork and bake the pie for 45 minutes. Remove from the oven and pour the cream through the centre hole into the pie.

Bake for 15 minutes more. Sprinkle with sugar and serve with a bowl of whipped cream or custard or ice cream.

Poires en Manteau

*Pears filled with raisins, flavoured with rum and wrapped in a thin
pastry shell*

A favourite dessert for buffets and family meals.

For 8 people

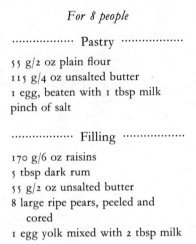

··············· Pastry ···············

55 g/2 oz plain flour
115 g/4 oz unsalted butter
1 egg, beaten with 1 tbsp milk
pinch of salt

··············· Filling ···············

170 g/6 oz raisins
5 tbsp dark rum
55 g/2 oz unsalted butter
8 large ripe pears, peeled and
    cored
1 egg yolk mixed with 2 tbsp milk

Place the flour in a large mixing bowl and mix in the butter and
egg beaten with milk. Add 3 tablespoons of water and salt and
blend quickly with one hand as you gather the dough into a mass.
Press the dough into a ball. It should not be sticky. With the heel
of one hand, press the pastry down on the table away from you.
Gather the dough into a mass, kneading for a few more minutes.
Sprinkle with flour and wrap in greaseproof paper or a kitchen tea-
towel. Let stand for 1 hour.

Place the raisins in a bowl, sprinkle with rum and let marinate,
stirring once or twice, for 1 hour.

Preheat the oven to 190°C/375°F/Gas Mark 5.

Divide the butter into 8 equal pieces. Fill each pear with raisins,
then close the hole with a piece of butter.

Place the dough on a floured board. Knead it briefly into a flat
circle. Roll it out with an even stroke, back and forth. It should be
8 mm/⅓ in. thick. Cut 8 large squares. Place each pear in the centre
of a square and pinch the corners so the pear is tightly wrapped in

its coat. It should look like a hut. Brush the pastry with the egg-yolk-and-milk mixture. Place the 8 pears in a buttered ovenproof dish and bake for 25 minutes. Serve warm or lukewarm with fresh cream.

Pommes Sévigné

Cooked apples covered with a light custard and a soft meringue

The beautiful Madame de Sévigné was the most brilliant observer of the court of Louis XIV. She was also the most *gourmande* of women.

For 8 people

8 large apples (preferably Granny Smith), peeled and cored	450 ml/16 fl oz milk
1 tsp cinnamon	4 eggs, separated
1 clove	1 tbsp grated black chocolate (or nutmeg)
6 tbsp granulated sugar	

Cook the peeled and cored apples with the cinnamon and clove, 6 tablespoons of water and the sugar in a covered pan until soft. Let them cook in the syrup, then drain them, setting the syrup aside, and place them in the centre of a large, shallow serving dish.

Meanwhile, stiffly beat the egg whites. Heat the milk in a large frying-pan and poach the egg whites, 1 tablespoon at a time, in the milk for about 2 minutes on each side. Drain on kitchen towels.

Pass the milk through a sieve. Beat the egg yolks into the syrup and pour into the warm milk, stirring constantly over low heat. When the mixture coats the spoon, pour it over the apples. Place the cooked egg whites around and sprinkle the whole dish with grated black chocolate or a little nutmeg.

Le Pouding

A creamy pudding, flavoured with lemon and caramel

A delicate, warm dessert.

For 8 people

peel of 2 lemons	55 g/2 oz unsalted butter
680 ml/1⅕ pt milk	85 g/3 oz flour
200 g/7 oz granulated sugar	4 eggs, separated

Preheat the oven to 180°C/350°F/Gas Mark 4.

Bring the lemon peel, milk and half of the sugar to a boil. Mix together the butter and flour and add the warm milk mixture, stirring vigorously. Remove the lemon peel. Bring the mixture to a boil and remove from the heat. Cool for a few minutes. Meanwhile beat the egg yolks and, in another bowl, beat the egg whites until they are stiff. Stir the egg yolks into the milk mixture, then fold in the egg whites.

Put the remaining sugar and 1 tablespoon water in a mould and pour the pudding mixture into it. Place the mould in a large dish with about 5 cm/2 in. of water around it and bake for 50 minutes.

Let stand for 10 minutes, unmould and serve lukewarm.

Pouding de Pain d'Épice

Gingerbread, raisin, lemon and orange peel, egg and rum pudding

The trouble with *pain d'épice* is that the stale slices become very hard. This recipe solves that problem.

For 8 people

450 ml/16 fl oz warm milk	peel of 1 orange, grated
3 eggs, well beaten	peel of 1 lemon, grated
450 g/1 lb *pain d'épice* (or gingerbread), sliced	115 ml/4 fl oz dark rum
125 g/4½ oz raisins	2 tbsp granulated sugar

Pour the milk over the eggs and add the *pain d'épice*. Preheat the oven to 170°C/325°F/Gas Mark 3.

Butter a round ovenproof dish. Place the raisins on the bottom, pour in half of the *pain d'épice*–milk–egg mixture, add the orange and lemon peel, rum and sugar, and pour in the rest of the mixture.

Place the dish in a large pan with 115 ml/4 fl oz water around it and bake for 1½ hours.

Unmould. Sprinkle with sugar and a few drops of rum. Serve warm with perhaps a bowl of plain vanilla ice cream or a compote.

Raisin à l'Eau de Vie
Grapes in brandy

900 g/2 lb grapes, very ripe and
    firm, black or white, washed
    and dried, with 12 mm/½ in. of
    stem left on
225 g/8 oz sugar

2 cloves
4 peppercorns ·
2 5-cm/2-in. strips of orange peel
2 5-cm/2-in. strips of lemon peel
good brandy to cover

Wash and dry the grapes. Place them in a large glass jar with the rest of the ingredients. Leave in a dark place, turning the jar upside down every month. They will be ready around the sixth or seventh month.

Serve on vanilla ice cream, with *Rigodon* (p. 251), or in small glasses after a meal.

Raisiné
Pears and quinces cooked in the juice of fresh grapes

A beloved dessert in Burgundy, this is served with crisp lemon biscuits (p. 220) or a bowl of whipped cream. For a medieval or *nouvelle cuisine* taste, it is also a splendid accompaniment to roast duck or pork.

2.75 kg/6 lb very ripe white grapes
900 g/2 lb tasty ripe pears, peeled,
   cored and quartered
2 large ripe quinces, peeled, cored
   and sliced

sugar to taste (omit entirely for a
   tart *raisiné*)

Crush the grapes through a sieve. Bring their juice to a boil and let it reduce, uncovered, for 30 minutes. Remove the froth on the surface with a slotted spoon.

Add the pears and quinces and let them cook over a low heat for 1 hour, uncovered, stirring from time to time. Add sugar to taste, if you wish, and cook for 10 minutes more.

Let cool and pour into glass jars. Cover the jars and keep in a dry place.

Rigodon
A light pudding enriched with nuts and served with stewed fruit

A classic of Burgundy recipes. A sweet dessert served with stewed fruit.

For 8 people

900 ml/1⅗ pt milk
150 g/5¼ oz granulated sugar
pinch of salt
pinch of cinnamon
115 g/4 oz stale brioche, diced
7 eggs, beaten
2 tbsp arrowroot (or cornflour)

10 hazelnuts, finely chopped
10 walnuts, finely chopped
25 g/1 oz unsalted butter
140 g/5 oz peaches stewed with
   red wine or stewed apricots,
   cooked apples, jam or *Coulis de
   Fruits* (p. 000)

Bring the milk, sugar, salt and cinnamon to a boil and turn off the heat. Preheat the oven to 180°C/350°F/Gas Mark 4.

Place the diced brioche in a large bowl. Pour a little of the warm milk on it, add the eggs, arrowroot and remaining milk, stirring vigorously. Add the nuts.

Pour into a deep, buttered ovenproof dish, dot with butter and bake for 30 minutes.

Serve cold or lukewarm unmoulded, covered with a thick layer of stewed peaches or stewed fruit, warm jam, or a *coulis* of fruit.

Note: Some people add sliced apples or pears to the mixture before baking it.

Sorbet au Marc
A tangy brandy sherbet

It is important to choose a good brandy, since cold increases all flavours, bad or good. This dessert is wonderful after a hearty meal.

For 8 people

1.4 kg/2⅝ oz granulated sugar	4 egg whites
peel of 1 lemon	115 ml/4 fl oz marc (brandy)
juice of 4 lemons	mint leaves

Heat 985 g/2 lb 3 oz of the sugar and 900 ml/1⅗ pt of water for 1 hour, uncovered, to make a thick syrup. Add the lemon peel and juice and cook for 30 minutes. Let cool. Remove the lemon peel.

Pour the liquid into ice-cube trays, place in the freezer and let it set but not freeze.

Beat the egg whites with the remaining sugar until stiff, add the marc and pour over the partially congealed liquid. Return to the freezer until ready. Stir well before serving.

Serve in a bowl with mint leaves stuck in the centre or in individual glass dishes.

Soupe à l'Abricot
An apricot dessert

The dukes of Burgundy loved this, and it is one of the prettiest desserts. Use very ripe, plump apricots or peaches. If you cannot find any that have enough flavour, use canned fruit.

For 8 people

24 ripe whole apricots
225 ml/8 fl oz red wine
85 g/3 oz granulated sugar
peel of half a lemon, grated
10 *croûtons*, fried in butter

Place the whole fruit in a thin-bottomed saucepan. Cover with the wine and 2 tablespoons of water and cook until soft (about 10 minutes). Pass the fruit through a sieve into a saucepan, discarding the pits. Stir in 50 g/1¾ oz of the sugar and the grated lemon peel. Bring to a boil and cook for 2 minutes.

Serve warm or cold with the *croûtons* and sprinkled with the remaining sugar.

Soupe au Vin en Dessert
A wine, egg, raisin and spice dessert

This is a most unusual soup, which should be served after a rather light meal. It is a rich medieval dessert and quite heady.

For 8 people

5 slices home-made or good bread, crusts removed and diced
70 g/2½ oz unsalted butter
6 eggs
1.7 l/2⅖ pt red wine (hearty Burgundy type)

3 tbsp granulated sugar
1 tbsp Spanish saffron
70 g/2½ oz raisins
1 tsp cinnamon

Sauté the diced bread in the butter until golden, tossing for about 5 minutes.

Beat the eggs lightly, then slowly add the wine and 225 ml/8 fl oz of water. Cook over low heat, stirring. Add the sugar, saffron, raisins and cinnamon and cook for about 10 minutes. This should be served warm with the crisp bread cubes.

Tarte aux Pommes

An apple dessert flavoured with orange, lemon and raisins

This unusual apple dessert can be served with plain cream or with a light orange custard.

For 8 people

3 eggs
200 g/7 oz and 2 tsp granulated
    sugar
115 g/4 oz plain flour
300 ml/10½ fl oz double cream
130 g/4½ oz unsalted butter,
    softened

900 g/2 lb (about 4) tart apples
    (such as Granny Smith), peeled
    and sliced
2 tbsp orange peel, grated
2 tbsp lemon peel, grated
70 g/2½ oz raisins (preferably
    Malaga type)

Preheat the oven to 200°C/400°F/Gas Mark 6.

Beat the eggs and 200 g/7 oz of sugar until light and foamy. Add the flour and cream, stirring vigorously. Add the butter and stir. Add the apples, orange and lemon peel and raisins. Pour into a buttered mould and bake for 15 minutes. Then raise the temperature to 220°C/425°F/Gas Mark 7 and cook for about 15 minutes. Cool for a few minutes and serve lukewarm, sprinkled with 2 teaspoons sugar, along with cream or custard.

Tarte aux Prunes

A plum and cinnamon–almond custard tart

This is a very tasty dessert made with either little yellow mirabelle plums or tart green plums, or with pale yellow ones. You can use canned fruit if it is tasty and firm. The *tarte* may be served warm or cold.

For 8 people

·················· Pastry ··················

155 g/5⅓ oz plain flour
170 g/6 oz unsalted butter,
   softened
1 egg, beaten

1 tsp salt
1½ tsp granulated sugar
2 tsp milk

·················· Filling ··················

3 eggs
7 tbsp granulated sugar
25 g/1 oz ground almonds
pinch of cinnamon

75 g/2¾ oz plain flour
450 ml/16 fl oz hot milk
40 g/1½ oz unsalted butter
680 g/1½ lb plums, pitted

Place the flour on a table. Make a well in the centre and place the butter and egg in it. Mix well with your hands. Sprinkle with salt and sugar and mix a few minutes longer, working with the tips of your fingers. Then push away from you with the palms of your hands and add the milk to the dough. Gather the dough into a ball, cover with a piece of wet cloth and let it rest for an hour or overnight in a cool place.

Prepare the filling. In a saucepan, beat together the eggs, 3 tablespoons of the sugar, the almonds and cinnamon. Beat in the flour and stir with a whisk.

Bring the milk to a boil and stir it quickly into the egg mixture. Place over low heat and stir continuously for 4–5 minutes to make a custard. Remove from the heat and cool.

Preheat the oven to 200°C/400°F/Gas Mark 6.

In a large frying-pan heat the butter and add the remaining sugar and the plums. Cook over low heat for about 5 minutes and cool.

Roll out the dough on a floured table to 6-mm/¼-in. thickness and place it in a buttered mould. Pour in the cooled custard, arrange the plums, skin side down if possible, and bake for 35 minutes. Cool before serving.

You can sprinkle the tart with a little sugar and plum brandy a few minutes before it is ready to serve.

Tarte Lyonnaise aux Miettes

*A crisp pastry shell filled with breadcrumbs, almonds, eggs, and orange
and lemon peel, and covered with meringue*

A classic dessert in Lyon, this pretty and light tart is always a
children's favourite.

For 8 people

······················· Pastry ·······················

340 g/12 oz plain flour
2 eggs, beaten
225 g/8 oz unsalted butter,
   softened

100 g/3½ oz sugar
1 tsp salt

······················· Filling ·······················

1 tbsp milk
70 g/2½ oz bread or biscuit
   crumbs
8 tsp ground almonds
2 eggs, whole
2 eggs, separated

peel of 1 orange, grated
peel of 1 lemon, grated
115 g/4 oz granulated sugar
3 tsp unsalted butter, softened
2 tbsp kirsch (optional)
2 tbsp icing sugar

Prepare the pastry. Working quickly with the tips of your fingers,
mix all the ingredients together on a well-floured board. Pound and
stretch the dough away from you with the heel of your hand to be
sure all ingredients are well blended. Shape the dough into a ball,
cover with a clean cloth and leave for 2 hours at room temperature.

To make the filling, mix the milk and breadcrumbs in a saucepan
and heat for a few minutes. Pour into a blender and add the
almonds, the whole eggs, egg yolks, orange and lemon peel, 100 g/
3½ oz granulated sugar, butter and kirsch. Blend until the mixture
is smooth. Beat the egg whites with the remaining granulated sugar
until stiff.

Preheat the oven to 190°C/375°F/Gas Mark 5.

Spread the pastry as thinly as possible in a buttered mould. Prick
it all over with a fork. Spread the filling over the pastry and cover
with the beaten egg whites. Sprinkle with the icing sugar and bake
for about 30 minutes.

Les Boissons de Ménage

Home-made Beverages

In the Middle Ages only young wines, beer and *hypocras* were drunk, and it was only in the sixteenth century that brandy became popular, along with liqueurs made with sugar, cinnamon and various flavours.

In France blackcurrant bushes grow wild in places where there is chalky, dry soil. Until the eighteenth century the fruit was used in Burgundy mostly for medical purposes. Leaves were crushed and used in herb teas; berries were cooked with sugar, crushed into juice and used by doctors, priests and housewives to treat a variety of ailments – fever, plague or simply digestive problems. In the nineteenth century the famous liquor made from blackcurrants was first concocted and was to become one of France's most popular drinks.

Blackcurrants grow in Burgundy wherever there is good wine. They are the complementary crop of wine-growers, and in July the blackcurrant picking is as important as the grape picking a few months later. The fruit is a staple in Burgundy and the berries are used in compotes, desserts of all sorts, jellies, preserves, candies, syrups, sherbets and a variety of drinks, including the famous kir.

I have included here only the Burgundy recipes agreeable to the modern palate. They can be served as aperitifs before meals, with dessert or between meals.

Crème de Cassis

1.25 kg/3 lb very ripe
  blackcurrants
1.8 l/3⅕ pt red wine
1.8 kg/4 lb sugar (approximately)
225 ml/8 fl oz brandy

Wash the blackcurrants and crush them coarsely. Add the wine and marinate for 48 hours in a covered bowl.

Pass through a sieve and add 2 lb of sugar for each 900 ml/1⅗ pt of juice. Bring to a boil, stirring, and boil for 5 minutes. Let cool. Pass through a sieve and add the brandy while stirring. Keep in tightly closed bottles. It will keep indefinitely.

Eau de Coing
Quince water

Grate a few unpeeled quinces when they are yellow, ripe and fragrant. Leave them in a bowl for 3 days, then add the same quantity of brandy and 225 g/8 oz of sugar for each 900 ml/1⅗ pt liquid.

Keep in a dark place for a year before drinking it.

Hypocras

Some medieval treats like *vespétro* were made with angelica seeds, coriander, cinnamon and sometimes with bitter orange and spices. This was one of the favourites until the sixteenth century.

pinch of cinnamon
pinch of crushed vanilla bean
1 clove
70 g/2½ oz sugar
2.7 l/4¾ pt dry white wine

Mix everything and keep for 3 weeks in a closed jar. Pass through a sieve and keep in well-closed bottles in a cool place.

Kir

Chanoine Kir, the mayor of Dijon in the 1950s and also a left-wing canon who was a highly controversial figure, may be best remembered for inventing what has become almost a national drink – *le Kir*.

For each person

1 tsp blackcurrant liquor or
    blackcurrant crème
1 glass of dry white wine
    (preferably Bourgogne Blanc
    Aligoté or Pouilly Fuissé)

Serve chilled. Kir can be made with champagne instead of wine, and is then called a 'royal'; or with red wine, and is then called a 'cardinal'.

Liqueur de Cassis

1.25 kg/3 lb blackcurrants
140 g/5 oz raspberries (optional)
pinch of cinnamon
1 clove

2–3 blackcurrant leaves
900 ml/1⅗ pt brandy
450 g/1 lb sugar

Wash the currants (and if desired, the raspberries) and place them in a large bowl. Add the cinnamon, clove, currant leaves and brandy. Cover and keep in a cool place for 45 days.

Drain the fruit. Combine the sugar with 225 ml/8 fl oz of water and add to the juice. Keep in tightly closed bottles and drink after 2 months.

Liqueur Rouge
Red liqueur

900 ml/1⅗ pt brandy
450 g/1 lb wild cherries
450 g/1 lb redcurrants
450 g/1 lb raspberries

115 g/4 oz blackcurrants
pinch of cinnamon
1 clove
450 g/1 lb sugar

Mix everything except the sugar and keep for 6 weeks in a closed jar. Pass through a sieve. Add the sugar and 225 ml/8 fl oz water and keep in bottles.

Ratafia de Cassis

4.5 kg/10 lb blackcurrants
8 l/1¾ gal brandy
pinch of cinnamon
10 cloves
1.25 kg/3 lb sugar

Crush the currants coarsely and place them in a large container. Add the brandy, cinnamon and cloves. Leave the mixture in the sun for 50 days.

Pass the mixture through a sieve. Dissolve the sugar in 225 ml/8 fl oz of water and add to the juice. Keep in tightly closed bottles. It can be used after 2 months.

Ratafia de Framboise
Raspberry ratafia

This is delicious made with wild strawberries, too.

900 g/2 lb raspberries, cleaned and trimmed
900 ml/1⅗ pt brandy
400 g/14 oz sugar

Marinate the raspberries in the brandy in a closed jar for 2 months, stirring with a wooden spoon from time to time. Pass the fruit through a sieve, crushing it with a spoon. Add the sugar and 115 ml/4 fl oz of water and bring to a boil. Remove from the heat at once. Cool. Add the brandy in which the berries have marinated. It is now ready to drink.

Ratafia de Genièvre
Juniper ratafia

This can also be made with sloes, cranberries, dog rose berries, wild cherries and blueberries.

> 85 g/3 oz juniper berries, crushed
> 900 ml/1⅗ pt brandy
> 300 g/10½ oz sugar

Crush the berries in a mortar or blender. Bring them to a boil with 3 tablespoons of water. Let boil for 3 minutes. Cool. Add the brandy. Put in a closed jar and leave for one week in a dark place. Pass through a sieve, pushing with a wooden spoon. Heat the sugar and 4 tablespoons of water until the mixture becomes syrupy. Add it to the berry juice. Pour into bottles and keep for 1 month before tasting it.

Ratafia de Noix
Walnut ratafia

A hearty drink to prepare in the early summer, when both the beige walnut shells and the green kernels are still so soft that the entire fruit can be pierced by a knitting needle.

50 green walnuts
4 cloves
1 tsp freshly grated nutmeg

4 stamens of Spanish saffron
1.8 l/3⅕ pt good brandy
900 g/2 lb sugar

Put all the ingredients except the sugar in a closed glass jar and leave in a dark place for 2 months. Pass the liquid through a sieve. Add the sugar and keep in the closed jar in a dark place for 3 months more. Pour into bottles.

Ratafia de Raisins

Grape ratafia

There are many *ratafias*. Some are made with cherry juice, brandy, clove and wild cherry; some with bitter lemon, coriander, cinnamon and brandy.

This *ratafia* is served before a meal or as a sweet afternoon wine with biscuits and is easy to prepare.

> about 1.25 kg/3 lb black or white
> grapes
> 900 ml/1⅗ pt marc (brandy)

Crush and pass the grapes through a sieve. Mix 900 ml/1⅗ pt of the juice with the marc. Keep for a few weeks in a wooden cask before bottling.

Vin Chaud

Red wine simmered with spices

1.4 l/2⅖ pt hearty red wine
225 g/8 oz sugar
1 lemon, unpeeled, cut into thin
  slices

1 clove
5 sprigs of thyme
1 bay leaf

Heat the wine and sugar to the boiling point. Add the lemon, clove, thyme and bay leaf. Remove from the heat after 5 minutes and serve at once.

Vin de Genièvre

Juniper wine

85 g/3 oz juniper berries, crushed
900 ml/1⅗ pt dry white wine
100 g/3½ oz sugar

Place the crushed berries in a jar with the wine and sugar. Close tightly and leave for 3 weeks in a dark place. Pass through a sieve. It is now ready to enjoy.

Vin de Noix

Green walnut wine

This comes from Dauphiné, a region to the east of Burgundy, famous for its large walnuts, which are picked in June, when the shell is still tender and can be pierced with a pin.

2.7 l/4¾ pt hearty red wine
450 ml/16 fl oz good brandy
900 g/2 lb sugar
14 green walnuts, quartered
1 unpeeled orange

Mix everything and leave in a jar for 40 days, shaking it from time to time, then pass it through a sieve into bottles.

Close tightly and keep in a dark place for a few months so the flavour will mellow.

Le Vin

Wine

From its beginning wine has always been accepted as a present from the gods. It is as old as civilization, and wine grapes have been growing in the rocky soil of Burgundy for over two thousand years. Here it is a part of daily life. It has been the core of rituals, pagan as well as Christian, since around the second century of our era, when mine workers grew fond of Greek wines. Later a grape was developed that could bear cold winters, and soon vineyards spread along the Rhône Valley and found their favourite place in Burgundy.

Wooden barrels replaced earthenware amphorae, and honey and spices were added to the wines to cover their acidity. Wine was not yet wine as we know it, since it was drunk very young. But it was widely enjoyed and soon became a highly profitable commodity. In the sixth century the king of Burgundy gave vineyards to the monks, and by the early Middle Ages the Church was the principal producer of wine. It was whispered that the monks expended as much effort on tending to their wine as they did on spreading the gospel.

Philip the Bold, 'First Great Duke of the West, Lord of the Best Wine of the Christian Kingdom', regulated the methods of selecting, growing and tending the vines and the wine. Later the kings of France, all very fond of Burgundy wine, kept a vigilant eye on the quality of the region's crops.

After the Revolution the vineyards were taken away from the Church by the state and sold to the people, hence a pattern in Burgundy of small ownership that still prevails. In the nineteenth

century the vineyards were decimated by phylloxera. But American plants became immune to it, and soon, by growing on American rootstock to replace the old vines, the vineyards were replenished.

The production of wine in Burgundy is small compared with that of Bordeaux – only twenty-eight million gallons a year – but it is rich in quality and diversity.

The land and the vine are important, but the devotion of the wine-growers (more than 33,000 in Burgundy now) is essential. Fine wines come from pruning and growing the vines, then tending and ageing the wine. This work starts in the autumn after the harvest, when the soil has to be ploughed and cleaned. In winter, pruning has to be done, and in spring, ploughing and removing of excess buds. In summer, there are two more ploughings, training and spraying, and in the autumn there is finally the harvest.

Good wine comes mostly from good management and technique.

Made by the fermentation of grape sugar, it needs elaborate care. The yeast grows in fresh juice and produces enzymes, which convert the sugar to alcohol and carbon dioxide. The grape skins give tannin, colour and even flavour to the wine. The difference between red and white wine does not stop at the colour but comes from the tannin that passes from the skin to the juice during vatting.

Red wine is made with black grapes fermented with their skins, crushed and vatted for six to seven days. The skins and pulp of the grape floating on top of the juice are called the *chapeau* (hat) and may be as much as one metre/three feet thick. The *chapeau* must be punched down a few times a day during fermentation, or the wine may be pumped through a hose over the *chapeau*.

Then the wine is drained and poured into oak barrels to age. The oxygen, which enters through the wood and cork, helps to 'mature' the wine. The colour deepens, and the taste becomes less harsh as it ages. Particles settle to the bottom. Twice a week more wine is added to the barrel to make up for the evaporation, so there is no space for bacteria to develop.

During the first year the wine is cleaned ('racked') about four times, and during the second year, about twice more. It is during this second year that the wine mellows and develops its bouquet. The third year the wine is cleared of any suspended particles left and undergoes a *collage* (a fining) with white of egg, blood or gelatin. After that the wine is bottled in the typical squat, slope-shouldered Burgundy bottle and aged for two to ten years.

White wines are made without grape skins, pressed as soon as possible and poured into barrels to ferment. The fermentation must be cool and slow, and here oxygenation plays a much smaller role than it does with red wines. The barrels are only partially filled, since the must (the not yet fermented juice) expands and the grape particles rise to the top. The temperature is kept at 15–21°C/60–70°F, and one racking is done after the first fermentation.

After twelve to eighteen months in the barrel, dry white wine is bottled. It is the fresh early taste of grapes that gives white wine its flavour, so it should be drunk quite young; it does not improve with age.

When the sun is not warm enough to provide the requisite sugar, *chaptalisation* – the addition of sugar to the must – is needed. This gives the wine a higher alcoholic content and sometimes even improves its flavour. Its use is widespread in Burgundy but always under strict government control.

The greatest wines of Burgundy come from the slopes of the Côte d'Or, a low range of hills along the western edge, beginning in Dijon and ending south of Santeny. The region is divided into two main parts. In the north, the Côte de Nuits, a narrow strip of hills, provides great red wines, such as Nuits-Saint-Georges, Vougeot, Gevrey-Chambertin, Vosne-Romanée, Musigny, which must be aged between five and ten years. South of this, Côte de Beaune offers splendid white wines, such as Meursault, Montrachet and Volnay, and a delicate red wine, Pommard.

Then there are the Hautes-Côtes, with Bourgogne Aligoté and Passe-Tout-Grains, fruity pleasant wines.

Farther south, Côte Chalonnaise gives good red and white wines, such as Givry, Mercurey and Montagny, and the Côte Mâconnaise has its delicious Pouilly-Fumé and Mâcon. Beaujolais, a light and pleasant wine, and Morgon and Brouilly come from the area near Lyon.

The main vine in Burgundy is the Pinot Noir, which produces red wines. The Gamay makes a light Beaujolais and plain red wines. The main vine for white wines is Chardonnay, which is the source of all the great white wines. Pinot Blanc and Aligoté provide pleasant light white wines.

The identity of a Burgundy wine comes from its vine and what is described on the bottle as a *climat*, which means a place whose soil and climate give the wine its quality. There are 419 *climats* in Côte de Nuits and about 900 in Côte de Beaune. A *climat* may belong to different owners. The finest are the fifty *Premier Crus* and the eighteen *Grand Crus*. As Talleyrand observed, 'When one is served such a wine one takes the glass respectfully, looks at it, inhales it, then having put it down, one discusses it.'

To the east of Burgundy, in Savoy, Dauphiné and Jura, there are many pleasant and fresh wines – dry light wines, sparkling wines and a delicious yellow wine prepared with grapes that have dried on straw for three months before being pressed, fermented and aged for four years. It is a sweet natural wine served with dessert and is called *vin jaune*.

Wines should please the palate, match the food they are served with and also balance one another. Usually, therefore, one starts the meal with a dry white wine, which is followed by a red one, then a great red wine, and, finally, sweet wines with desserts and champagne with fruit.

Light white wine tastes best with fish, ham, chicken, snails, crayfish, sausages; light red wine, with light soups and mild cheese; hearty red wine with peasant soups, vegetables, meat, game, highly flavoured cheese and some fowl dishes. But all these rules may be broken according to what tastes best to the host.

Menus

Menus

To entertain is a serious matter. In the eighteenth century women of quality were given three funeral orations – one by a philosopher and two by regular guests at her table.

Choosing a menu requires taste and imagination. Clichés – pigeon with peas, veal with noodles, duck with turnips – should be avoided. It is better to serve such combinations as lamb with a purée of butter beans, veal with onion *confits* or chicken with melted leeks. One should remove the commonplace from the menu; otherwise the conversation can also become trite and ruin the feast.

As in all good marriages, the different dishes must keep their own personalities. The different flavours should offset or enhance one another, answer to one another, associate but never be absorbed. There must be contrasts – warm and cold, creamy and dry, sweet and salty – to bring balance and liveliness to a meal.

A meal is eaten first with the eyes, so, of course, a veal cream dish should never be followed by a pale custard dessert, nor should a *rouget* fish be served before rare beef or a beetroot salad and a strawberry cake.

I have chosen here a few menus to convey the Burgundy spirit.

Le Déjeuner entre Amis
Lunch

Salade de Céleri
Filets au Safran
Le Paillasson
Pommes Sévigné

Potage de Porée à la Ribelette de Lard
Le Saladier Lyonnais
Coeurs à la Crème

Le Déjeuner Elégant

Oeufs en Meurette
Poulet au Fromage
Gâteau de Pommes de Terre
Salade de Nevers
Fruits Cuits au Vin

Délices d'Endives
Côte de Boeuf Bourguignonne
Gratin d'Oignons
Champignons de Dijon
Salade de Pissenlits
Raisiné et Massepains

Le Dîner entre Amis
Dinner

Soupe Nevers
Saupiquet I
Gratin Rouge
Crépinette aux Marrons
Laitue Bourguignonne
Gouerre au Cirage

Le Régal Aillé
Boeuf Bourguignon
Pâtes Fraîches
Purée de Fenouil
Salade à la Menthe
La Cervelle de Canut

Le Dîner Elégant

Saumon aux Herbes
Jambon à la Saulieu
Gâteau au Céleri
Gratin Trois
Sorbet au Marc

Chèvre Chaud
Canard à la Menthe
Petits Navets en Ragoût
Raisiné
Salade aux Griaudes
Framboises à la Neige

Le Pique-nique
Picnic

·········· Salé (*salty dishes*) ··········

Fricandeau
Tarte Bourguignonne
Terrine de Canard
L'Enchaud
Délice de Fromages

·········· Sucré (*sweet dishes*) ··········

Nonnettes
Massepains
Noeuds d'Amour
Pogne

Le Buffet
Buffet

·········· Froid (*cold dishes*) ··········

Terrine de Canard
Saumon aux Herbes
Filets de Harengs
Fromage Fort du Beaujolais
Bersaudes
La Cervelle de Canut
Jambon Persillé
Corniottes
All the salads
All the desserts

········ Chaud (*hot dishes*) ········

Saupiquet I and II
Ravioles
Boulettes Dorées de Montagne
Croquettes aux Herbes
Tarte Bourguignonne
La Gougère
Les Petits Paniers
Saucisson Chaud Lyonnais
Petits Poissons à la Bourguignotte

Le Goûter
Snack

········ Sucré (*sweet dishes*) ········

Biscuit de Savoie
Nonnettes
Lait de Poule
Pain d'Épice
Pogne
Caramels

Le Machon
Snack

········ Salé (*salty dishes*) ········

Filets de Harengs
La Gougère
Fricandeau
Délice de Fromages
La Cervelle de Canut
Fromage Fort du Beaujolais

La Moutarde

Mustard

In 400 BC Aristophanes mentioned the taste of a stew seasoned with mustard. The Romans used a mixture of seeds and vinegar called *sinapis*, and they introduced the Gauls to this condiment, which they believed to be also a medicine.

Burgundy became the centre of the preparation of mustard; in the fourteenth and fifteenth centuries it was eaten not only with meat and fish but also with soups. When the cardinal of Euze became pope, he named one of his cousins 'first *moutardier*', whose official attire was a green suit worn with a necklace; with an allowance of 1,000 ducats, he enjoyed a cosy life in exchange for keeping a vigilant eye on the mustard situation in the papal palace. 'I tickle the mouth and I sting the nose' was the motto of this *moutardier*.

Philip the Bold, Duke of Burgundy, whose motto was *Moult me tarde* (I am impatient), is said to have ordered 82 kg/180 lb of mustard for one of his festive meals.

Mustard is an annual. It has yellow flowers, and the seed, round and purple-brown with a yellow centre when its shell is removed, holds all the active ingredients of mustard. The crushing of seeds (of the species *Brassica nigra* or *Brassica juncea*, or a mixture of both) is done in a mill, and the crushed seeds are mixed with the juice of unripe grapes or with grape must or with vinegar or wine. Salt, sugar, spices and herbs may be added in small quantities.

The thick mixture is put through a sieve and pulverized. The soft, smooth paste that results is kept in large containers, where its flavour is developed for about ten days before it is ready for sale.

Mustard enhances the taste of food and is said to be good for the digestion. One can understand why Louis XI used to go out to dinner carrying his own pot of mustard for fear of having to do without.

Until the sixteenth century mustard makers sold their product in the streets. The quality of the mustard plant growing in Burgundy, as well as the excellence of the *verjus*, or wine vinegar, produced there, made Burgundy mustard the most famous in the world. Each mill crushed its own mustard seeds, and since the seventeenth century, mustard makers have joined together in corporations with specific trademarks and regulations.

Today the preparation of mustard is severely regulated and follows certain fundamental rules: for example, the taste of the seeds must never be overpowered by herbs that are too strong or by vinegar that is too heavy.

Spécialités

Special Treats

A truffle is a truffle is a truffle wherever it is eaten. A carefully prepared *boeuf bourguignon* can taste as good in Dundee, Durham or Denbigh as it would in Dijon. But there are a few dishes that do not cross the Channel, and to taste them we either have to cross it ourselves or read and dream about them.

Why are such special treats untransportable? The reason is that some depend on local products – a special cardoon, a musky mushroom, a plump snail that cannot be found outside of Burgundy and is too fragile to be shipped. And some dishes are prepared or eaten in ways that would be hard to enjoy here. So I mention them here only to show the diversity and inventiveness of Burgundy cooking:

Stuffed veal ears seasoned with butter, brandy and breadcrumbs, deep-fried in batter.

A leg of wild boar wrapped in its fur, placed in a deep hole in the ground, covered with embers and cooked for a day, then served with redcurrant jelly.

The *ferchusse*, a mixture of pork lungs, heart and liver sautéd with onions and garlic, cooked with red wine and traditionally eaten on the day the pig is killed.

Sanquette, coagulated chicken blood sautéd in chicken fat with onions, seasoned with vinegar, tarragon and parsley.

Beef or veal brain cooked in red wine and served with onions, mushrooms and *croûtons*.

Tripe filled with spices, garlic and onions and cooked with wine and carrots.

Gratins of pig's feet and pork rind cooked with white wine and herbs.

Salads of sheep's feet and sheep's testicles.

A wild boar's head cooked in water and vinegar, sautéd with onions, garlic, juniper and red wine and thickened with fresh blood.

The *gruotte* made of the lungs, liver and head of baby boar, sautéd with onions, herbs and wine – a favourite of hunters.

Roasted suckling pig stuffed with chopped heart, liver, kidney, garlic and sage and simmered in white wine.

Beef heart marinated in wine and herbs, then cooked for twelve hours.

There are all kinds of sausages prepared in different ways in Burgundy and, mostly, in Lyon: blood sausages made with onions, spinach, cinnamon, sage and rice and either cooked with chestnuts or fried apples and cream, or seasoned with mustard and tarragon; Lyon pistachio sausage, Morteau smoked sausage flavoured with aniseed; Seaulieu raw cured sausage eaten with plain potatoes or cooked in a stew; *andouille*, made with pork stomach marinated in spices, mustard and vinegar, then eaten grilled with lemon and mustard or sautéd with shallots and white wine and accompanied by beans and pig's ears.

There are smoked, cured and boiled hams, prepared in endless ways.

Cheese preparations are often startling. Blue cheese is left in an earthen pot to mature. Sprinkled with dry white wine, it is stirred every day. Then goat cheese is added to it and the mixture is kept in a warm place and eaten between summer and autumn. There is also fresh goat cheese mixed with ewe cheese and butter cooked slowly together and seasoned with sugar; Gruyère cheese, goat cheese, butter, brandy and wine melted together and spread on toast; cheese, wine, walnut oil and brandy, left to ferment and eaten on warm toast; fresh cheese wrapped in vine or chestnut leaves, sprinkled with brandy and kept in a cellar for three weeks; cheese mixed with flour, milk and egg and eaten in a pie.

Matefaims, thick pancakes, true 'hunger killers', are spread with jam. *Galette à la sermouille*, a pie made of semolina, is served with double cream. Chestnut, clove, fennel and egg custard is sprinkled with pistachios, and there are endless desserts based on pumpkin. Cooked blackcurrants are used with crêpes, sponge cakes and sweet omelettes. Blackcurrant and barberry jam, watermelon jam and verjuice jam are spread on *rigodon* and other pastries. Endless amounts of fritters in the shape of bows, butterflies, ribbons and balls are made with semolina or wheat flour or potato flour and flavoured with fruits and liqueurs. A Lyon delicacy is fritters of carp roe, seasoned with lemon juice. Fritters of marinated frogs' legs, sprinkled with garlic and parsley, are served with a cream-and-chives sauce.

And, finally, *trempe au vin*, a curious mixture of bread moistened with a hearty red wine and sugar, is given to sea and river mariners and newlyweds for energy.

Index

anchovies 8
Anguille en Matelote 70–71
aniseed 13
appetizers 28–43
  aspic of ham 36–7
  celery with ham and cheese
    sauce 41–2
  cheese and ham cubes,
    deep-fried 38
  cheese and mint pork rolls 40–41
  cheese blend with white
    wine 214–15
  cheese pastry 35–6
  cheese sticks, deep-fried 213
  chicken liver, pork and
    herb-spiced patties 33
  chicken-liver soufflé 34–5
  chicory and ham with poached
    egg 30–31
  duck pâté 42–3
  fried cakes of pork and
    chestnuts 29–30
  garlic treats 40
  kippered herring fillets,
    marinated 32
  pork and herb patties 31–2
  pork spread 29
  sausage with potatoes, white
    wine and mustard 42

  stuffed dumplings 38–9
apples
  applesauce fritters 218
  cabbage with sausage, sage
    and 160
  cake with 253–4
  custard, meringue and 248
  duck roasted with mint
    and 112–13
  gratin of cabbage, ham, meat
    and 171
  pancakes with rum and 227–8
  sausages, prunes and 110–11
  soufflé with 242–3
  tarts with orange, lemon and
    raisins 254
  warm dessert of 230
apricots
  cake with walnut rum
    and 235–6
  dessert soup of 252–3
artichokes 156
  sauce for 62
asparagus 156
  sauce for 62
aspic
  ham 36–7
  marinated beef and vegetables
    107–8

Baguettes 213
bay leaf 13
beans, broad, in mixed
    vegetables 182
beans, dried 157
  lentils in salad with vegetables,
    herbs and bacon 48–9
  lentils with toast, pâté and
    bacon 185–6
  red kidney beans with wine and
    spices 178
  white bean purée 189
  white beans with wine and
    shallot sauce 177
beans, green 158
  with cream sauce 179
  salad with shallots, mushrooms
    and 48
  sauce for 57–8
beef
  balls of cheese, onions, herbs
    and 111–12
  Boeuf Marinière I 106
  Beoeuf Marinière II 107
  chopped, in stuffed
    dumplings 38–9
  fondue of 200
  gratin of, with onions and
    herbs 101
  marinated, with vegetables in
    aspic 109–10
  marinated, with wine and
    vegetable sauce 101–2
  Pot-au-Feu 204–7
  rib steak with wine sauce 119–20
  sauce for 58, 59
  sautéd, baked with vegetables,
    herbs and wine 103
  stew of 108
  stew, of Burgundy 198–9
  T-bone steak with cream
    sauce 149
  T-bone steak with wine sauce 104

  wine, onions and 104–6
  see also veal
beetroot, salad with peppers, celery
  and 54
Beignets à la Crème 216–17
Beignets au Caillé 217–18
Beignets de Compote 218
Bersuades 29
Beurre Bourguignonne 57–8
Beurre d'Escargot 58
beverages, home-made 257–63
  with blackcurrants 258–60
  grape ratafia 262
  green walnut wine 263
  Hypocras 258–9
  juniper ratafia 261
  juniper wine 263
  Kir 259
  quince water 258
  raspberry ratafia 260–61
  red liqueur 260
  red wine with spices 262
  walnut ratafia 261–2
Biscuit de Savoie 219
Biscuits au Citron 220
blackcurrants
  beverages with 258–60
  pâté of 244
Blanquette de Veau 100
Boeuf à la Mâcon 101
Boeuf à Sauvage 101–2
Boeuf aux Légumes 103
Boeuf Beaujolais 104
Boeuf Blond 104–6
Boeuf Bourguignon 198–9
Boeuf en Daube Charollaise 108–9
Boeuf en Gelée Vézulienne 109–10
Boeuf Marinière I 106
Boeuf Marinière II 107
boiled dinner
  pork and vegetable 207–8
  Pot-au-Feu 204–7
Bonnet de Chou 160

Boudin Blanc et Pruneaux 110–11
Boulettes Dorées de Montagne 111–12
bouquet garni 8
bread 9
breadcrumbs 9
   leeks, cheese, spices and 184
   omelette of cream, herbs and 94
Brochettes, Petites 38
Brussels sprouts, soup with 25–6
Bugnes Lyonnaises 220

cabbage 156
   baked, with sausages, apples and
      sage 160
   gratin of apple, ham, meat,
      shallots and 171
   purée of 121–2, 188
   salad of sautéd 46
   soup with carrots, turnips
      and 19–20
   soup with rice and 23
   stuffed, with fruit and
      sausages 161–2
cake *see* desserts
Canard à la Menthe 112–13
Canard Sauvage à la Diable 113–14
capers 13
Caramels 221
cardoons 157
carp
   sauce for 64–5
   sautéd 71–2
Carpes en Meurette 71–2
carrots
   cake with mushrooms, cheese
      and 166–7
   in mixed vegetables 182
   with mustard and butter 162–3
   soup with cabbage, turnips
      and 19–20
   soup with onions, turnips, sorrel
      and 25
Cassolettes Meringuées 221

cayenne pepper 13
celery 157
   gratin of parsley, egg and 166
   salad with lettuce, egg, ham,
      cheese, walnuts and 53–4
   salad with peppers, beetroot
      and 54
   sauce for 62
   walnuts, cheese and 47
   wrapped in ham with cheese
      sauce 41–2
Cervelle de Canut, La 214–15
Champignons de Dijon 160–61
Châtaigne, La 222
cheese 9, 211–15, 278
   blend of, with white
      wine 214–15
   celery with walnuts and 47
   dumplings filled with 224–5
   fritters with 217–18
   fruit purée with 224
   and mint pork rolls 40–41
   salad with melted 215
   soup with (smooth) 20
   spread of herbs, wine
      and 214–15
   spread of wine, broth and 214
   see also Gruyère cheese
cherries
   black, custard of 222–3
   black, with meringue 221
   cake of 223
chestnuts 9, 157
   fried cakes with salt pork
      and 29–30
   pie of 222
   purée of potatoes and 186
Chêvre Chaud 215
chicken
   baked, with tomatoes and cream
      under cheese crust 147
   baked, with wine and cheese
      sauce 140–1

chicken – *contd*
  gratin of, with onions, wine and
    herbs 101
  grilled, with wine sauce 139–40
  marinated, with cream and
    grapes 146
  marinated, with wine and
    vegetables 153–4
  Pot-au-Feu 204–7
  with prunes and wine 144–5
  sauce for 59
  sausages with prunes and
    apples 110–11
  sautéd, with mushrooms and
    walnuts 143–4
  sautéd, with onions and
    mushrooms 118–19
  sautéd, with vinegar, wine,
    mustard and cream 141–2
  sautéd, with wine, cream and
    prawns 142–3
  soup with cream, corn meal
    and 24
  soup with tomatoes and 18
  stuffed, with vegetables 137–8
  with wine and cream 138–9
  wine, vegetables, herbs and 131–2
  see also liver, chicken
chicory 157
  ham and, with poached egg 30–31
chives 13
  omelette of mustard, cream
    and 94–5
Chou Farci 161–2
Civet de Dinde 114–15
Civet de Porc 115–16
Clafoutis I 222–3
Clafoutis II 223
clove 13
Cochon de Lait Vigneron 116–17
cod, dried 10
  boiled and sautéd with onions
    and potatoes 79

fritters of 80
  gratin of 77–8
Coeurs à la Crème 224
Confiture au Potiron 225–6
Coq au Vin Bourguignon 118–19
coriander 14
corn meal, chicken soup with cream
  and 24
Corniottes 224–5
Côte de Boeuf Bourguignonne 119–20
Côte de Veau Dijonnaise 122
Côtes de Porc au Vinaigre 120–21
Côtes de Porc Farcies 121–2
Coulis de Fruits 226
Coulis de Tomates 58–9
Coupes aux Fruits 227
courgettes, pie of tomatoes, onions
  and 189–9
Crapìau de Pommes 227–8
cream 10
  chicken soup with corn meal
    and 24
  fritters with 216–17
  omelette of 93–4
  soup with cabbage, carrots,
    turnips and 19–20
  soup with vegetables and 19, 27
Crème aux Fruits 228–9
Crème de Cassis 258
Crépinette aux Marrons 29–30
Croquettes aux Herbes 123
Crousets 193
Croûtons 10
  omelette with 95
Crozets 193–4
cucumbers in mixed vegetables 182
custard
  apples, meringue and 248
  egg yolk, with broth 17–18
  fruit 222–3
  on fruit delight 227
  fruit with 228–9
  with lemon and wine 240–41

light, dessert 238
   tart with plums and 254–5

dandelion greens 157
   salad with bacon, croûtons
      and 51
   salad with vinaigrette sauce
      and 50–51
Daube d'Agneau 123–4
Délice de Fromages 214
Délices d'Endives 30–31
desserts 216–56
   almond and lemon wafers 239
   apple, warm 230
   apple and rum pancakes 227–8
   apple cake 233–4
   apple soufflé 242–3
   apricot soup 252–3
   black cherries with meringue 221
   blackcurrant pâté 244
   brandy sherbet 252
   caramel-flavoured cake 234–5
   caramelized fruits 231–2
   caramels 221
   cheese spread with herbs and
      wine 214–15
   cheese with fruit purée 224
   cherry cake 223
   chocolate mousse with orange
      peel 239–40
   dumplings filled with cheese and
      cream 224–5
   floating island with raspberry
      purée 230–31
   fruit delight 227
   fruit purée 226
   gingerbread 243–4
   gingerbread pudding 249–50
   grapes in brandy 250
   honey wafers 236–7
   lemon and caramel pudding 249
   lemon and rum cake 245
   lemon biscuits 220

lemon cake 219
   nut pudding with stewed
      fruits 251–2
   pears, quinces and grapes 250–51
   pumpkin jam 225–6
   pumpkin pudding 229
   raisin pastry 233
   stewed fruit 232
   stuffed honey and almond
      cake 241–2
   stuffed pears 247–8
   tangerines with brandy 238–9
   walnut rum and apricot jam
      cake 235–6
   wine, raisin and spice soup 253
   see also custard; fritters; pies; tarts
dried cod *see* cod, dried
duck
   baked wild 113–14
   fricassée of 126
   pâté of 42–3
   roasted, with mint and
      apples 112–13
dumplings
   dessert, with cheese and cream 224
   stuffed 38–9

Eau de Coing 258
eel
   sauce for 64–5
   wine, herbs and 70–71
eggs 86–98
   baked, with cheese 89
   baked, with mashed potatoes and
      cheese 88–9
   baked, with mushrooms and
      cream 91
   baked, with sliced potatoes and
      cheese 93
   baked stuffed 87–8
   fake snails 87
   fried, with onions, wine and
      herbs 88

eggs – *contd*
poached, with chicory and
ham 30–31
poached, with cream sauce 90
poached, with wine, onion and
herb sauce 91–2
salad with chicken livers,
herring, meat and 55–6
salad with lettuce, ham, celery,
cheese, walnuts and 53–4
sauce for 62, 64–5
see also custard; omelettes
Enchaud 31–2
Epaule d'Agneau Farcie 124
Escargots 72–3
Escargots au Vin Blanc 74–5
Escargots Bourguignonne 73–4
Estouffade de Carottes 162–3

Faux Escargots 87
fennel, purée of potatoes and 188
Filets au Safran 75–6
Filets de Brochet Mâcon 76–7
Filets de Harengs 32
Filets de Poisson aux Pâtes 77
fish 68–85
anchovies 8
baked, with wine and cream
sauce 80–81
baked fillets 75–6
baked fillets with sorrel 77
carp, sautéd 71–2
chicken sautéd with wine, cream
and large prawns 142–3
eel with wine and herbs 70–71
frogs' legs, with sauce 78–9
pike, marinated and baked 76–7
salmon, marinated 84
salmon with mint and
tomatoes 83–4
sauce for 60–61, 62, 64–5
sliced, with mustard, wine and
cream sauce 82

stew of 203–4
trout, stuffed 84–5
whitebait, grilled and
marinated 81
wine, vegetable and bacon sauce
with 82–3
see also cod, dried; herring; snails
Flamous 229
Flamusse aux Pommes 230
*Flan de Pommes de Terre à la
Bourguignonne* 163–4
flour 10
Foie de Porc Bourguignonne 125
Fondue Bourguignonne 200
Fondue Savoyarde 200–201
Framboises à la Neige 230–31
Fricandeau 33
fricassee, goose or duck 126
Fricot d'Oie 126
Frites à la Crème 164–5
fritters 279
applesauce 218
with cheese 217–18
codfish 80
cream 216–17
light 220
love knots 241
frogs' legs with sauce 78–9
Fromage Fort du Beaujolais 215
fruits *see* desserts; specific fruits
*Fruits Caramélisés au Vin
Rouge* 231–2
Fruits Cuits au Vin 232

Galette aux Pommes de Terre 165
Galette de Goumeau 233
Galette Grand-mère 233–4
garlic 10, 157
garlic treats, 40
Gâteau au Caramel 234–5
Gâteau au Céleri 166
Gâteau aux Noix et au Rhum 235–6
Gâteau de Carrotes 166–7

Gâteau de Foies Blonds 34–5
Gâteau de Pommes de Terre 167–8
Gaufrettes au Miel 236–7
gherkins 11
Gigot Boulangère 126–7
ginger 14
gingerbread 243–4
    pudding 249–50
goose
    braised 133
    fricassee of 126
Gouerre au Cirage 237
Gougère, La 35–6
grain dishes *see* pasta and grain
        dishes
grapes
    in brandy 250
    chicken with cream and 146
    pears, quinces and 250–51
    ratafia 262
Grapiau 168–9
Gratin Daupinois I 169–70
Gratin Dauphinois II 170
Gratin de Chou 171
Gratin de Morue 77–8
Gratin de Potiron 172–3
Gratin de Verdure 173–4
Gratin d'Oignons 171–2
Gratin Forestière 174–5
Gratin Rouge 175
Gratin Savoyard 175–6
Gratin Trois 176–7
Gratinée Lyonnaise 202–3
green beans *see* beans, green
Grenouilles au Vin Blanc 78–9
Gruyère cheese 9
    baked eggs with 89
    baked eggs with sliced potatoes
        and 93
    balls of beef, onions, herbs
        and 111–12
    carrot cake with mushrooms
        and 166–7

cubes of, with ham,
    deep-fried 38
fondue of 200–201
leeks, breadcrumbs, spices
    and 184
omelette of ham, cream and 96
pasta filled with 195–6
pastry of 35–6
potato and flour sticks
    with 193–4
potato cake with herbs and 167
potato gratin with onions, garlic
    and 175–6
salad with lettuce, egg, ham,
    celery, walnut and 53–4
soup with 21
soup with vegetables, salami
    and 26–7
sticks of, deep-fried 213
sticks of potatoes, flour and 193–4
tomatoes stuffed with shallots
    and 191
see also cheese

ham 10
    aspic of 36–7
    baked 130
    baked, with cream sauce, vinegar
        and vegetables 209–10
    baked, with vegetables, wine and
        cream sauce 208–9
    boiled 127–8
    celery with cheese sauce 41–2
    chicory and, with poached
        egg 30–31
    cubes of, with cheese,
        deep-fried 38
    gratin of cabbage, apples, meat,
        shallots and 171
    gratin of meat with onions and
        herbs 101
    gratin of turnips, herbs
        and 190–91

ham − *contd*
 omelette of *Gruyère* cheese, cream
  and 96
 omelette of mushrooms and 97
 potatoes with onions, cream,
  eggs and 163–4
 salad with herbs, vinegar
  and 52–3
 salad with lettuce, eggs, celery,
  cheese, walnuts and 53–4
 spinach baked with cream sauce
  and 129–30
 with tomato sauce and
  cheese 128–9
 vegetables and, in pie 149–51
 with vegetables and mustard and
  cream sauce 136
 see also pork; salt pork
Haricots Blancs au Vin Rouge 177
Haricots Rouges 178
Haricots Verts a la Crème 179
herring
 marinated kippered fillets 32
 salad with boiled eggs and 49–50
 salad with chicken livers, eggs,
  meat and 55–6
Hypocras 258–9

jam, pumpkin 225–6
Jambon à la Saulieu 128–9
Jambon au Torchon et au Foin 127–8
Jambon Chaud Chablisienne 129–30
Jambon Grand-mère 130
Jambon Persillé 36–7
juniper
 ratafia of 261
 wine of 263

Kir 259

lace fat or pork caul 12
Lait de Poule 238
Laitue Bourguignonne 45

lamb
 baked, leg of 126–7
 stewed 123–4
 stuffed, shoulder of 124
leeks 158
 breadcrumbs, cheese, spices
  and 184
 soup with potatoes and 17
lentils *see* beans, dried
lettuce
 salad with creamy sauce 55
 salad with egg, ham, celery,
  cheese and walnuts, 53–4
 salad with garlic, butter and
  lemon 45
 salad with mint 45
 salad with walnuts, lemons,
  mustard and cream 47
Lièvre de Pâques 131
Liqueur de Cassis 259
Liqueur Rouge 260
liver, chicken
 in omelette 96
 patties of salt pork, herbs and 33
 salad with eggs, herring, meat
  and 55–6
 in soufflé 34–5
liver, pork, marinated 125
liver in duck pâté 42–3

Mandarines a l'Armagnac 238–9
Marinade 59
Massepains 239
Matelote de Pommes de Terre 179–80
mayonnaise 63–4
meats 99–154; *see also* specific meats
menus 269–73
 buffet 272–3
 dinner 271
 lunch 270
 picnic 272
 snack 273
Meurette de Poulet 131–2

mint 14
  duck roasted with apples
    and 112–13
  rolls with cheese, pork
    and 40–41
  salad with lettuce and 45
  salmon with tomatoes and 83–4
  sauce with 60
Morue à la Lyonnaise 79
Morue en Beignets 80
Mousse au Chocolat 239–40
Mousse au Citron 240–41
mushrooms 156
  baked eggs, cream and 91
  cake with carrots, cheese
    and 166–7
  chicken sautéd with onions
    and 118–19
  chicken sautéd with walnuts
    and 143–4
  with Dijon sauce 160–61
  gratin of potatoes, onions
    and 174–5
  in mixed vegetables 182
  omelette of ham and 97
  salad with green beans, shallots
    and 48
  sautéd, with French fried
    potatoes and sauce 164–5
mustard 11, 274–6
  sauce I 65–6
  sauce II 66
  sauce with egg, butter, lemon
    and 65

Noeuds d'Amour 241
Nonnettes 241–2
noodles 194–5
nutmeg 14
nuts 11; *see also* specific nuts

Oeufs a la Dijonnaise 87–8
Oeufs au Civet 88

Oeufs au Nid 88–9
Oeufs Crémés 89
Oeufs en Cassolette Dijonnaise 90
Oeufs en Cocotte 91
Oeufs en Meurette 91–2
Oeufs Savoyard 93
Oie à la Moutarde 133
Oignons aux Épinards 180
oil 11–12
omelettes
  apple 242–3
  breadcrumb, cream and herb 93
  chicken liver 96
  cream 94
  croûton 95
  Gruyère cheese, ham and cream
    96–7
  ham and mushroom 97
  mustard, cream and
    chive 94–5
  onion, cream and vinegar 98
  snail 97
Omelette à la Crème 94
Omelette à la Mie 93
Omelette à la Moutarde 94–5
Omelette aux Croûtons 95
Omelette aux Foies 96
Omelette aux Pommes 242–3
Omelette de Savoie 96
Omelette d'Escargot 97
Omelette du Morvan 97
Omelette Machon 98
onions 158
  beef, wine and 104–6
  braised, with raisins, herbs
    and wine 183
  chicken sautéd with mushrooms
    and 118–19
  fried eggs with wine, herbs and
    88
  gratin of 171–2, 175
  gratin of potatoes, garlic and,
    with cheese crust 175–6

onions – *contd*
 gratin of potatoes, mushrooms
  and 174–5
 omelette of cream, vinegar
  and 98
 pancake of potato, egg, cheese
  and 168–9
 pie of tomatoes, courgettes and
  189–90
 pork, wine, herbs and 215–16
 potatoes and, with herbs and red
  wine 179–80
 sautéd, with potatoes 186–7
 sautéd, with potatoes, vinegar
  and herbs 187
 soup with carrots, turnips, sorrel
  and 25
 soup with eggs, cheese, wine and
  202–3
 soup with leeks, potatoes and 17
 in stuffed dumplings, 38–9
 stuffed, with spinach, cream,
  cheese, eggs 180
 turnips, herbs, garlic and 182–3
orange-flower water 12

Paillasson 181
Pain d'Épice 243–4
Paniers, Les Petites 38–9
parsley 14
pasta and grain dishes 192–7
 cheese-filled pasta 195–6
 Crousets 193
 home-made noodles 194–5
 potato and flour sticks with
  cheese 193–4
 rice with herbs 197
pâté
 duck 42–3
 lentils with toast, bacon and
  185–6
Pâté de Cassis 244
Pâtés Fraîches 194–5

Pauchouse 203–4
pears
 pie of 246
 quinces, grapes and 250–51
 stuffed 247–8
pepper 14
peppers, salad with beetroot, celery
  and 54
Perche à la Charollaise 80–81
Petites Brochettes 38
Petits Légumes 182
Petits Navets en Ragoût 183
Petits Oignons à la Bourguignonne 183
Petits Paniers 38–9
Petits Poissons à la Bourguignotte 81
pies
 chestnut 222
 meat and vegetable 149–51
 pear 246
 prune 237
 tomato, onion and
  courgette 189–90
 see also tarts
pike
 marinated and baked 76–7
 sauce for 64–5
plums, tarts with custard and 254–5
Pogne 245
Poirat, Le 246
Poireaux à la Savoyard 184
Poires en Manteau 247–8
Poisson à la Moutarde 82
Poisson en Meurette 82–3
Pommes de Terre aux Herbes 184
Pommes de Terre Lyonnaise 186–7
Pommes Sautées 187
Pommes Sévigné 248
Porc au Vermouth 134
Porc aux Haricots Rouges 135
Porc Dijonnaise 136
pork
 boiled dinner of vegetables
  and 207–8

cheese and mint rolls with 40–41
chops stuffed with ham, cheese
   and sage 121–2
chops with garlic, herbs and
   onions 120–21
gratin of meat with onions and
   herbs 101
liver of, marinated 125
loin of, with vegetables 134
onions, wine, herbs and 115–16
patties of herb and 31–2
roast of, marinated 147–8
sauce for 59, 65–6
spareribs 135
spareribs and herbs 151–2
stuffed suckling pig 116–17
with vegetables and cream
   sauce 136
see also ham; salt pork; sausage
pork caul or lace fat 12
Potage de Porée à la Ribelette de
   Lard 17
potatoes 159
baked eggs, cheese and
   mashed 88–9
baked eggs, cheese and sliced 93
cake of herbs, cheese and 167–8
cake of salt pork and 165
crisp patties of 181
French-fried, with sautéd
   mushrooms and sauce 164–5
gratin 176–7
Gratin Dauphinois I 169–70
Gratin Dauphinois II 170
gratin of mushrooms, onions
   and 174–5
gratin of onions, garlic and, with
   cheese crust 175–6
onions and, with herbs and red
   wine 179–80
pancake of onions, eggs, cheese
   and 168–9
purée of chestnuts and 186

purée of fennel and 188
salad of, warm 52
sausage and, with white wine and
   mustard 42
sautéd, with ham, onions and
   cream 163–4
sautéd, with herbs and cream
   sauce 184–5
sautéd, with onions 186–7
sautéd, with onions, vinegar and
   herbs 187
soup with leeks and 17
sticks with flour, cheese
   and 193–4
Pot-au-Feu 204–7
Potée aux Lentilles 185–6
Potée Bourguignonne 207–8
Pouding 249
Pouding de Pain d'Épice 249–50
Poule-au-Pot Bourguignon 137–8
Poulet a la Crème Charollaise 138–9
Poulet à la Moutarde 139–40
Poulet au Fromagw 140–41
Poulet au Vinaigre 141–2
Poulet aux Crevettes 142–3
Poulet aux Noix 143–4
Poulet aux Pruneaux 144–5
Poulet aux Raisins 146
Poulet Surprise 147
Pouti 186
prawns, chicken sautéd with wine,
   cream and 142–3
prunes
chicken, wine and 144–5
pie of 237
sausages, apples and 110–11
pumpkin 159
gratin of 172–3
jam of 225–6
pudding of 229
soup with 21–2
Purée of Choux 188
Purée de Fenouil 188

Purée de Haricots Blancs 189
purées
    cabbage 121–2, 188
    chestnut and potato 186
    fennel and potato 188
    fruit 226
    fruit, with cheese 224
    raspberry, with floating
        island 230–31
    white bean 189

quince
    beverage of 258
    pears, grapes and 250–51

rabbit
    marinated, with cream and
        grapes 131
    sauce for 59
Raisin a l'Eau de Vie 250
Raisiné 250
raisins
    braised onions with herbs, wine
        and 183
    pastry with 233
    soup with wine, spice and
        253
    tarts with apples, oranges,
        lemons and 254
raspberries
    purée of, with floating
        island 230–31
    ratafia 260–61
ratafia *see* beverages, home-
    made
Ravioles 197
Régal Aillé 40
rice
    with herbs 195
    soup with cabbage and 23
Rigodon 251–2
Riz aux Herbes 195
Rôti de Porc de Beaune 147–8

Roulade au Fromage 40–41
Roulades au Céleri 41–2

saffron 15
Salade à la Menthe 45
Salade au Chou 46
Salade aux Griaudes 46–7
Salade aux Noix 47
Salad de Céleri 47
Salade de Haricots Verts 48
Salade de Lentilles 48–9
Salade de Lyon 49–50
Salade de Nevers 50–51
Salade de Pissenlits 51
Salade de Pommes de Terre 52
Salade des Vendangeurs 52–3
Salade Dijonnaise 53
Salade Rouge et Verte 54
Salade Verte a la Crème 56
Saladier Lyonnais 55
salads 44–56
    cabbage, sautéd 46
    celery with walnuts, cheese and
        vinegar 47
    chicken liver, egg, herring,
        meat, herbs and vinaigrette
        sauce 55
    dandelion greens with bacon and
        croûtons 51
    dandelion greens with vinaigrette
        sauce 50–51
    diced salt pork with vinegar and
        herbs 46–7
    green, with ham, herbs and
        vinegar 52–3
    green, with herring and boiled
        eggs 49–50
    green bean, with shallots and
        mushrooms 48
    green pepper and red beetroot
        with celery and shallots 54
    lentil, with vegetables, herbs and
        bacon 48–9

lettuce, egg, ham, celery, cheese
   and walnut 53
lettuce, seasoned with garlic,
   butter and lemon 45
lettuce, with creamy sauce 56
lettuce, with mint, garlic and
   wine vingegar 45
lettuce, with walnuts, lemons,
   mustard and cream 47
melted cheese with 215
warm potato 52
salami, soup with vegetables,
   Gruyère cheese and 26–7
salmon
   marinated 84
   mint, tomatoes and 83–4
salt 12
salt pork, lean 11
   chestnuts and, in fried
      cakes 29–30
   diced, in salad 46–7
   patties of chicken liver, herbs
      and 33
   patties of pork, herbs and 123
   potato cake with 165
   potatoes with onions, cream,
      eggs and 163–4
   salad with dandelion greens,
      croûtons and 51
   salad with vinegar, herbs
      and 46–7
   sauce with red wine, onion
      and 61
   soup with leeks, potatoes and 17
   spread of 29
   vegetables and, in pie 149–51
   see also ham
Sauce à la Menthe 60
Sauce au Beurre Rouge 60–61
Sauce Bourguignonne 61
Sauce Bourguignotte 62
Sauce de Sorges 62
Sauce Dorée 63

Sauce Mayonnaise 63–4
Sauce Meurette 64–5
Sauce Mousseline Dijon 65
Sauce Moutarde I 65–6
Sauce Moutarde II 66
Sauce Tomate Crue 67
sauces 57–67
   butter, garlic, shallot and
      parsley 55–6
   egg, butter, lemon and
      mustard 65
   herb, with egg, mustard and
      lemon 62
   marinade, 59
   mayonnaise 63–4
   mayonnaise, seasoned 63
   mint 60
   mustard I 65–6
   mustard II 66
   red wine and butter 60–61
   red wine, bacon and onion 61
   red wine, butter and herb 63
   red wine, vegetable and
      herb 64–5
   snail butter 58
   tomato, raw 67
   tomato, warm 58–9
Saucisson Chaud Lyonnais 42
Saumon aux Herbs 84
Saumon en Papillote 83–4
Saupiquet I 208–9
Saupiquet II 209–10
sausage 278
   baked cabbage with apples, sage
      and 160
   cabbage stuffed with fruit
      and 161–2
   potatoes and, with white wine
      and mustard 42
   Pot-au-Feu 204–7
   with prunes and apples 110–11
   soup with vegetables, *Gruyère*
      cheese and salami 26–7

shallots 12, 159
sherbet, brandy 252
snails
    baked 73–4
    butter sauce for 58
    fake 87
    marinated 74–5
    omelette for 97
    preparation of 72–3
    sauce for 57–8
Sorbet au Marc 252
sorrel
    baked fish fillets with 77
    soup with onions, carrots,
        turnips and 25
    soufflé
    apple 242–3
    chicken-liver 34–5
Soupe à la Bressane 18
Soupe à l'Abricot 252–3
Soupe à l'Oeuf 17–18
Soupe Arlequin 19
Soupe au Chou 19–20
Soupe au Fromage 21
Soupe au Potiron 21–2
Soupe au Riz au Chou 23
Soupe au Vin 23–4
Soupe au Vin en Dessert 253
Soupe aux Gaudes 24
Soupe Dauphinoise 25
Soupe Nevers 25–6
Soupe Savoyard 26–7
Soupe Verte 27
soups 16–27
    apricot dessert 252–3
    broth with custard 17–18
    Brussels sprouts 25–6
    cabbage, carrot and turnip 19–20
    cheese (hearty) 21
    cheese (smooth) 20
    chicken, with cream and corn
        meal 24
    leek and potato 17

    onion, carrot, turnip and
        sorrel 25
    onion, with eggs, cheese and
        wine 202–3
    pumpkin 21–2
    rice and cabbage 23
    tomato and chicken 18
    vegetable, creamy 19, 27
    vegetable, *Gruyère* cheese and
        salami, 26–7
    wine and vegetable 23–4
    wine, raisin and spice
        dessert 253
special treats 277–9
spices and flavourings 13–15
spinach 159
    gratin of 173–4
    ham baked with cream sauce
        and 129–30
    onions stuffed with cream,
        cheese, eggs and 180
squash, pie of tomato, onion and
    courgette 189–90
staples 8–13
Steak à la Moutarde 149
stewed fruit 232
    with nut pudding 251–2
stews
    beef 106–10
    beef, of Burgundy 198–9
    chicken 131
    fish 203–4
    lamb 123–4
    Pot-au-Feu 204–7
    turkey 114–15

tangerines with brandy 238–9
Tarte aux Légumes 189–90
Tarte aux Pommes 254
Tarte aux Prunes 254–5
Tarte Bourguignonne 149–51
Tarte Lyonnaise aux Miettes 256
tarts

almond, orange and lemon, with
    meringue 256
apple, with orange, lemon and
    raisins 254
plum and custard 254–5
see also pies
Terrine de Canard 42–3
Terrine de Navets 190–91
Tomates au Fromage 191
tomatoes
    baked chicken with
        cream and, under cheese
        crust 147
    pie of onion, courgettes
        and 189–90
    salmon with mint and 83–4
    sauce of, raw 67
    sauce of, warm 58–9
    sauce of, with ham and
        cheese 127–8
    soup with chicken and 18
    stuffed, with cheese and
        shallots 191
Travers de Porc aux Herbes 151–2
trout
    mint sauce for 60
    sauce for 64–5
    stuffed 84–5
Truite Farcie aux Herbes 84–5
turkey
    marinated, and cooked with
        cream and grapes 131
    marinated with wine and
        vegetables 153–4
    stewed, in wine and
        herbs 114–15
turnips 159
    gratin of ham, herbs and 190–91
    in mixed vegetables 182
    onions, herbs, garlic and 183
    in poultry fricassee 126
    soup with cabbage, carrots
        and 19–20

soup with onions, carrots,
    sorrel and 25

veal
    chops baked with onions and
        wine 122
    sauce for 65–6
    sausages with prunes and
        apples 110–11
    sautéd, with onions and
        wine 153
    sautéd, with wine and
        mustard 152
    vegetables with wine, herbs,
        eggs, cream and 100
    see also beef
Veau à la Moutarde 152
Veau Meurette 153
vegetables 155–91
    baked ham with, and cream
        sauce 208–9
    boiled dinner of pork
        and 207–8
    marinated beef in aspic
        and 107–8
    mixed 182
    pie of meat and 149–51
    pork with cream sauce and 136
    Pot-au-Feu 204–7
    sauces for 65–6
    sautéd beef with 103
    soup with cream and 19, 27
    soup with *Gruyère* cheese, salami
        and 26–7
    soup with wine and 23–4
    in stuffed dumplings, 38–9
    veal with wine, herbs, egg, cream
        and 100
    see also salads; specific vegetables
vermouth 12
Viande aux Baies 153–4
Vin Chaud 262
Vin de Genièvre 263

Vin de Noix 263
vinegar 12

waffles, honey 236–7
walnuts
    cake with rum, apricot jam
      and 235–6
    celery with cheese and 47
    chicken sautéd with mushrooms
      and 143–4
    ratafia of 261–2
    salad with lettuce, egg, ham,
      celery, cheese and 53–4
    salad with lettuce, lemons,
      mustard, cream and 47
    wine of 263

whitebait, grilled and marinated
    with herbs, wine and vinegar
    81
wine 13
    green walnut 263
    juniper 263
    preparation of 264–8
    sauce with bacon, onion
      and 61
    sauce with butter and 60–61
    sauce with butter, shallots, herbs
      and 63
    sauce with vegetables, herbs
      and 64–5
    soup with vegetables and 23–4
    with spices 262